About the Author

Eleanor Agnes Berry is the author of 24 published books and says her first brush with literature was when she broke windows in Ian Fleming's house at the age of eight. 'He struck me as being a singularly disagreeable man, with no understanding of children,' she recalls. Of Welsh ancestry, she was born and bred in London. She holds a BA Hons degree (a 2:2) in English.

Eleanor specializes in black humour. In many of her books, there is a firm of funeral directors called Crumblebottom and Bongwit. The works of Gorky, Dostoevsky, Gogol, Edgar Allan Poe, James Hadley Chase, George Orwell, Joe Orton and William Harrison-Ainsworth have strongly influenced her writings. While at university she completed an unpublished contextual thesis on the Marquis de Sade (whom she refers to as 'de Soggins'). In her spare time she wrote a grossly indecent book, entitled, *The Story of Paddy*, which she had the good sense to burn, and inadvertently set a garage on fire.

After leaving university she worked as a commercial translator, using French and Russian. She then worked as a debt collector for a Harley Street specialist, namely the late Dr Victor Ratner, and has since worked intermittently as a medical secretary. She was unfairly sacked from St Bartholomew's Hospital in London because she had been a close friend of the late Robert Maxwell's. (She had worked there for five years!)

Two of her novels are available in Russian and a third, which she refrains from naming, is currently being made into a film.

Eleanor is the author of numerous articles in *The Oldie* magazine and has appeared on television and on radio several times, including Radio California. Her interests include Russian literature, Russian folk songs, Irish rebel songs, the cinema, amateur piano playing, sensational court cases, the medical profession, entertaining her nephews, to whom she is extremely close, and swimming across Marseille harbour for kicks. When she dies, she will have her ashes scattered over Marseille harbour, her favourite place.

Eleanor Berry is the maternal niece of the late, famous, self-confessed gypsy author, Eleanor Smith, after whom she was named. Sadly, Eleanor Smith died before Eleanor Berry was born.

Books by Eleanor Berry

The Story of Paddy (A pornographic book – not published)
Tell Us a Sick One Jakey (Out of print)
Never Alone with Rex Malone (A black comedy about Robert Maxwell's alleged relationship with a crooked funeral director – Out of print)
Someone's Been Done Up Harley
O, Hitman, My Hitman!
The Adventures of Eddy Vernon
Stop the Car, Mr Becket! (Formerly *The Rendon Boy to the Grave Is Gone*)
Robert Maxwell as I Knew Him (Out of print)
Cap'n Bob and Me (Out of print)
McArandy was Hanged on the Gibbet High
The House of the Weird Doctors
Sixty Funny Stories
The Most Singular Adventures of Sarah Lloyd
Alandra Varinia – Sarah's Daughter
The Rise and Fall of Mad Silver Jaxton
By the Fat of Unborn Leopards
The Killing of Lucinda Maloney
My Old Pal was a Junkie (Available in Russian)
Your Father Had to Swing, You Little Bastard! (Also available in Russian)
An Eye for a Tooth and a Limb for an Eye (A Story of Revenge)
Help me, Help me, It's Red!
Come Sweet Sexton, Tend My Grave
My Face Shall Appear on the Banknotes
My Unique Relationship with Robert Maxwell – The Truth At Last
My Father Was a Newspaper Man

Reviews

Tell Us a Sick One Jakey
'This book is quite repulsive!' Sir Michael Havers, Attorney General

Never Alone with Rex Malone
'A ribald, ambitious black comedy, a story powerfully told.'
Stewart Steven, *The Daily Mail*

'I was absolutely flabbergasted when I read it!' *Robert Maxwell*

Robert Maxwell as I Knew Him
'One of the most amusing books I have read for a long time. Eleanor Berry is an original.' Elisa Segrave, *The Literary Review*

'Undoubtedly the most amusing book I have read all year.' Julia Llewellyn-Smith, *The Times*

'With respect and I repeat, with very great respect, because I know you're a lady, but all you ever do is just go on and on and on and on about this bleeding bloke!' *Reggie Kray.*

Cap'n Bob and Me
'A comic masterpiece.' *The Times*

'As befits the maternal granddaughter of F.E. Smith (famous barrister who never lost a case) Eleanor Berry has a sharp tone of phrase and a latent desire for upsetting people. Campaigning for her hero, Robert Maxwell, in a General Election, she climbed to the top of the Buckingham Town Hall and erected the red flag. Eleanor Berry fits into the long tradition of British eccentricity.' Stewart Graham, *The Spectator*

Someone's Been Done Up Harley
'Eleanor Berry's dazzling wit hits the Harley Street scene. Her extraordinary humour had me in stitches.'
Thelma Masters, *The Oxford Times*

O, Hitman, My Hitman!
'Eleanor Berry's volatile pen is at it again. This time, she takes her readers back to the humorously eccentric Harley Street community. She also introduces Romany gypsies and travelling circuses, a trait which she has inherited from her self-confessed gypsy aunt, the late writer, Eleanor Smith, after whom she was named. Like Smith, Berry is an inimitable and delightfully natural writer.' Kev Zein, *The Johannesburg Evening Sketch*

McArandy was Hanged on the Gibbet High
'We have here a potboiling, swashbuckling blockbuster, which is rich in adventure, intrigue, history, amorous episodes and above all black humour. The story Eleanor Berry tells is multi-coloured, multi-faceted and nothing short of fantastic.' Angel Z. Hogan, *The Daily Melbourne Times*

The Adventures of Eddy Vernon
'Rather a hot book for bedtime.' the late Nigel Dempster, *The Daily Mail*

Stop the Car, Mr Becket! (formerly The Rendon Boy to the Grave is Gone)
'This book makes for fascinating reading, as strange, black-humoured and entertaining as Eleanor Berry's other books which came out before it.' It is to be noted that Eleanor is embarrassed by parts of this book. *Gaynor Evans, Bristol Evening Post*

Sixty Funny Stories
'This book is a laugh a line.' Elisa Segrave, writer and diarist

The House of the Weird Doctors
'This delightful medical caper puts even A.J. Cronin in the shade.' Noel I. Leskin, *The Stethoscope*

The Most Singular Adventures of Sarah Lloyd
'A riotous read from start to finish.' Ned McMurphy, *The Irish Times*

Alandra Varinia – Sarah's Daughter
'Eleanor Berry manages to maintain her raw and haunting wit as much as ever.' Dwight C. Farr, *The Texas Chronicle*

The Rise and Fall of Mad Silver Jaxton
'This time, Eleanor Berry tries her versatile hand at politics. Her sparkling wit and the reader's desire to turn the page are still in evidence. Eleanor Berry is unique.' Don F. Saunderson, *The South London Review*

'This is a dark, disturbing but at the same time hilarious tale of a megalomaniac dictator by the always readable and naughty Eleanor Berry.' The late Sally Farmiloe, award-winning actress and author

By the Fat of Unborn Leopards
'Could this ribald, grisly-humoured story about a right-wing British newspaper magnate's daughter, possibly be autobiographical, by any chance?' Peggy-Lou Kadinsky, *The Washington Globe*

'Fantastically black. A scream from beginning to end.'
Charles Kidd, Editor of *Debrett's Peerage*

The Killing of Lucinda Maloney
'This is the funniest book I've read for months,' Samantha Morris, *The Exeter Daily News*

My Old Pal was a Junkie
'Eleanor Berry is to literature what Hieronymus Bosch is to art. As with all Miss Berry's books, the reader has a burning urge to turn the page.' Sonia Drew, *The Texas Times*

Your Father Had to Swing, You Little Bastard!
'A unique display of black humour which somehow fails to depress the reader.' Craig McLittle, *The Rugby Gazette*

'This book is an unheard of example of English black humour. Eleanor Berry is almost a reincarnation of our own beloved Dostoevsky.' Sergei Robkov, Russian magazine, *Minuta*

An Eye for a Tooth and a Limb for an Eye: A Story of Revenge
'Words are Eleanor Berry's toys and her use of them is boundless.' Mary Hickman, professional historian and writer

Help Me, Help Me, It's Red!
'Despite the sometimes weighty portent of this book, a sense of subtle, dry and black humour reigns throughout its pages. The unexpected twist is stupendous.'
Stephen Carson, *The Carolina Sun*
'This is grim humour at its very best. The most challenging and most delightful novel I have read in six months.' Scott Mason-Jones, *The New York Globe*

Come, Sweet Sexton, Tend My Grave
'Breathtakingly black, a treasure to read from beginning to end.'
Grace Ponsonby, *Newsweek*

My Face Shall Appear on the Banknotes
'Tightly paced and bitter-sweet throughout throughout.'
Alexis Lawrence, *The Cork Evening News*

'A satisfying and fantastic read in all ways.'
George Cullen

My Unique Relationship with Robert Maxwell – the Truth at Last
'A scholarly, moving but at the same time, delightfully comic work, seeped in black humour – a genuine page-turner.'
'This is the most entertaining book, I have read so far about the controversial Mirror Magnate and Eleanor Berry's friendship with him.'
'So far we have only heard negative things about him, but Eleanor has shown his human, kind and compassionate side, hitherto unknown to the British public.'
John Cohen, *The Oxford Times*

MY FATHER WAS A
NEWSPAPER MAN

Eleanor Berry

www.eleanorberry.net

Also available on You-Tube and

Amazon

The Book Guild Ltd

First published in Great Britain in 2021 by
The Book Guild Ltd
9 Priory Business Park
Wistow Road, Kibworth
Leicestershire, LE8 0RX
Freephone: 0800 999 2982
www.bookguild.co.uk
Email: info@bookguild.co.uk
Twitter: @bookguild

Typeset in Baskerville

Printed and bound in Great Britain by CPI Group (UK) Ltd, Croydon, CR0 4YY

ISBN 978 1913551 827

British Library Cataloguing in Publication Data.

A catalogue record for this book is available from the British Library

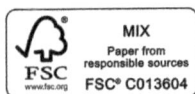

MIX
Paper from
responsible sources
FSC
www.fsc.org
FSC® C013604

In Memory of Bashir

.

Introduction

It has taken me some time to write this book, which is an autobiography. Although many of its pages naturally relate to me, I have also written about my father, my mother, my childhood, my education, my adulthood and my beloved Peachey, the love of my life, now dead.

I have also told some humorous anecdotes, about isolated incidents in my life.

I have cited some extracts from sensational court cases, which I have attended as a hobby. These have held an enormous fascination for me. I confess that I have inherited this gene from my maternal grandmother, who attended the trial of Dr Crippen, much to the annoyance of her husband, F.E. Smith, who represented Ethel le Neve, Crippen's mistress. He finally got her off!

I have described some of my experiences at university, where I spoke with a heavy Irish accent, to hide my own accent, and my situations following my graduation.

I worked as a freelance translator, using French and Russian, and later as a temporary medical secretary, in National Health hospitals, all over London, for many years.

In the end, I realised I was cut out to be a writer. Writing runs throughout my family. It is my passion and it is by far the only occupation I enjoy.

I have spoken about my father's two newspapers, *The Daily Telegraph* and *The Sunday Telegraph*, as well as all the printers' strikes which certainly shortened his life.

In addition, I have spoken about my mother, Pam, and her side of our family. She was the youngest daughter of F.E. Smith, a brilliant barrister, who apparently never lost a case. He was also a distinguished statesman,

Secretary of State for India, Earl of Birkenhead (from whence he had hailed) and finally he became Lord Chancellor. This had been his ambition since his early boyhood. (See the biography of him, written by his eldest son, Freddie.)

F.E., for such was he known to his friends, died in 1930. My mother, who was his youngest daughter, was only sixteen at the time.

F.E. strongly believed in working like a dog and playing hard as well. Apart from the extraordinary workloads he carried on his shoulders, he returned to his home, Charlton, in Northamptonshire on Fridays. He played several sets of tennis at weekends. He was devoid of snobbery, and often invited Mr Rainbow, his gardener, to make up a four. At other times, he galloped through the undulating Northamptonshire countryside.

I have briefly mentioned my mother's elder sibling, Freddie, who, like his sister, Eleanor, was a prolific writer. He went to Oxford. It was thought at first that Pam, had failed to put pen to paper.

However, despite Eleanor's and Freddie's enjoyment of the written word, Freddie has also stated, in his funny and moving memoir of his late sister, Eleanor, that, Pam, too, had written a saucy book in her teens.

The book was extremely raunchy throughout. In fact, her shocked elder brother commented that her prose would have brought a "blush to the cheeks of James Hadley chase!"

I admit that this was the only "book" to be penned by my mother. As she would understandably have failed to find an appropriate publisher, her book cannot be regarded as a formal literary work.

I have covered my father's side of the family as well. He was a Welshman. More importantly, I have described his eminent career as a newspaper proprietor, his gentle and witty personality, his kindness, generosity and modesty.

With great reluctance, I have spoken about the incomprehensible and tragic sale of both his newspapers to a certain Conrad Black, who is said to have had a somewhat tawdry reputation, as well as a custodial sentence behind him.

There appeared to be no one around to give my father decent advice, and he believed in doing everything himself. This could have been his main weakness. I feel that, had my mother been alive, the papers would not have been sold.

My father, Michael Berry, was a man of varied interests, other than newspaper publication. He was fascinated by planting trees, which started off by being very small, and finally growing to substantial heights over the years.

A cousin of his was invited by my father to look at his trees.

The man turned out to be very rude. My father pointed to one of his trees and identified it by a long Latin name.

The visitor kicked the tree, let out a guffaw and remarked, "No, it's not. It's ash and it's dead!"

Despite this humiliation, my father continued to enjoy working on trees, as well as fixing fuses in plugs. He had long, slender fingers and was very good with his hands. He also restored paintings and made them look like original masterpieces.

This book may not be without its faults, but none of it is dull. After much thought, I have entitled it, *My Father Was a Newspaper Man*, which I consider to be apt.

I was born in London on 6th of May, 1950, at 27 Welbeck Street. I had two brothers and one living sister, all older than me. I was the only one to be born after World War II. I was named Eleanor Agnes. I don't like the name Agnes, which came from my paternal grandmother. My sister, Harriet, an exemplary, but somewhat bossy, elder sister, was five at the time of my birth. She was christened Harriet, Mary Margaret.

Harriet loved playing with dolls and was overjoyed when I was born. She told everyone that I was a "living doll which had been sent straight from heaven". Her personality, namely that of a somewhat fierce advisor but loving protector, has not changed. We bickered a lot when we were children, and still do at times, although, on the whole, we get on reasonably well.

"How dare you?" I used to shout at her.

"I don't know how I dare. I just do," she replied.

I am fairly dependent on my sister, although we do not always see eye to eye.

We had a beloved Norland Nanny, whose name was Nina Lawrence and she hailed from Southampton. She had a heart of gold, and we all adored her. My mother, too, was devoted to her and so was my father.

Even in later years, Harriet's personality has remained basically the same. Not long ago, she booked us both into a ghastly hotel somewhere in Dublin. We had a room to ourselves. Each room was dark and was obscured by leafy trees, making it impossible to see the sky.

The temperature was ninety degrees in the shade. I left my room and walked towards the lift, which was out of order. Harriet was waiting impatiently outside the lift.

"The milk, which was brought to my room, is sour. The orange juice is off. The room is haunted. There's no air conditioning, and the bloody lift is out of order!" I complained vehemently, adding, "I really don't find any of this at all amusing!"

Harriet was exasperated. "Oh, I do wish you'd stop being such a *fucking* old woman!" she shouted.

* * *

When Harriet was much younger, she cracked a black-humoured joke, regarding the death of King George VI, who had died in his sleep. He had cancer in both lungs, and the news of his death was circulated all over the world. Sir Winston Churchill's special code, for some reason, was "Hyde Park Corner". A pot of tea was about to be brought to the supine King's bed on a silver tray. The staff at Buckingham Palace seemed more concerned about the tea than about the deceased King. Nicky, Harriet and Nanny sat solemnly round the breakfast table.

"Who drank the tea?" asked Harriet, in a deep, reverent tone of voice.

* * *

Long before the King's death, a surgeon came into his Majesty's bedchamber.

"Sire, I have tragic news," he said.

"What news is that?" asked the King.

"I am afraid there are massive growths in both your lungs. You only have a short time to live."

The King frenziedly lit a cigarette!

* * *

Sometime after I was born, Harriet used to climb onto a chair, several times a day, and help Nanny to change nappies.

Unlike Harriet, I am not at all domesticated. I refer, particularly, to my hatred of cooking. There is a deep-rooted reason for this. When I was ten, we were renting a villa in the south of France. My mother spoke to me forcefully and said, "If you don't learn to cook, you will never find a husband. The way to a man's heart is through his stomach and also through vigorous exercise. If you fail to marry, you will be very lonely in old age."

My nephew Jonathan listened attentively to her in later years. And, although his words had little to do with those of my mother, he said something very cheeky, which was part of his charm. He knew what a phenomenally bad skier I was and always had been, also what a poor athlete and gymnast I am. He calls me British bullet!

Whenever we happened to be on the ski slopes at the same time - I, on the nursery slopes of course, and he just coming off his customary black run, accompanied by his father Adrian, he liked to tease me before frequenting the cafes.

My mother was anxious for me to take vigorous exercise everyday which I hated. Even when fanatical fuckers in mud-splashed knee-high socks, were jogging along country paths, my mother slowed down lowered one of the windows of her Mini Clubman Estate and called out to me, her voice as loud as mine,

"Oh, can't I put you out to jog alongside this charming looking gentleman darling? The exercise would do you a world of good."

"No thanks," I replied. "I don't think he would like it much either. After all, I don't even know him."

I will never know to this day, whether my mother was joking or not!

Although my mother's words were wise indeed, even if they had been uttered as far back as 1960, I am pleased to say that times have changed. A lot of men prefer to cook these days. My mother gave me some lamb cutlets, tomatoes, peas and potatoes. She told me to go to the kitchen and cook dinner, having briefly explained what she wanted me to do. There was a gas cooker in the kitchen. I lit all four rings with a match and tried to carry out her instructions.

Suddenly, there was a terrifying explosion. I was thrown to the other side of the kitchen, and plaster from one of the walls came down on top of me. My face was covered with soot. My reaction was to become frightened and very bad-tempered. Although this was an accident, the members of my family were pretty pissed off. We had to rent another villa that evening, and my father paid for the damage which had been done to the kitchen in the previous villa. On top of that, I have a morbid fear of poisoning others.

I will never ever try to cook again. Why should I do so? I'm a prolific writer. I tell this story to any man I go out with, and many of these men understand my words.

My late brother Nicky (Nicholas William) is two years older than Harriet. My eldest sibling is my late brother Adrian (Adrian Michael).

Nicky doted on me. We were very close. When we grew up, we shared a flat in London for almost ten years.

I used to collect skulls to put my wigs on to. Unlike me, Nicky hated morbidity. I inherit the macabre streak from my maternal grandmother. I will say more about this later.

"For Christ's sake, get all these *fucking* skulls out of here, woman!" Nicky used to say, his voice raised.

It was he who introduced me to Robert Maxwell, whom I regard as a God-like figure, even though he is deceased. I regarded Nicky as being the Pope and Maxwell as a deity. I felt at ease in Nicky's presence, because he hated displays of emotion, and never tried to get into my head.

There is a room in my parents' Buckinghamshire house, once known as the "North Library" where we all used to play as children. It was there that Nicky taught me to sing *God Save the Queen* as well as *The British Grenadier*. It is now a "Playroom", which was used by Harriet's sons. The room has always been very popular with children. Sometimes I sleep there because of my arthritis.

To return to Nicky's countless wishes not to be psychoanalysed, or to be questioned about Freudian matters, let me tell you an amusing story:

Harriet Crawley, a well-known, very clever and rather daring writer, whom I will refer to later on in this book, leant across the dinner table, sometime in 1973, in a smart London restaurant, her blue eyes wide, and said, "Nicky, what, in your opinion, is the true meaning of life?"

Nicky was furious and looked exasperated and raised his eyes to the ceiling. He rapidly transferred his napkin from left to right.

"Oh, for God's sake, Harriet [Crawley], how the hell do you expect me to answer a whacky question like that?"

"I think you're being bloody rude!" she replied, as her eyes filled with tears.

Although I have always liked her, I considered her behaviour really intrusive, and akin to reading someone's diary.

I found the situation embarrassing. I changed the subject and referred to the Marquis de Sade, about whom I was doing a contextual thesis at university. I quoted a ribald passage from his prose in French.

To give another example of Nicky's disdain for emotional attitudes of any kind, he once spoke to me about D.H. Lawrence's tragic, but beautifully written, novel, *Lady Chatterley's Lover* and other works by the same author. I was due to write an essay about this book, and I wanted a quick synopsis of *Lady Chatterley*, in particular, as, at the time, it was my favourite.

"It was damned amusing, but in the end, things got a bit dicey," said

Nicky, not really giving me the information I wanted. Harriet, on the other hand, found the book distressing.

Because I had been upset by parts of the book, especially by the snobbery and class divide, Nicky's matter-of-fact language caused me to snap out of my despair.

I wrote a book which was entirely based on Nicky, entitled *An Eye for a Tooth and a Limb for an Eye*, about my view of the necessity of revenge. Nicky was the main protagonist I called him "Silas Buckleshott", and I appeared as his devoted younger sister, Rhoda, who planned to take the most terrible revenge on her employer, by sacking her. Very regrettably, Nicky was not amused by the book.

I'm afraid, he and Harriet failed to get on. This may have been because Harriet is emotional and analytical. She tends to be tactile, unlike Nicky. Harriet always warmly expressed her love for my father. The fact that she was so loving towards him, bonded them until his death. I could never have shown such love openly, but that does not mean it didn't exist.

Perhaps, I can be compared with Cordelia, in Shakespeare's *King Lear*. Someone foolishly took me to see this play after my father's death, and I had a psychotic episode.

Harriet married a very amusing and brilliant Argentinian writer called Martin Cullen (pronounced Martine Cuzhin), and her temperament became more "Latin" than it had been before her marriage.

* * *

They have two sweet, very clever sons, Miguel and Domingo (nicknamed "Mingo"). When Mingo was about eight, I overheard him saying to a friend of his, "I've got this aunt, and she writes these books, but we're not allowed to read them!"

Both Harriet and Martin are great scholars, or intellectuals, I should say. They are phenomenally clever and well-read. Harriet loves to travel and explore, but I am of a more sedentary disposition. For some reason, I become depressed when I travel. I also suffer badly from arthritis.

Harriet is extremely analytical, as I said earlier, particularly of other people's personalities, and their reasons for being what they are. Despite their different personalities, I have always been very devoted to Harriet and Nicky, as well as Adrian. I was particularly close to Nicky, with whom I lived.

Nicky got on amazingly badly with my mother, but not my father. My mother had a tendency to be very bossy, as the late Robert Maxwell pointed out once. She was forever telling others what to do. Staggeringly, Maxwell found my mother "formidable."

My mother died of breast cancer, and was ill for six weeks. As she lay on her deathbed, in January, 1982, my father used extremely tactful language and told Nicky to leave the room, in case my mother witnessed his presence and saw it as "heralding a real deathbed scene". My father, as will be shown in my long passage about him later on in this book, was exceptionally sensitive, and diplomatic. "Kennedy over Cuba." That's the way I've always thought of him as being!

On the whole, I got on reasonably well with my mother, particularly during the last few years of her life. When she was struck down, I rang her up most days, and she said how sweet I was to do so. She needn't have said this, but she did. I also took the day off work to drive her to hospital, when she needed to have some tests. She really appreciated this. Once more, she was abundantly grateful.

She died shortly before the Falklands War. Apart from the terrible effect that her death had on my father, it was not entirely untimely.

My mother was a fanatical supporter of the British, but was far from being a royalist, and Martin, was strong supporter of the Argentinians. Harriet would have been left in the middle, and she and her husband might easily have had to emigrate to Argentina, to save their marriage. They were genuine Montagues and Capulets.

Their first son, Miguel, the Spanish name for "Michael", was named after my father. He was born on 2nd of March, 1982. There is a photograph of him, as a baby, holding a Union Jack in one hand and the Argentinian flag in the other.

Nicky really played his cards badly, where his relationship with my mother was concerned. Although she was obviously much older than he, he was forever having rows with her. In the end, she cut him out of her will. Nicky became an astute businessman, however, and a tycoon later on in life. Even so, my mother's action of cutting him out of her will, could easily have been avoided, had he gone out of his way to be a bit more tactful and polite to her.

Nicky got married in a hurry. My mother took the phone call, announcing his girlfriend's pregnancy. She slammed the phone down and rushed into the room next door. "Oh, my God, it's a shotgun!" she shouted.

Where my mother was concerned, I was really quite fond of the old bat, and my behaviour towards her was much more sensible than Nicky's had been.

* * *

Robert Maxwell once said to Nicky, "Sometimes, I see myself in Eleanor." I've never quite understood what he meant by that remark.

* * *

My mother could be vindictive, jealous and obsessive. Indeed, she suffered from obsessive-compulsive disorder, like myself, but she had many human qualities. She was devoted to Adrian's children, Jessica and Jonathan, and to Nicky's two sons, William and Alexander, although she continued to get on badly with their father. It is a shame that she never lived to meet Miguel and Mingo, Harriet's sons. Harriet was heavily pregnant when my mother died. She was expecting Miguel.

"Oh, the poor, poor, poor, little mite!" my mother exclaimed repeatedly from her deathbed. "Whatever is to become of him?" (It was known that Harriet was going to have a son.)

Nothing was too much trouble, where my mother's grandchildren were concerned, and she was forever buying them presents and taking them on outings, as I mentioned earlier.

Despite her many faults, no one can deny that there was a strong streak of kindness in her heart, and she was well-meaning towards those who suffered, such as unhappy children, widows and those who were ill, unfortunate or bereaved.

However, if anyone slighted her, even if in a very minor way, her vengeance towards that unfortunate, knew no parallel. Once she got her knife into her victim's flesh, she continued to twist it, and had to be physically forced to remove it.

My mother had an elder sister called Eleanor, as I stated earlier. She died a few years before I was born, and I was named after her. Nobody really knows the cause of her death, other than to say that she died in her house in London, during World War II. She was not bombed by the Germans. She died in her bed.

Some say that she died of "flu"; some say that she died of appendicitis; others say that she died of colitis. As I understand it, colitis is quite an easy disease to cure nowadays, although this was not the case during the War.

Eleanor had a morbid fear of doctors and hospitals. Whenever a doctor visited her house, she refused to let this unfortunate in. Her death was a mystery, unlike her remarkable, but short, life. As I said, she was a prolific writer, who had penned eight books, about gypsy life and travelling circuses. These subjects fascinated her from about the age of twelve onwards.

In fact, her obsession about gypsies and their lives, lasted until she was laid in earth. On one occasion, when she was in her teens, she walked all the way to a field, in which gypsies had encamped.

She invited them to her home, in quantities, having bribed them with buns and lemonade. She led them to her father's austere dining room, in which he had received statesman and other dignitaries, its walls dark and uninviting. Once her new guests had sat down noisily at the equally dark table, she fed them, even more liberally, with food obtained from the kitchen.

Her father did not take long to come into the dining room to find out where the noise was coming from.

"What do you think you're doing?" he demanded mildly.

"You told me once that I was partly gypsy," she replied defiantly. "Why do you think I like doing this sort of thing?"

"Because you're mentally unstable!" shouted her father.

Like my mother, she could be vicious and vindictive. If anyone crossed her path, she would declare vehemently, "I will write them a letter!" I'm afraid there are no copies of any of these letters in existence. Like my aunt, Eleanor, I always write punitive letters if I am provoked.

Eleanor's surname was Smith, as she was the daughter of F.E. Smith. Naturally, my mother's surname was Smith as well, until she married my father, Michael Berry. Like me, my mother was born under the sign of Taurus, the Bull. Her birthday was on 16th May, and woe betide any luckless party who forgot it! I have inherited many of her genes, and it would therefore be hard for me to spit on her grave.

* * *

My mother was not devout, although she became furious if anyone cracked irreligious jokes in front of me when I was underage. When Harriet was about twenty, she told a famous joke, which I think first appeared in the Russian newspaper, *Izvestia*, in the 1950s.

The joke describes a non-believing wartime pilot, and a believing wartime co-pilot, flying in the same plane. The non-believing pilot crosses himself, when the plane is about to land. After landing, he is questioned by the believing co-pilot about his confusing gesture, and his colleague replies, "I need to check that everything is ready, before we land: spectacle, testicle, wallet and watch."

My mother was incandescent with rage, and gave Harriet a hell of a ticking-off. This was because I was present and she didn't want me to be corrupted at a young age. However, Harriet did not appear to be at all humiliated by my mother's rebuke.

Adrian, who was also there, slapped his thigh and let out a guffaw. My mother ticked him off as well.

"Don't blame me. I didn't say a word," he replied.

A similar incident occurred when my mother, Adrian and I were visiting the Holy Land in 1964. We were in a hired car, on the way to Damascus. Adrian was asleep and my mother woke him.

"We are on the road to Damascus, Adrian," she said.

"By Jove, do you think we'll get a vision?" asked Adrian theatrically.

My mother wasn't very pleased. "Not in front of Eleanor!" she shouted. I was fourteen!

* * *

On another matter, I had an illustrious christening in Saint Margaret's Church, Westminster, about two months after I was born. The christening took place in July, 1950.

Among my godparents were Sir Cecil Beaton, the gay photographer, and the prolific writer, Nancy Mitford, the sister of the infamous Nazi, Unity Mitford. Nancy Mitford lived in Paris all her life, and Unity boasted that she had had a baby by Hitler! She had no connection whatever with any members of my family. Also, it was proved after the War that Hitler had been unable to have children, either by Unity or any other mother.

Whenever I wrote to my godparents, thanking them for gifts, my mother told me to address them as "Dear Godfather Cecil" and "Dear Godmother Nancy". I can't deny that I was well brought up.

The late Robert Maxwell had not been chosen, however. To me, he was my real godfather, and I am proud to have been his friend. When I wrote to him, which I did on many occasions, I addressed him in Russian, as "Dear Comrade Bob", due to my Russian connections at the time, and my having taught myself Russian, against my parents' wishes. They wanted my third language to be Italian, for some reason, and sent me to Florence. I was quite happy to spend my days on the Ponte Vecchio, with my head buried in my Russian primer.

At roughly the time of my christening, my parents had a ghastly next-door neighbour. He was the actor, John Gielgud. My father used to call him "Stinker", because he owned a parrot, which recited, "*To Be or Not to Be*", from about two o'clock in the morning onwards. The actor kept the horrible bird in his garden.

My mother wheeled me in a pram into our garden, and left me by the fence, dividing John Gielgud's garden from ours, from about ten-thirty in the morning onwards. Predictably, I made an awful noise, crying and screaming. Gielgud was unable to learn his lines and called the police.

Apart from the noise made by Gielgud's parrot, my christening went according to plan, apparently, and my parents had been able to get a reasonable night's sleep beforehand.

* * *

Adrian was thirteen and at Eton when I was born. He was not dissimilar to me, in that he was literary, original and eccentric.

"Call the baby Carlotta!" he wrote forcefully to my parents. I have no idea why he wanted me to be given such a frightful name.

In later years, I accompanied my mother to Sir Cecil Beaton's funeral, and was unaware, at the time, that he had been as queer as a nine-bob note.

"Where is his widow?" I asked, my voice raised, during the service.

"Shut your trap!" said my mother loudly.

When I was about thirteen, I drafted a letter to Sir Cecil Beaton, which read, "The costumes in *My Fair Lady* were really quite good." My mother wasn't very impressed.

Like her father, my mother was considered to be good-looking, particularly when she was young. It is not known whether she had actually had lovers, although she was thought of as having been somewhat flirtatious at times.

My father found out about her alleged dalliances, whether they had been real or merely imagined. It was my late Uncle Seymour, on whom Nicky and I doted, who foolishly told my father, that he suspected, if erroneously, that my mother might possibly have been "naughty" at times. No-one knows. My father believed Seymour, who was his favourite brother.

My mother was furious with Seymour and vehemently disapproved of any of her children staying in his house. He had a manor house called "Hackwood", in Hampshire. There was a cinema there, as well as an indoor swimming pool.

After I had passed my driving test, I gained access to a Mini Clubman Estate. When I wasn't visiting the Maxwells' house, I went to Hackwood most weekends, in order to annoy my mother. I have always been a rebel. Also, Nicky was often there.

The Macaulays, a large Irish family, stayed at Hackwood as well most weekends. Billy, a farmer and the proud owner of a number of racehorses in Ireland, was head of the Macaulay family. He and his wife, Diana, were horse-crazy.

Billy spoke with a thick Irish accent, and Diana, the youngest of one of my father's sisters, spoke with a refined English accent.

Billy was a fantastically good-looking, mischievous but inclined to be hot-tempered at times. Curiously, he was militantly opposed to the presence of the British in Belfast, so he paid his small daughters sixpence each to sing Irish rebel songs outside the rooms occupied by British soldiers staying at Hackwood as well.

It was Seymour who enjoyed inviting the British soldiers to Hackwood, whenever Billy was visiting, and he did so for purely perverse motives, namely to cause his Irish guest to fly into a rage. Billy reacted in the way Seymour wished him to react.

Billy printed the words of famous Irish rebel songs, in capitals, on A4 paper, to enable his daughters to sing them to the wretched soldiers, disturbing their sleep at seven o'clock each morning.

Among the songs was "*The Wearing of the Green*", "*The Burning of Father Murphy*" and "*The Hanging of Kevin Barry*", which the girls were only able to sing to the tune of "*Clementine*", in maddeningly piping voices.

The comatose soldiers were incensed. By the time they had scrambled to their doors, to find out what was on the other side of them, dragging on their uniforms, the girls had run away.

The Macaulays were a dysfunctional family, in that Diana was said to have had a "drinking problem". When I stayed in their house in Ireland, on several occasions, I never noticed her drinking alcohol. All she consumed was Coke and lemonade. Her daughters resented the problem, however. Billy flew into rages and stated that their mother's drinking habits were "none of their bloody business!"

I will not comment. After all, I was a guest in Diana's house, although I frequently flirted outrageously with Billy, when I was about twenty. Sometimes, I called out, "God you look sexy!" whenever he got out of the swimming pool at Hackwood. He was delighted by my remarks!

I am happy to say that Billy had quite a *penchant* for me. He always rang me up on my birthday, and once, he sent me a saucy letter, saying, "I hope your sex life is proceeding satisfactorily, and that you are keeping a sharp eye to AIDS!"

Also, I wrote a raunchy book, which was based on a character modelled on me and another character modelled on Billy. The book was entitled *The Most Singular Adventures of Sarah Lloyd.* The two characters have violent sex on the floor of Billy's study, in his house in Ireland, when he goes so far as to lick her clitoris!

* * *

William, the eldest, was one of Billy's favourite sons. He was a jockey who rode his father's horses. Before William was about to visit his father's study for inspection, Billy called his son's name.

"Would you be getting your hair cut, son!" commanded Billy.

"Jesus Christ wore his hair long, so why shouldn't I!" retorted the boy.

Billy banged his fist on his desk in a rage, displaying his heavy Irish accent. "Jaysus Chroist may have worn his hair long, but Jaysus Chroist didn't happen to be royden' any of my fockin' hosses!" he shouted.

This story has found its way into both Macaulay folklore and Berry folklore.

Diana had a lover called "Dominic Filmasanki". They often had sex in the back of his sports car. On one occasion, Billy found them, wrenched him out of the car and savagely beat him up. When I heard the story, I couldn't help being impressed by Billy's virility.

Nineteen sixty-eight was a year I remember well. It was not a happy year either, mainly because of recurrent printers' strikes on my father's papers *The Daily Telegraph* and *The Sunday Telegraph*. The conversations between my parents at the dinner table were edged with gloom and fears that our family firm was about to go bust.

Many events occurring during 1968 were major. Some were only minor.

I had just had my eighteenth birthday, and my parents had given me a latch key to open the front door of 18 Cowley Street.

I frequently lost my key and had to stay in other people's houses, which greatly irritated my mother.

I applied for a job as a nanny, in 1968. I was due to work for a family in Bayswater Road, but I was sacked after ten minutes. A stout woman, of about forty-five, let me into her house, without even introducing herself. I gave her my name.

The premises stank of leaking gas, which I pretended to ignore. The woman was wearing a short, pale green, floral dress and plain tights.

"I'm your new nanny," I announced, adding, "Would you please call your children?"

There were only two children. They were aged between thirteen and fifteen. They had been playing football on the lawn, but their ball hit the kitchen window, breaking the glass. They were wearing muddy boots and blustered into the kitchen, knocking crockery over as they ran.

"Would you please take up your positions against the wall, and give me your names. (I had recently seen the film *The Sound of Music*.) Also, please refrain from breaking any more windows and knocking your mother's crockery about, unless you intend to replace it with your pocket money."

"I'm Eric," said the fifteen-year-old. "My brother's name is Joe. He's thirteen and a half."

"Your services are no longer required," said the house owner curtly.

"Why are they no longer required?"

"I don't wish to discuss the matter. Kindly leave now."

"You haven't even sampled my services yet," I said.

The house owner took a while to pick up her contact lenses. She had allowed them to fall onto her dirty linoleum floor. "Would you please leave now! I don't intend to repeat myself, yet again," she said forcefully.

The only pleasant event of 1968, was my introduction to a man to become my dear friend, Robert Maxwell, at his house, Headington Hill Hall, on the outskirts of Oxford.

The date was 10th of June, which was his birthday. I had no idea that his favourite son, had recently been killed in a road accident. It appeared that he saw me as a replacement for his son, who had blonde hair like myself.

This was perhaps why he invariably granted me special favours, which he did not bestow on his other children, with whom he was quite strict.

He, his wife Betty, a very kind-hearted lady, and his many children, lived in a large Bath-stone house, overlooking a sloping lawn, in the centre of which was a circular swimming pool. Next to that, was a sauna, and a hut, in which bathing suits were kept.

Maxwell asked me to call him "Bob". Nicky was particularly interested in him from a business point of view, as he was then Business Correspondent of *The Daily Telegraph*. Bob was a well-known publisher and owner of a company known as *Pergamon Press*, which was up the hill in the same area as his house. Years later, he became the proprietor of *Mirror Group Papers*, encompassing *The Daily Mirror*, which he owned until his death.

Nicky had driven me to his house, accompanied by a rather strange woman called Anne, by whom he was besotted. He wanted to marry her, but she married someone else – a man called David Metcalfe.

Nicky was incensed and turned up at the wedding, and scowled at the bridegroom throughout the service, and made sure that the bridegroom noticed.

Following the wedding, Nicky had lunch with Anne, once a week, in London, and took me with him, to give himself moral support. Also, he was of the opinion that Anne quite liked me. We often went skiing together.

To return to Bob, he was always friendly and welcoming. He danced with me for a while, told me the names of his wife and children, and asked me to put on a "nice, tight-fitting bathing suit!"

"Can you swim, Pussycat?" he asked.

I told him I could, so he picked me up and threw me into the water.

Thereafter, he was particularly kind to me, and asked for nothing in return. Betty, his wife, was also exceptionally good to me.

When I told him I was trying to teach myself Russian, against my parents' wishes, he very kindly gave me an expensive *Pergamon Press* intensive Russian course. It must have cost him an arm and a leg! It was more than what I wanted.

Whenever I saw him, I told him about *The Daily Telegraph*'s and *The Sunday Telegraph*'s printers' strikes and the effect that this had on my home life. I also told him that my mother repeated, over and over again, the possibility of the firm going bust.

"Don't worry. That won't happen," said Bob.

"Why not?"

"It's a complicated matter, I know, and your mother is of a rather hysterical disposition. Just take it from me. Your dad's firm will not go bust. Also, you can stay in my house, at any time, when you feel things are getting rough."

"Thank you so much, Bob."

* * *

It was also in 1968 that there was a vigorous campaign throughout Buckinghamshire to prevent another airport being built. Had it been built it would have been an eyesore. There were several emotive rallies, stretching over a myriad of fields.

The singer Eartha Kitt sang lustily at one of these rallies, and reduced one farmer, after another, to floods of tears.

"We shall not, we shall not be moved…
"They shall not put concrete on our own dear land.
"We shall not be moved!"

The rally was not unlike a Nuremberg rally. The atmosphere was electric.

Generous donations were handed out, by other inhabitants of Buckinghamshire.

My father knew about my friendship with Bob and persuaded me to go to his house and ask him for another donation. He was aware of the fact that Bob would have been more willing to donate to me than to my father.

"How much money do you want?" I asked casually

"Well, a lot of people are giving £5,000."

"I don't think Bob will be prepared to give as much as that. He's not

Onassis you know. However, I will go, daddy. Besides, if I go, there'll be a good chance I'll be given plenty of tea."

"You will? That's really sporting of you! That's my girl!" he replied.

I still hadn't passed my driving test, so the legendary Mr Taylor (name changed as always) drove me to Headington Hill Hall. As Mr Taylor had a rather explosive personality, he and Bob failed to get on. Bob got on badly with most men, although he invariably got on well with women.

I got out of the car and found Bob at the bottom of the drive outside his house. He was even better-looking than before, and I fainted. This delayed the journey home to my parents' house, as I had had to lie down. Finally, I went down to the drawing room, a light, airy room, containing a grand piano and a harp.

"Here's the cheque for your dad," said Bob.

Before I left the house, I surreptitiously went into the downstairs bathroom, and opened the envelope. Because Bob had been so nice, I will not quote the enclosed amount, other than to say it was a bit on the naughty side.

I said, "Goodbye," to Bob and Betty, thanked them and got into Mr Taylor's car. I started a conversation with him, He was angry because he had missed *Dad's Army*.

"What did you think of Mr Maxwell, Mr Taylor?" I ventured.

Mr Taylor seemed pissed off and ground the gears. "No comment!" he rasped.

My father was sitting in front of a log fire, its timbers dwindling. He looked concerned. "What took you so long?" he asked.

"I was delayed. Bob is so extraordinarily good-looking, that I fainted. I had to go to bed for a while."

"Cor-lover-duck!" said my father obscurely, adding, "you women are always fainting. Have you got the money?"

I handed him the envelope containing the cheque, which I had already seen.

"This falls cheekily short of the money which I had been expecting," said my father. "I wanted £5,000 pounds for the bloody Airport Fund."

"It was you yourself who taught me never to extort money with menaces," I replied.

There was a short silence which I broke by quoting the famous song, *Wernher von Braun*, "If ze rockets go up, who cares where zay come down. It's not my department, said Wernher von Braun."

"Tell Wernher von Braun I'd like a word with him about his bloody rockets," said my father tersely.

* * *

In the spring of 1968 Enoch Powell, a dowdy-looking nutcase, whose Birmingham accent was even thicker than a bowl of pea soup, made a lengthy, racist speech, in which he encouraged the expulsion of blacks from Britain, particularly from Birmingham and Wolverhampton, where there had recently been a large influx of black immigrants.

His demented speech (known as his "River of Blood" speech), caused blacks and whites to loathe each other, to such a terrifying extent that the country was almost on the verge of civil war. When speaking about my mother (Lady Pamela Berry), on one occasion, Enoch Powell said: 'One needs a long spoon!"

Enoch Powell is dead now, thank God! He had dementia. Mercifully, most memories of his insane, not to mention dangerous, rantings have faded into obscurity.

The late, and well-known journalist, Peregrine Worsthorne, had been employed by my father to write for *The Sunday Telegraph*. He had written articles of considerable length, each Sunday. Among these was an incredibly ill-judged article, suggesting that he was in favour of most of Enoch Powell's opinions!

It was at this point that my mother came into her own, with all guns blazing. "Peregrine Worsthorne's a Mosleyist!" she shouted at lunch one Sunday.

At one of her *soirées*, to promote my father's trade, she approached Perry, as he was known, and gave him a hell of a ticking-off, while he struggled nervously to put part of a lobster, diced with *mayonnaise*, into his mouth. I stood near them and listened to the one-sided conversation.

Harriet was furious with me. She said I had shown an unhealthy interest in someone else's embarrassment. I thought it was most unwise of Perry to have attended the *soirée* just after he had written the batty article. The beleaguered journalist did not retaliate, and stood to attention with his head lowered. Obviously, he had not expected to be reprimanded so vehemently by his boss's wife. Looking back, I'm surprised my father failed to sack him, taking into account that he had written the article for what was meant to be a "family newspaper".

I won't deny that I had always liked Perry, but I had no idea what the wretched man thought he was doing when he took up his pen and finally handed in his "copy" on that unfortunate occasion. Perhaps he was terribly despondent for some reason, and had deliberately been looking for enough rope to hang himself with.

It is possible, when he had been in his cups, that he might have had an altercation with a black man in a downmarket pub. Alternatively, he could have received a hostile letter from his bank manager.

Also, at about that time, his wife had been suffering from a brain tumour. I can't really imagine him as a genuine racist. He was too meek and gentle for that description.

He and I had a lot of amusing conversations, at launches of Adrian's books in Daunt's Bookshop. Perry was livid when Dominic Lawson sacked him from *The Sunday Telegraph* following so many years' service. He used unbelievably obscene and abusive language, to describe Lawson's personal appearance, which unfortunately, libel laws prevent me from quoting.

The genial journalist and I discussed (just for fun) how best to bump Lawson off. Perry suggested erecting a series of machine guns outside his front door. I suggested (also in fun) on writing the following words on a wall in the gents of an IRA pub, in Kilburn, with a thick felt pen: "Dominic Lawson pleasures himself while eating Irish Catholic babies for breakfast!"

Perry laughed, became very animated, and asked me where I'd got that "extraordinary" idea from. He added, very obscurely, in a pronounced Eton accent, "I say, are you terribly left-wing?"

* * *

I can't possibly write this book, without speaking about my hero, Robert Maxwell, and stating the enormous part he played in my life. Because of his kindness towards me, Bob has permanently been on my mind and in my thoughts until the end of his life. So, for that matter, was my beloved Peachey.

I spoke to Bob's son, Ian, quite recently. He stated that his father had been terrified of my mother! I may have mentioned this before. So far, I thought that the only person Bob had been really terrified of had been his father, Mehel Hoch. The formidable Czechoslovakian peasant had once rubbed his son's face, in his own vomit!

Mehel Hoch frequently beat his son, whose original name was Jan Ludwig Hoch. When the young Hoch was only three, and was desperately trying to race against another child across a stormy river, Hoch lost the race and was gutted.

Added to his humiliation, his father was incandescent with rage, because he had to pull his son out of the water, and get soaking wet, wearing the only clothes he possessed! He gave his son a savage hiding.

I think there was something distinctly *Freudian* about this distressing incident. Years and years later, Bob became morbidly obsessed by Rupert Murdoch of all people, and tried, over and over again, to outsmart him.

Murdoch is hardly a robustly-built figure in the way Bob was, but even so, it is not unlikely that Murdoch could well have represented the child who swam faster than he in the stormy river, in the wilds of Czechoslovakia that day, and got the better of him.

Bob's preoccupation with the unprepossessing, puny, Australian was incomprehensible, not to mention pathological. On one occasion he was informed that Murdoch would be playing poker in a salon in New York. Bob hired the next private jet, and joined his astounded nemesis at the poker table, having insisted on dealing the cards himself.

He won the game several times but still was not satisfied. He took the next plane to London, where he insisted on giving a television broadcast, in which he stated forcefully that *The Sun*, (owned by Murdoch) had always been a "lying newspaper". Again, a psychologist would surmise that he was returning to his childhood, when he was beaten by the faster swimmer. No wonder he said on more than one occasion, "I think I see myself in Eleanor."

This could take us back to Wuthering Heights. "I am Heathcliff."

"Are you still having trouble with Rupert Murdoch?" I asked him once, to jolly him along when he was low spirited. We were sitting by his swimming pool in Oxford.

"Not a chance," he replied vehemently. "Rupert Murdoch is having a lot of trouble with me!"

Very sadly, something in his psyche deteriorated, when his secretary, by whom he was absolutely besotted, buggered off with another member of his staff and wrote a particularly unpleasant book about his boss, after his death. Can you imagine the sheer cheek and cowardice of this person!

His obsession regarding Murdoch grew even worse after that, and somehow, he went bust. I don't know anything about high finance and try as I do to understand this complex and complicated subject, I cannot begin to fathom the agony behind the fall of this giant, ever-giving colossus.

I desperately wanted to see him again, but his family members and members of his staff, dissuaded me, without giving me a reason for his inability to see me.

I will never know exactly what happened before the tormented Hoch boy reached his grave, in the *Valley of the Blessed*. His son, Ian, informed me of a grief suffered by his father during the last week of his life.

He was watching a harrowing Holocaust film through a pair of binoculars, for some reason.

"What are you doing, Dad?" ventured Ian, as he came into the room.

"I'm looking for my mother, and I'm trying to find the train she was put on, when she was taken to Auschwitz," replied Bob.

I don't like to think of Bob being in this terrible state of mind. I like to remember him as the hero who saved my life, by carrying me out of an operating theatre, unscrubbed, like a babe in arms, the hero who showered me with gifts, and the hero who showed me round *The Mirror* holding my hand.

According to her book, Betty was apparently a virgin when they married, and his style was forceful. He wept throughout the act because he regretted the pain he was inflicting on her.

Such an eminently human man he was, despite his faults, so brave, so Churchillian, so kind. I could go on but won't other than to say he was my true Messiah

Education: Prebendal School, Godstowe School, Wycombe Abbey, Sussex University and Joining the Communist Party

Prebendal School, in Aylesbury, Buckinghamshire, was an appalling school from an academic point of view. As in American schools, there were boys and girls in the classrooms. I disapprove of this, because at co-ed schools, pupils tend to be distracted and to be overtly preoccupied with members of the opposite sex, rather than with their studies.

I was very young when I attended Prebendal School, and there were roughly twenty pupils in our class. The teacher was a blowsy, scruffy-looking woman called Mrs Crook. She was about forty-five. She always wore a royal-blue twin set and pearls, and her grey hair looked as if it had been dragged through a hedge.

She was a lousy teacher. One morning, for some reason, best known to herself, she told us all to stand up and give three cheers for the Russians! I think the Russians may have completed some astronomical feat or other. A number of parents complained to the headmistress about Mrs Crook's extraordinary behaviour.

There was little discipline in her class. On one occasion we were asked to read a passage about the life of the poet, Wordsworth, but not once were we told who he was or what he had written.

Mrs Crook's conduct was totally unprofessional. Sometimes, it was almost comical. She was speaking in an exceptionally vague manner about French history, and she appeared to be pretty pissed. In her own words, she referred to "a certain Napoleon Bonaparte", with her speech markedly slurred. Suddenly she rushed from the classroom, to the nearest bathroom.

I nearly always sat next to a lovely-looking, cherubic boy called Simon Derby-Ball, who had a violent reputation in the playground. He frequently knocked smaller boys over, and hit them with sticks, although he never hit girls. He invited about six girls to form what became known as "Simon's gang". I was very keen on Simon, and he chose me to be his "moll". I had a schoolgirl crush on him at the age of nine.

He button-holed younger boys and ordered them to take their shorts off. I am ashamed to say I helped him. We were all reported to the headmistress, a fat, unprepossessing-looking woman, with a long, black moustache. Her name was Miss Duncan.

Miss Duncan called us into her study and told us to line up in front of her. She began by saying, "Where does one normally take off one's clothes?"

"In the lavatory," replied a gang member inanely.

"*In the lavatory?*" repeated the headmistress theatrically. After a few seconds, she asked, "Would you like me to phone your parents, and tell them what you've been doing?"

A particularly impertinent gang member, called Sheila Dart, answered the question. "It would take you far too long to phone our parents, and you would also have a very large phone bill on your hands!" replied Sheila.

In the end, Miss Duncan became bored and dismissed us.

I insisted on sitting next to Simon at lunch every day, and I threw a tantrum whenever I was unable to do so.

* * *

All in all, I despised the Prebendal School, apart from the opportunities I had of sitting next to Simon at lunch and being with him in the playground.

"Do you think I will get into Wycombe Abbey?" I once asked Mrs Crook.

"No," she replied. "You haven't got a chance of doing so." She failed to suggest ways in which I could have bettered myself. I stayed at this dreadful school until the end of the summer term.

* * *

While I was there I was very lonely in the evenings, after I had done my homework. The only children I could play with were my father's chauffeur's son, a boy called Dave Taylor, and the gardener's daughter, Ruth Swithenbank.

It was in later years, when I was about fourteen, that I used to give Dave Taylor hand-jobs in the bushes. He was circumcised and very well endowed. He was about fifteen. We also indulged in minor sexual activities.

Dave's father, Tom Taylor, was gnome-like in appearance, was in his fifties and was basically very kind-hearted, although he had a formidable temper. It gave me enormous pleasure to pour a handful of gravel into his bowl of clean oil, which he was about to pour into my father's car. His rage was superb. When luckless workmen came to do repairs in the house, I liked to jump on top of their cars and loved the sound of cracking metal. They lined up their cups of tea in a row, on top of a plank. I turned each cup upside down. This made a terrible mess on the dustsheets covering the carpets. It also caused an awful smell. The workmen, who had been deprived of their cups of tea, were livid.

* * *

The news regarding Dave Taylor's and my sexual activities with him in the bushes eventually reached my father's ears. He summoned Tom Taylor, Dave's father, to the drawing room. I must admit Dave was very good-looking, particularly as he grew older. It was Nicky who informed me about my father's interview with Mr Taylor. He had been listening from the room next door.

"You sent for me, sir," said Tom, his head lowered and his cap in his hand.

"Yes, it has been brought to my attention that your David has been engaging in sexual activities with Miss Eleanor in the bushes," said my father.

Apparently, the otherwise fiery Tom Taylor shifted from one foot to the other and cleared his throat. "I certainly wasn't aware of that, sir," he eventually managed to mutter.

"I want this behaviour to be stopped immediately!" said my father forcefully.

"I can assure you that this will not happen again, sir. I'll have a word with my son when I get home."

There was little more to be said. Mr Taylor shuffled out of the room.

He himself was very much a ladies' man. All my parents' employees were aware of his dalliances, and they frequently laughed and joked about them.

Mr Taylor had a very timid wife, called Mary, who bitterly resented her husband's promiscuity. Mary was my mother's maid for a while, and went into her boss's bedroom one morning, crying. My mother was rubbing cream onto her face, with a cosmetic smoothing iron, and reading *The Daily Telegraph* at the same time. She knew what her maid intended to talk to her about and didn't want to enter into a discussion about Mr Taylor's sex life. My mother was embarrassed because he had often driven her to the nearest town, which was Aylesbury.

My mother looked briefly from the newspaper's printed page. "Pull yourself together, dear, he'll soon come to heel," she muttered.

Dave Taylor, even as a boy, was a raving sex maniac, like his father, Tom, who was my father's and mother's chauffeur, most of the time. Tom gave his son a blue-painted bicycle for his birthday, and it had a loud, tinkling bell on its handlebars.

Dave used to ride his bicycle up and down the lane, outside his parents' house. The bell made a loud noise, which could be heard by other people who were walking up the lane. He was then about twelve and liked to shout at the top of his voice, "I say, do you know what a gentleman does to a lady, when he wants to have a baby?"

Many members of his unfortunate audience were elderly ladies on their way to the cemetery where they planned to lay flowers on their loved one's graves.

Sometimes, Dave went even further: "Would you like me to roll you in the grass, when you've laid down your flowers?"

Whenever Dave behaved in this manner, Tom spanked him.

* * *

My mother employed another member of staff in our country house. Her name was May Amendie and she used to pass plates round the table. May Amendie was universally disliked. Adrian made the mistake of borrowing money from her, when he was fifteen, and bribing her with sixpence, in return for her addressing him as "sir", when he was only nine.

On one occasion, May tripped over my mother's dog, Max, when she was serving lunch. Potatoes, peas and carrots were spilt all over the floor.

"Oh, Max, oh, my poor, poor, poor little dog, are you alright?" asked my mother, who was deliberately trying to annoy the woman.

"No one asked me if I was alright, madam!" said May.

Like the Taylors, May was also highly sexed. She frequently called out an electrician, having deliberately damaged all the plugs. She used to have sex with him, in a broom cupboard, just outside my mother's bedroom, but my mother was so engrossed in reading *The Daily Telegraph* that she seldom realised what was going on.

After my mother's death, she wrote an offensive letter to my father, saying how much she had disliked my mother.

"May Amendie never made amends!" I joked, after having consumed a few gin and tonics. I thought my joke was brilliant, but my father did not share my opinion.

Harriet and Nicky edited a magazine about the sex lives of members of my parents' workforce. It was printed once a week and it became more and more racy each time. In the end, my father read it. He asked Harriet and Nicky to close it down!

* * *

It's just as well my parents took me away from Prebendal and sent me to Godstowe School, a boarding school, although during my first two weeks there, I was very homesick. I was ten.

I continued to be a naughty child, and I received quite a few detentions each term. I liked the school after I'd settled down, and it was a good school academically.

I was in the "C" stream at first (i.e. the bottom stream), but after I had been coached during the holidays, I was promoted to the "B" stream and finally to the "A" stream, which was the top stream.

Before I went to Godstowe, Harriet taught me the Facts of Life. I was in a dormitory with about six other girls.

The lights had not been turned out. We were sitting on our beds, wearing pyjamas. It was quite cold. It was September 1960.

The girl occupying the bed next to mine was about eleven, and was forthright in her speech and her ways. I could tell that she had been at the school for at least a year.

"Our mothers told us something, before they brought us here. Did your mother tell you anything?" she asked me rather aggressively. I had some idea what she was referring to.

"My mother didn't," I replied, "but my sister did."

"I see. Tell us what your sister told you."

"You're referring to the Facts of Life, aren't you?" I said.

"Yes. Go on. What did your sister tell you?"

I repeated Harriet's words to the girls, speaking loudly so that they could hear my voice. It appeared that Harriet had left something out, however.

"What do you know about menstruation?" asked the eleven-year-old.

"I've never heard of that," I confessed. Because I knew nothing about this subject, I was regarded as a pariah.

"You'd better write to your sister, and ask her what menstruation is!" said the eleven-year-old girl. "Otherwise, you can't be one of us. What school does she go to?"

"Westonbirt. That's in Gloucestershire."

I tried to find out what menstruation was by going through an older girl's drawers during break the next day. Unfortunately, I was caught by the housemistress, Miss Reynolds, whom I will speak about later.

"I've found out something about you which isn't very pleasant," she said obscurely.

* * *

We had a strange headmistress called Miss Webster. She looked like Abraham Lincoln and her fat, black sausage dog, scuttled behind her, wherever she went.

Every day, after lunch, I approached her and begged her to ring for a taxi to take me home.

The first time I did this, she was pleasant and sympathetic, although she gently explained gently that boarding school rules were boarding school rules, and had to be adhered to.

I refused to give up. On about the fourth or fifth occasion, she became angry and told me to go to whatever class I was meant to be attending.

Once I had been at Godstowe for about two weeks, I managed to shake off my depression and settled down. I was particularly good at French, Latin and English, and at the end of the first term, I was top of the class in most of these subjects. Latin was my best subject. I did particularly well because of my coaching during the holidays.

Our house was called Walker House. I made quite a few friends, one of whom was called Rebecca Roberts. Rebecca was very glamorous, and always gave me the audience I craved. She told me about menstruation and prevented me from being a pariah in the dormitory. Like myself, she was in the "A" stream. A vibrant, Persian girl, called Mariam Siassi, was also a good friend of mine. She had thick, wiry, black hair, and large, enquiring brown eyes.

Mariam was obsessed by Elvis Presley, and never stopped putting his records on, and dancing to them, which drove us all potty. She danced seductively in a room known as the "house study" when she wasn't doing her prep.

Her father, Dr Ali Siassi, had retired. He lived in a small, very depressing, north London flat, with his son, Paraviz. Dr Siassi was divorced from Mariam's mother, who looked like a fashion model. Occasionally, she visited Godstowe and Mariam showered her with hugs and kisses.

Mariam's father was short, bald and hot-tempered. Her brother, Paraviz was chinless and had an irritatingly limp handshake. Unlike his vivacious sister, he was a terrible bore, seldom spoke and permanently looked at the floor.

Mariam had a formidable temper, like her father's. She lost it whenever any of the girls referred to her parents' divorce. She got on very well with me but beat Rebecca up at a later date, because she (Rebecca) had flirted with a boy she was keen on, whom she had met at a party.

The Latin teacher, Miss Stainer, was a really good teacher. We were lucky to have been taught by her. This did not deter us from outrageous and mischievous behaviour, however. Rebecca, Mariam, myself and a few others, occupied the dormitory immediately underneath her small and attic-like bedroom. This was during my second term at Godstowe.

Miss Stainer was visited by her boyfriend, John, every night. The acoustics were such that we could hear every sound they made, including the creaking of the mattress, which became faster and faster. We invented a rhyme about this unfortunate woman:

> *"Please put a penny in the old man's hat.*
> *Miss Stainer is conceiving in the upstairs flat."*

One Saturday night, when we thought Miss Stainer would be away for the weekend, we went up to her bedroom to read her love letters from John. These were tied up with red ribbon.

I was accompanied by Rebecca, Mariam and two others, called Anne Welsh and Hélène Biddle. Rebecca was the first to untie the bundle of love letters, which she found in Miss Stainer's top drawer. One of them read:

"Dearest, darling, Brenda,
"I think you are hot, hot, hot! Even when you are in your underwear, I still think you are hot, hot, hot!"

Suddenly, we heard footsteps on the spiral staircase leading to Miss Stainer's bedroom. Rebecca froze and stood still in terror. The rest of us scrambled under the bed. Miss Stainer asked Rebecca what she was doing in her bedroom.

"I was just making sure the room was warm enough."

"A likely tale! Get out of here, you little brat!"

Miss Stainer sat at her dressing table and took about ten minutes to apply her makeup. She rose to her feet, turned the light off and left the room, having complained out loud about the fact that she had not been issued with a key.

We waited for about five minutes, got out from under the bed and went back downstairs.

I didn't find out until years later that Rebecca's sole reason for working so hard, both at Godstowe and Wycombe Abbey, was her fear of being ignored by her father. She worshipped her father, who had suffered from heart trouble for years.

Rebecca had me to stay in her parents' house in Farnham, Surrey, on countless occasions. At that time, I was learning to play the recorder, which is a flute-like instrument, and which makes a terrible noise. The only tune I could play at the time was *"Three Blind Mice"*, which, in my innocence, I thought I played brilliantly.

I am sorry to say that Rebecca's father, George Roberts, did not share my opinion.

Every time I arrived at his house, he left a note in his room, stating, in capitals, "THREE BLIND MICE IS BACK. HAVE GONE FISHING!"

* * *

Every Christmas, Rebecca's parents gave her a New Year party at a hotel called the Hog's Back, somewhere in Farnham, Surrey. By this time, I was still about ten, or eleven, and had met quite a few of Rebecca's friends. I was determined to show off. I need an audience in the way a Chinaman needs rice.

"Three Blind Mice" was no longer the only tune I could play on the recorder. I also played *"Clementine"*, *"London's Burning"*, *"Jingle Bells"* and several others.

I clambered up on top of the grand piano, wearing a pink silk dress with a round white collar. I played all these tunes, but it was impossible for the pianist to make himself heard. In the end, he reached up and lifted me to the floor.

* * *

Mr Roberts finally returned to his family's house after his fishing trip. However, there was one thing and one thing only which endeared him to me. He had found out that I was F.E. Smith's maternal granddaughter. He adulated F.E. Smith, due to his physical beauty, brilliance, unique statesmanship and wit, as well as the many qualities which I have mentioned earlier.

Once Mr Roberts was privy to this information, he became very friendly towards me. Instead of calling me "Eleanor" he called me "Elly".

On one occasion, after I had seen a film which had excited me, I became roused and flirted outrageously with Mr Roberts at breakfast one morning. I was wearing see-through pyjamas and made a series of seductive movements, while looking him in the eye and winking at him.

"I say, Elly!" muttered Mr Roberts. Rebecca sat at the end of the table, giggling. Her mother had left the house early, to work in a citizen's advice bureau.

* * *

When I was at Godstowe, my parents forced me, against my will, to have riding lessons on Saturday mornings. Horses and I have never got on, because they are bigger than I am, as I may have said earlier. My parents wanted me to gain social graces later on in life. I never refused these lessons, because I was afraid of being called a "coward".

Unfortunately, a horse knows when it's got a dickhead on its back. I frequently fell off. Sometimes, I really hurt myself.

The best part of the morning was the welcome journey, back from the riding school, to Godstowe. I was euphoric on these occasions. One day, I completely lost it and repeatedly hit the driver on the head with my riding crop, in time to the catchy piece of music being played on the car's radio.

The driver was ill-prepared and swerved into a ditch. He radioed for another driver to take his place. Later that day, he had a massive heart attack, which killed him outright. I was nearly sent to a borstal, but I was spared this ordeal, because the luckless driver's death coincided with the date of President Kennedy's assassination. Everybody's interest was focused on that subject alone, and not on the driver's demise. I will always remember him. His name was Mr Bowler.

"We'll drink a toast to Lee Harvey Oswald!" I said to some of the girls who had been in the taxi with me, but only lemonade was available. We could hardly have expected alcohol at Godstowe. Don't think I wasn't guilty about the taxi driver's death. I was, and always have been.

Miss Reynolds, the housemistress of Walker House, had severe psychiatric issues. She had forty girls to look after and was unable to cope most of the time. A therapist might easily have diagnosed schizophrenia in this disordered woman. She could also have suffered from bipolar disorder, which I think was more likely. She permanently looped up and down, and her abrupt mood changes must have had a terrifying effect on the children in her care, particularly the very young ones.

She had tight, white curls, and a very witch-like face. She repeatedly delivered inappropriate punishments to many of her girls. For instance, on one occasion, I decided to drink my evening's milk through a chocolate-coated straw. She flew into a rage and forced me to forgo the end-of-term party.

On another occasion, Hélène Biddle, whose name I have mentioned already, was using a torch to read one of Agatha Christie's novels under her bedclothes. Miss Reynolds ordered her to get out of bed, get dressed and walk in the dark to Miss Webster's flat.

Although it was ten-thirty at night, and raining hard, Miss Reynolds made no allowances for whether or not Miss Webster had gone to bed. Hence, Hélène walked outside for about ten minutes, before returning to the house. She told Miss Reynolds that Miss Webster had turned her away because of the lateness of the hour. The following morning, Miss Reynolds appeared to have forgotten the incident.

She had a superb phrase – or sentence, I should say – which she was forever shouting at the top of her voice when any of her girls misbehaved, even if the offence was only minor.

She caught me eating a Mars Bar in the dormitory, after the lights had been turned out. I was then able to hear her wonderful words, which were like pure nectar to my ears, and which she shouted at the top of her voice: "I think you're downright dirty, mean and stinking rotten!"

Due to the fact that these words were often inappropriate, no one took this woman seriously. We all thought she was absolutely barking. She once confessed to Mariam that she was fifty-three, but she looked at least eighty-three. We assumed she was a virgin, and that she had never had any contact with men. To show her ignorance about this sort of thing, she confiscated Mariam's copy of *The Agony and the Ecstasy*, thinking that this book was about the sex act!*

We had a terrific maths teacher at Godstowe. She was superb. Her name was Mrs Thein, and she was a large, Burmese lady with curly, dyed, black hair. She made us work hard and we respected her.

There was something captivating about her. Also, she helped me to get into Wycombe Abbey, together with the coach, whom my parents had hired.

Strangely, Mrs Thein addressed us by our surnames.

"You'll have to pull your socks up, Berry!" she said once.

I took her words seriously and did as I was told for a change.

Mrs Thein also had a burning sense of the difference between right and wrong. If someone had been persecuted, she came crashing down on that person's persecutors. There was a matron at Walker House, called Miss Miller. For some perverse reason, I tormented this wretched woman, by putting up notices which read, "I hate Matron Miller," all over the place.

I really didn't mean to do her any harm, although, sadly, Miss Miller had a nervous breakdown, and left Godstowe at the end of term, in December, 1962, shortly after the Cuban Crisis.

I was not the only person who ruined poor Miss Miller's life. There were others. Mrs Thein gave us all a very stern talking-to and accused us of unprovoked cruelty towards an innocent party.

I felt dreadful about my cruelty to poor Miss Miller, which had originally been delivered in fun. I have tried in vain to find out where she has been buried, if only for an opportunity to lay flowers on her grave.

On another matter, we were forced to read *David Copperfield* during English lessons. I hated it. I sat at the back of the class, reading Gogol's novel, *Taras Bulba*.

---

* *The Agony and the Ecstasy* is the title of Irving Stone's biography of Michelangelo.

The teacher was incensed. "What do you want to be when you grow up?" she demanded.

"A striptease artist," I replied. I was asked to leave the room and was given a detention!

* * *

When Miss Webster told me the glorious news that I had passed my Common Entrance and had got into Wycombe Abbey, I was so bowled over with joy that I leapt onto her back, bringing her to the floor, while her fat, black sausage dog sniffed anxiously around her supine body. She was visibly shaken, and it took her quite some time to get to her feet.

"I'm sending a *frightful* report about you to Wycombe Abbey," she eventually managed to mutter.

There were two reasons why it was vital for me to get into my senior school. One is that most of my friends were there. The other was that my mother had said she would send me to a convent in the Pyrenees, had I failed the exam. Apparently, only French was spoken at the convent, and the girls there were extremely catty. After I had passed the exam, I asked my mother whether she really would have sent me to this awesome place. She replied that she would certainly not have done so, but would have tried to get me into Wycombe Abbey a second time.

She admitted that sending me to a convent in the Pyrenees would have been cruel beyond belief, even bordering on sadism, and that she had only threatened me in this way in order to make me work harder. She stated that all she wanted for me was a decent education, unlike the one she had received.

* * *

Wycombe Abbey, a Protestant school, is in High Wycombe, Buckinghamshire. I was known as "Elly B" there, and was very happy, although many of my contemporaries were not. I worked industriously and got good end-of-term reports. The only subject I was bad at was chemistry. I was very popular but continued to be an attention-seeker, despite my permanent hard work.

There was a universally hated monitor called Hilda Swain (name changed). She was a Shakespeare buff and a terrible bully. She played *Hamlet* in an end-of-term production and acted the part amazingly badly. She looked like an oily skinned dragon, had unnaturally curly hair and was about five foot eight inches tall.

She was too big for her boots and was forever bullying younger girls. She was fiercely ambitious and more than anxious to make her debut in London's West End. The first play she appeared in was *Romeo and Juliet*, which was shown at the Aldwych. She was about nineteen at the time.

As she lay on her back pining for Romeo, an ambulance, with its siren blaring loudly, stormed down the street outside the theatre. Hilda was livid. She had no sense of humour whatsoever. If she had, she would have made a comic gesture of some kind, and had her audience in stitches.

I approached her at a school reunion at a much later date. Even then, a few girls were still adulating her, as if she were a goddess-born. I could not forget the manner in which she had bullied younger girls, who did not have sufficient vocabularies to retaliate.

I poked her in the ribs. "I hear you had a bit of trouble with your *Juliet*, up at the Aldwych!" I said, and laughed loudly. A few other girls of my age joined me, including Rebecca. Hilda sneered at us but was unable to find words crushing enough to sting us.

Years earlier, when Hilda had been a monitor at Wycombe Abbey, I confess that I was not exempt from her despicable bullying. She was seventeen and I was only about fourteen. I am pleased I got my revenge, if only in later years. Had Sir Winston Churchill not believed in revenge, the Germans would probably have won the war.

I was writing an essay about the Jacobite Rebellion. It was a Saturday, and I had been asked to hand it in first thing on Monday morning.

I was at my desk in a room known as the "house study" when Hilda approached me.

"I want you to wash up the tea things," she said curtly.

"I can't. I've got to hand in my history essay, first thing on Monday morning."

"Your history essay does not concern me. It's time you pulled your weight for a change."

"If I fail to hand it in on time, I'll get a detention," I said.

"You haven't heard a word I said, have you?"

"My parents are paying for me to get a decent education," I said. "They're not paying for me to wash things up, which is what the kitchen staff are meant to do."

"You'll do as you're told, if you know what's good for you," said Hilda.

"Sorry, Hilda, I'm afraid I won't, for the reason I gave you."

"You'd better come and see me in the monitors' room," she demanded.

"Not till I finish my essay about the Jacobite Rebellion. Then, and only then, will I agree to see you in the monitors' room," I replied.

Unfortunately, I relented. I never forgave myself. She gave me a savage ticking-off. She had a tongue like an adder.

I was very nearly in tears, but I was determined not to cry in front of her. "You're a bully," I said.

"Would you mind repeating that, please?"

"You heard me."

I walked out. Once I had reached the corridor outside, I cried, but all my friends were waiting for me, supported me and told me how brave they thought I was.

That is why I took my revenge against Hilda at the school reunion in later years, and I remembered my brother Adrian's legendary words: "No sister of mine takes a blow without retaliating."

Incidentally, Hilda's "*To Be or Not to Be*" speech was a miserable and ghastly failure. She sounded like a combination of a debutante giving instructions to a downmarket hairdresser, and a private, pleading not to be executed. The speech was even more deplorable than the speeches she recited throughout the rest of the play. Some of the girls in the audience were in stitches. Their parents were embarrassed beyond belief.

Poor old Hilda simply couldn't act, even though acting had always been her ambition. After her *Romeo and Juliet* disaster, she abandoned the theatre altogether, and got married. Shortly after that, she was accounted for as "getting mixed up in a really sordid divorce". God knows what this entailed!

Hilda had a friend of her own age, another monitor called Margaret Jones (name changed), who was also a Shakespeare buff. She was popular, clever, modest and kind. Younger girls often asked her for her autograph.

Hilda's parents took Hilda and Margaret to a production of Richard III. Hilda sat next to her parents and Margaret sat on Hilda's right-hand side. A highly sexed young man fondled Margaret's thighs. She told Hilda about this in a whisper. Hilda flushed like a housemaid. "Oh, do let me change places with you!" she pleaded.

Margaret had been rather embarrassed by the young man's attention to her and willingly changed places with Hilda. However, once Hilda sat next to the man, and pulled her tights up, hoping that he would fondle her thighs, he showed no interest in her!

Margaret was not catty in any way, but she couldn't resist telling this story to most of the girls in the house, seniors and juniors alike. Hilda had become a laughing-stock, both at school, in her subsequent career, and in her failed sex life.

* * *

My best subjects were French, Latin and English, as they had been at Godstowe. I made up my mind to work hard from the beginning of my career at Wycombe Abbey in order to get decent grades at O Levels. I planned to take my A Levels elsewhere, particularly as Russian was not taught at the school. I was interested in studying Russian even then.

There were too many chapel services, which I avoided. I used the time to devote myself to my studies. I was always unfit, as I still am, and I skipped games as well. I had a particular loathing for lacrosse and tennis but enjoyed cricket because this meant we could sit on the grass and gossip.

I feel most strongly that there should have been compulsory current events classes and newspaper-reading classes. I was very shocked on learning that one of the girls didn't know who the President of the United States was, and she was fifteen! Also, when I was at Godstowe, no one said anything to us about the Cuban Missile Crisis of 1962.

To say that it was not a school's policy to scare the tiny tots is fair enough. Why were we not told, once the crisis had come to an end? When the Cuban Crisis was over, I really shocked my father by saying, in devastating ignorance, "I hear there's been a major war between Russia, Cuba and America!"

* * *

In January 1965, Sir Winston Churchill died, after a short illness. He was ninety. Although I rarely invited my friends home, as I was ashamed of my riches, I brought Rebecca to 18 Cowley Street, so that she and I could watch the funeral cortege from the balcony attached to *The Daily Telegraph's* offices in Fleet Street.

It was a memorable and wonderful occasion. Randolf, Sir Winston's son, followed the coffin down Fleet Street, in the freezing January weather. All my family members were in my father's offices, and when the cortege came past, Rebecca and I wept. Even Nicky, who invariably kept a stiff upper lip, was slightly emotional.

What made the occasion even more moving were the solemn looking men who raised their hats as the cortege passed by, as well as the lowering of the cranes, and the black edges surrounding the railway tickets.

I would like to say a lot more about Sir Winston Churchill's funeral, but I was happy enough to be able to watch parts of it from my father's offices.

Had I had grandchildren, I would have been delighted to tell them what I had seen on that historic day. Rebecca has grandchildren, but I will never know, to this day, whether she has told them about the funeral or not.

What struck me, as well as my family, however, was the shocking way in which the British public turned against the glorious saint, who had saved, not only their country, but most of their lives as well.

* * *

I was fifteen. A certain Suzie Flint was a "friend" of mine, so called. I had no idea that she was a professional conniving and social-climbing liar. I have changed her name, of course. She had once met Nicky and had developed a crush on him. She sucked up to me from one day to the next, pretending to be interested in all the things that interested me.

She told me that she knew my pin-up at the time, the actor, Peter O'Toole, personally, and that she frequently went to his house for tea on Sundays. She also said that he had asked her to bring her friends with her. Being very gullible, I believed her lies.

Finally, I reluctantly invited her to 18 Cowley Street for dinner. Nicky was there, with a girlfriend of his, in whom he was obviously interested.

On returning to Wycombe Abbey, Suzie completely ignored me.

"Have I said something offensive?" I asked her. She didn't answer. We were in the house study. I can remember that she was carrying a ghetto blaster, which was playing Petula Clark's song *"Downtown"*, with its volume turned up. As I walked towards Suzie, she backed out of my presence, singing this dreadful song in time to the music.

Never trust a woman unless she proves herself to be trustworthy, say I!

Later, I asked one of my proper friends, Rebecca, Louise Spencer, Hella

Snelling, Gail Heseltine and Suzanne Corlett, why Suzie had been behaving in this way. "She keeps saying, 'She's so young and I'm so mature,'" I was told. Suzie had added, "All I really want is Nicky, and he's found someone else. Elly B's no longer of any use to me."

We put Suzie in Coventry for three weeks. On Saturdays and Sundays, we were allowed to wear our own clothes. Susie always wore a red woollen mini dress, which was her favourite. She said she had worn it in the presence of film stars, actors and actresses. We didn't believe her and hid the dress under a mattress, in one of the dormitories.

Susie was heartbroken but was too self-conscious to make inquiries. She asked us whether we had seen the dress anywhere. We all said "no". I'm sure she could easily remember what she had said about her wish to seduce Nicky, and use me for this purpose alone. My friends were fiercely loyal, and were incensed by the manner in which I had been dishonoured.

We made up a bonfire in the heart of a wooded area, and, as we got angrier and angrier, we burnt her precious dress.

Susie latched onto Rebecca, not knowing of her involvement in her dress's destruction, and tried unsuccessfully to poach some of her boys.

Susie also loved to be top of the class particularly in English literature, and told everyone that by the time she left Wycombe Abbey, she would know at least five Shakespeare plays "brilliantly". Not a chance. She was expelled!

What really troubled Susie most of all was the fact that Rebecca had been invited to watch the passing of Sir Winston Churchill's cortege whereas she had not.

Later she concocted the most ridiculous story and boasted that she had a new boyfriend called "Dick", who favoured young women wearing lacy white underwear. She frequently imitated this young man's imaginary voice, and her reply. "Oh, kiss me, Dick," which she kept repeating *ad nauseam.*

During the holidays, Rebecca and I invited ourselves to Suzie's parents' flat near Victoria Station. We looked everywhere for signs and photographs of "Dick", as well as letters from him. We found nothing. Dick did not exist! When we returned to the school, Rebecca and I told everybody about this imaginary young man. We had everyone in stitches. Suzie had made a complete laughing-stock of herself.

I made friends with another girl at Wycombe Abbey. She was adopted and her new name was Rae McFarlane. She was tall and had long, black hair, taken back in a slide.

She was a Hungarian refugee, and in 1956, when the Russians invaded Hungary, her mother had tried to escape with her, holding her hand, across the Hungarian border, but in doing so, was shot dead by Russian soldiers.

Rae's original name was "Johannah Weilland", but her foster mother, a staid Presbyterian and Scot, who spoke with a pronounced Scottish accent, and who was permanently clad in dowdy tweeds, forced her to change her name to Rae McFarlane, after her sister.

The girl hated her foster mother. She had no siblings and there was no father figure in her meagre family either. "I do wish I had a daddy," she said on frequent occasions. I was so sorry for her.

She was raised on a farm in Tunbridge Wells, Kent. The unique thing about this girl was that she was a brilliant pianist and composer, which suggested that either her natural mother, or her natural grandmother must have been endowed with this remarkable gene.

Rae told everyone that she was descended from Brahms. This might well have been true, given her talents as a composer.

In later years, she bought a caravan and travelled across the North of England, having given birth to a certain David Millington, a charming young man, said to be the illegitimate son of a "bent copper!" Rae and David had a perfect relationship. She had gained a blood relation, which made her feel more secure, although Rae refrained from sending the boy to school, and preferred to educate him herself.

Strangely no one in our house liked Rae, except me. She was invariably loud and coarse, like a drunken peasant, and had the most dreadful table manners imaginable. Although bad table manners are an anathema to me, and always have been, I encouraged her to behave badly at the table, because her uncouth ways continued to amuse me.

Once, someone had spilt tea, which was trickling through a crack in a table, onto the floor, and causing puddle to form. The housemistress, Miss Donaldson, made a huge scene about this, referring to the puddle as being "hateful" and "revolting". Ray found the situation hilarious and had hysterical giggles.

"You have the manners of a Frenchman!" a monitor called out.

Rae was given a detention.

None of the other girls could identify with the vulgar Hungarian refugee. They went out of their way to avoid her, regardless of her musicianship.

Despite her crudeness, I found Rae fascinating. Not only did she give me free piano lessons, she was also very erudite. Her knowledge of literature was legion. She and I took pleasure in the summer months, sitting on the grass outside the drive, talking about books.

She got into the Royal Academy of Music but was thrown out because she had become addicted to heroin. She and I also fell out soon after that, but our quarrel had nothing to do with drugs. I have written about her in my novel, *My Old Pal Was a Junkie*, which is available all over Russia as well as Britain. Although Rae had been a friend of mine at school, she turned out to be a thoroughly bad lot. She had also been a friend of Rebecca's for a short period of time, but she disgraced herself in the Roberts' household. She flirted outrageously with two of Rebecca's boyfriends, and stole a gold pill-box into the bargain. She pocketed the pill-box on leaving the Roberts' house early one morning.

It was entirely Rae's fault that she and I fell out. I had not interfered with her drug-taking and had never poached any of her many boys. She told me, quite out of the blue, that she wanted nothing further to do with me, and that she never wished to see me or to hear from me again. I think this was because I reminded her of Wycombe Abbey, which she hated. I also attributed her behaviour to her unpredictable Slav blood.

My mother did not care for her either, although Rae had been well-mannered and had dressed smartly when they met . When I asked my mother what she did not like, about her particularly clammy handshake, she replied, "She must have a very heavy touch on the key-board," in her characteristic and low voice.

As I had not provoked Rae, I got my own back on her by writing the recently mentioned book and sending her a copy. It was not very flattering! I'm sure she received it, but she didn't acknowledge receipt of it. Nor did I expect her to do so.

* * *

The housemistress at Wycombe Abbey was called Miss Donaldson, and our house, Wendover. Although she was disliked, particularly by Miss Fisher, the headmistress, as well as by my mother, I think she basically meant well and intended to help the girls in her care.

Miss Donaldson was known to many of the girls as "Donalbain". She was about forty-eight, and was hardly a snappy dresser. She wore the same dull, grey dress, from one day to the next, suggesting that she had bought it in an Oxfam shop.

Her grey hair was cropped closely to her head, and she had staring blue eyes, but, redeemingly, a beautiful nose. Her voice was deep and military. When she was in a rage, she sounded like a cuckolded colonel.

Miss Donaldson found out that I had failed to keep a number of minor rules, and she called me into her study one evening at bed-time.

"I can just see it coming," she said, in a theatrical tone of voice.

"See what coming?" I asked.

"Years hence, I know I will pick up my newspaper, and will see the headline, 'Eleanor Berry in Prison'."

It took me a while to find an appropriate answer. "Which newspaper do you think you will be looking at?" I asked eventually.

On one occasion, when I had been given a detention, Adrian came to pick me up when it was over. He was going through a most eccentric phase of wearing a white, rubber mackintosh, thigh-high, black leather boots and a whip which he cracked at regular intervals. He stood in the hallway of Wendover House Hall, doing just that, for about half an hour. Because he was so good-looking, girls walked past him, ogling him. "That's Eleanor Berry's brother!" exclaimed some of them, "He's come to collect her after her detention."

Very regrettably, Miss Donaldson was forever imposing amateur psychoanalysis on many of her girls. She inadvertently caused some of them to develop mental illnesses when they grew older. She cross-examined Rebecca and me about our relationships with our fathers, and even went so far as to ask me whether my father had ever abused me! She had quite a lot to say about my relationship with Adrian, as well.

"Is that bitch giving you any more trouble?" Adrian asked me once, in a moving and brotherly way, just before the beginning of the summer term of 1967.

I told my parents about Miss Donaldson's *penchant* for the psychoanalysis of some of her girls, and in particular, the extremely improper question she had asked me. They were very angry. My father drove at speed to the school and asked to see Miss Fisher. After a ten-minute wait, his request was granted and Miss Donaldson was given a formal written warning.

* * *

Long after Hilda Swain's departure from the school, some of the older girls were looked up to and admired, if they had had sex or had indulged in any form of sexual activity. This was referred to as "scoring".

I told some of my friends about my dalliances with Dave Taylor, and my hand-jobs with him in the bushes. I walked arrogantly down one of the corridors, accompanied by several girls.

"Elly B's scored!" shouted one.

"With my father's chauffeur's son!" I shouted loudly.

"With her father's chauffeur's son!" some of the girls called back.

At that time, Rebecca and I, who were both about fifteen, were the only girls of our age who had "scored", and we were given film-star status.

I was regarded as a heroine, because I had broken the class barrier, like Lady Chatterley. Rebecca, on the other hand, had only indulged in upmarket sexual contacts. Her boyfriends were mainly Etonians. She was rather cross when I pointed this out to her, namely that I had broken the class barrier, whereas she had not.

"I dare you to strip down to your B squared* and knickers and recite lines from *Romeo and Juliet* in the drive!" she said confrontationally, adding, "I bet you can't do Juliet in the balcony scene."

I rarely say "no" to a dare. I had been made to learn passages from Shakespeare, whenever I had been naughty as a child, as we all had, but lines from *Romeo and Juliet* had never been my *forte*. I only know about six lines from the play, so I refused to accept the dare.

* * *

It was soon after that, that I joined the Communist Party. I was aged between fifteen and sixteen and had immersed myself in the study of Russian literature, because its moribund tones had always attracted me.

I read Maxim Gorki's pre-revolutionary novel *The Mother*, which describes

---

*   B Squared: was the slang word for "bra" at Wycombe Abbey.

young, vibrant, male factory workers in urban, late nineteeth century Russia, and their deeply protective relationship with a downtrodden, illiterate, old woman, known as *The Mother*.

She is the mother of Pavel Vlassov, one of the factory workers whose father was an old drunk. Working conditions in the factory are poor, and the workers, all of whom are of a heroic disposition, are copper-bottomed left-wingers.

I read the book twice, was profoundly moved by it, and became a starry-eyed Communist overnight! Being a socialist was not enough for me. I had to be a Communist. I found out the address of the Communist Party's offices and asked them to send me a form, which they did, almost immediately. I filled in the form straight away, and, using very flowery language, I pledged my allegiance to the party. Unwisely, I also supplied the address of my school, and within about a week, I received a very polite letter, worded as follows:

"Dear Comrade Berry,

"Try as we did, we were unable to find your house. We would be grateful if you could please give us clearer details about your whereabouts."

I didn't want these people to descend on a public school, so I wrote back to them, saying that I was not living at any fixed address, because I was travelling round the country, in order to get in touch with the proletariat.

Somehow, I received my membership card, even though the comrades still couldn't find my address.

I attended a few Communist Party meetings during my school holidays. These took place in a windowless hall somewhere in Westminster, near my 18 Cowley Street address.

Just before the meetings, I brushed my hair and caused it to fall untidily over my face, obscuring most of my features. I wore a shabby, old blazer with *The Thoughts of Chairman Mao* protruding from one of its pockets. I also carried a rolled-up copy of *The Daily Worker* under my arm.

I was still at Wycombe Abbey, although it was my last term. When I left the school, aged about seventeen, to do my A Levels, I was absolutely heartbroken. It was at Wycombe Abbey that I had been my happiest, because of the camaraderie of the other girls, and the opportunity to talk to them about Russian literature, and books in general.

I continued to attend Communist Party meetings a few times a week. Somehow, I don't know how, I was photographed in the *Tatler* (an upmarket fashion magazine), wearing my best clothes.

Ever since, my mother nicknamed me "*Comrade Tatler*", which she was forever teasing me about.

* * *

I continued to be friendly with Miss Fisher, the headmistress of Wycombe Abbey. She was about forty, tall and slim, and was the niece of the Archbishop of Canterbury.

Mercifully, she never found out about my having joined the Communist Party. Somehow, I thought it would have been disrespectful to her, were I to confess that I had done so.

Suddenly, she asked me, "Do men fall for you in droves?" I thought her question was most unusual. I did not wish to tell her about my sexual dalliances with Dave Taylor and my occasional one-night stands, so I said, untruthfully, that they didn't.

"I like you because you're so odd, and I'm sick and tired of being surrounded by people who are normal!" she exclaimed suddenly.

That does not alter the fact that she had once said that I was a "first-class pest" because of my habit of skipping games.

Some Events in My Mother's Life

My mother was known universally as "Pam". First, she was known as "Pam Smith", then, on marrying my father, Michael Berry, as "Pam Berry". Finally, she became "Lady Hartwell", because my father was granted a life peerage by a Labour government headed by Harold Wilson in 1968, and she also took the title. She had "Lady" in front of her name all her life, because her father, F.E. Smith, had become the Earl of Birkenhead, as I mentioned earlier.

In her adult years, she was a lover of the arts and a Trustee of the British Museum. She was also on the Committee of the English-speaking Union. She was formerly Chairman of the Incorporated Association of British Fashion Designers.

Her father, F.E. Smith, claimed that he had started his career at the bottom of the ladder. He was a fanatical sportsman, a huntsman, a keen tennis player and a lover of the chase. He was only fifty-eight when he died, which I have said before.

During his rather short life, he was reputed to be a famous wit, a brilliant barrister, who apparently had never lost a case, and a prominent statesman. He also became Secretary of State for India, and finally Lord Chancellor, which was his boyhood ambition, according to the biography written by his son Freddie.

Lamentably, he did not consider it important for pretty girls to go to schools with high academic standards. That is why my mother suffered so much humiliation in her later years, and spent her time reading "improving books" to better her mind.

Due to her inadequate schooling, she saw to it that her children received a decent education. She was both a bully and a tyrant, but had she not hired a formidable task master of a coach, who made me work for eight hours a day, during my school holidays, I would never have got into an academic school, such as Wycombe Abbey, and afterwards into Sussex University. I don't think I would have got a BA Hons degree (a 2:2) in English, and I certainly don't think I would have been able to write so many books, and derived so much pleasure from doing so.

My mother's second problem was her terror of my father's demise. He fainted once in the offices of *The Daily Telegraph* and she thought he had died. Later, she went to her room and sobbed all night. Only Harriet, who has a reasonably soothing effect on hysterical parties, was able to calm her down to some extent. This did not alter the fact that a doctor was asked to visit the house and give her a shot of *diazepam*.

Even when my father had a sore throat once, and lay under a blanket on a *chaise longue* outside the villa, on a balcony, she was in floods of tears and approached Adrian and me. We were sitting at a table, busily writing our books. Adrian was using a laptop and I, as always, was using a pen and paper. I hate laptops. I've got a phobia about them. I don't know why.

"He really isn't at all well," my mother said to Adrian. There were tears on her cheeks.

Adrian was irritated. He tapped his keys furiously. "He's perfectly alright. There's nothing wrong with him," Adrian replied, and continued to tap his keys.

Unfortunately, I inherit my mother's hysterical disposition and also her obsessive-compulsive disorder, as I'm sure I've said before. I kept looking at my father. First, I frenziedly looked at my papers. Then I stared at my father as before.

"Why the hell do you keep looking at him?" asked Adrian in an exasperated tone of voice. "Get on with your writing! Also, you're interfering with my writing."

Shortly after my mother's death, my sister-in-law Marina beckoned me into the room she shared with Adrian, and sat me down on the bed. She was very sympathetic and wanted to talk to me about her difficult, late mother-in-law, to whom she had invariably been very tactful.

"Do you think she was happy?" asked Marina.

"No," I replied.

* * *

When he was about fourteen, Adrian had been listening outside the drawing-room door in our London house. A row was taking place between my parents. It was Adrian who told me this story, to jolly me along.

"Did you spend the night with him?" shouted my father.

"Oh, no, no," replied my mother.

Apparently, they had been arguing about a certain Alastair Forbes, who had had some connection with *The Spectator* at the time.

"If I find out the truth, I'm going to divorce you!" threatened my father.

Adrian then explained to me the difference between love and lust. He told me that he had occasionally had extra-marital dalliances, and that Marina, too, had done so. "There's nothing wrong with lust, as long as it is not brought into the marital home, and as long as it's discreet," said my brother.

On this occasion, I felt very warmly towards Adrian. This conversation had taken place in 1986, when I was depressed because I was out of work. I hadn't started my writing career in a serious way, at that time.

My father, on the other hand, was a member of the old school. He did not approve of extra-marital dalliances.

In later years, my mother became an exemplary and loyal wife. She was strongly averse to ribaldry of any kind. Indeed, no one could have rebuked impropriety more vehemently than she.

Some time ago, I left a pornographic magazine on my bedside table in our villa in the south of France. It was entitled *Cock Rings, Fetters and Whips*. Its cover showed a few men in body-covering black leather; with their sex organs protruding from them. The cover was really erotic, in my opinion, particularly as their sex organs were erect.

My mother picked up the magazine and whitened. "All I want to do now is go and have a cold shower!" she exclaimed obscurely.

"There's no need. There's plenty of hot water in the house," I replied. She stormed out of the room, slamming the door behind her.

My mother had always been a compulsive pill-popper, as had my aunt Eleanor. Both sisters lined pills up in rows by their beds. A doctor was called out when my mother was ill and closely examined her many bottles, at my father's request. "There's only one bottle here which is actually harmful," said the doctor.

I too, am a "pill-popper", which is a hereditary trait, although none of my pills are recreational. My mother came into my bedroom, shortly before she died.

"Darling what in the world are all these pills?" she asked. "I mean what the Dickens are they all for?" She was merely projecting a side of herself onto me

F.E. Smith, too, had a pathological fear of illness, although there is no record in Freddie's book about his having pills lined up in rows by his bed.

* * *

Before my father met my mother, at an Oxford lunch party, he had a walk-about with a woman called Honor (Guinness, I think). My mother never stopped cross-examining my father, about the nature of his relationship with this woman. She appeared to be very jealous of her, even during later years.

"Don't push your luck!" she shouted, whenever my father mentioned her name.

When Honor died, my mother showed compassion, and said to us all, "We must be very nice to Daddy today, because Honor's just died."

At the beginning, and even during her marriage to my father, my mother was a voracious reader of "improving books", to better her general knowledge and to make up for her poor education. I have stated this earlier.

My father was impressed by her skills as a conversationalist, and also on hearing a story about her behaviour at the nursery table, aged eight.

"Little girls should only speak, when they are spoken to," her nanny had said forcefully.

"If everybody only spoke when spoken to, there wouldn't be any conversation, would there?" retorted the cheeky charge.

My mother had always been spoiled rotten by F.E. Smith, who had denied her nothing. She was his youngest child. She had two older siblings, called Eleanor and Freddie, as I mentioned earlier. My father, too, spoiled my mother to some extent, although there was a limit to his tolerance of her wayward behaviour.

On one occasion, they were in a hotel, where she locked herself in a bathroom and refused to emerge, until my father kicked the door down. She had long nails in those days, and clawed furrows on both his cheeks, making him look like a member of a bizarre African tribe. In return, he put her over his knee and spanked her.

Her elder sister, Eleanor was equally as wayward, when she wasn't bringing gypsies to her father's house. She used to sit on benches in other people's gardens, after their houses had been sold. Also, she and my mother fought continuously, and persisted on throwing used ashtrays at each other, in F.E. Smith's library.

"What was my aunt Eleanor really like?" I once asked my mother.

"Oh, she was a *very* queer lady!" my mother replied, her voice as low-pitched as ever.

The sisters' elder sibling, Freddie, had a dry sense of humour and a sardonic tongue. Sometimes, he could be as frightening as the very brushes of Hieronymus Bosch.

I was dining alone with Freddie on one occasion, and decided to talk to him about Russian literature, practically the only subject I knew anything about at the time.

I decided to kick off with Tolstoy and spoke about what I thought was one of his axioms. Freddie rocked backwards and forwards in his chair. This showed that he suffered from severe depression. I knew nothing about this, because no one had told me.

His action of rocking backwards and forwards was extremely unnerving. It reminded me of the way in which barristers walk up and down in court.

"I can't hear you," Freddie said eventually. "Speak up! You're not talking to an ant."

I raised my voice and repeated what I thought was Tolstoy's axiom.

He continued to rock backwards and forwards and had a swig of cider. "That's not Tolstoy, you ass! That's Turgenev!" he stated forcefully.

"Oh, I'm afraid I didn't know that. I'll make a note of it."

There were occasions when my mother put me on a diet. The copious tea trolley, was wheeled into the library at five o'clock.

"What will you have?" Freddie asked me. I took a modest celery stick.

"Don't be so damned wet!" He exclaimed. "Have some chocolate cake!"

Freddie was not a harsh person fundamentally. He could be very sentimental. He wept piteously all the way through the film *Lassie Come Home* whenever he saw it. He was known by his friends and acquaintances to be an extremely hospitable and generous host and a man of great charity. Apart from intellectual books, he loved reading about naked women.

There were times when his behaviour was outrageous. When lunch was about to be served, he frequently stripped off and dived into the swimming pool. However, he suffered from acute melancholia for most of his life, because he felt unable to live up to his father's gigantic image. I didn't know about his melancholia until after his death, which was caused by pneumonia.

He had occasional outbursts of alcoholism but usually confined himself to cider. On one occasion, when he had consumed something much stronger, he ended up, plastered, in a bedroom owned by a local cottager! His wife, Sheila, was very embarrassed and coaxed him home. She took one arm, and his butler the other. Apparently, Sheila married him because she was turned on by his gloomy fits. He reminded her of Mr Rochester!

Freddie and Eleanor loved travelling throughout Spain and sometimes Eleanor contributed towards amateur bull-fights, when she wasn't mixing with gypsies and scaring her family to death. Most of her books are about gypsies and travelling circuses, which were her passion.

Once, she told her bemused family that she had just got married, and she eagerly led them to a lion-tamer's tent in a circus. She told her family that the lion-tamer was her husband!

"You will all have to excuse me, I'm afraid I must go and feed my lions," said the baffled lion-tamer.

It was to my mother's and her sister, Eleanor's credit that they were both fiercely loyal to those whom they loved. They took up the cudgels for their dearest friends, when they felt they had been insulted or slighted.

This trait is shown in my mother's extreme loyalty towards her close friend, and former paramour, Lord Rothschild, whom she felt had been slighted.

I will cover this matter later on in this book.

* * *

As I mentioned earlier, both my mother and her father had fearsome tempers and were averse to impropriety of any kind.

To give an example of this characteristic, a friend of my late brother Adrian came to dinner at 18 Cowley Street and consumed a massive amount of *Pimms*, causing him to become absolutely legless.

The unfortunate guest had the misfortune to be sitting next to my mother. He was unaware of her explosive personality. "When I'm short of a woman, I just toss off into a sock!" he boomed vulgarly.

My mother was struck dumb. "Do you mind?" she shouted.

The above incident shows that my mother could sometimes be an awful tease towards Adrian's friends. Whether or not this trait was due to jealousy will never be known.

Adrian often brought his friend, the late writer, Dennis Wheatley, to 18 Cowley Street. I cannot for one moment, refer to Wheatley as a stunningly accomplished writer. His books are very long and his prose is questionable. His themes are concentrated on black magic and similar matters. He states in one instance, in a particularly banal manner, "The four friends held hands," presumably to keep evil spirits away.

Poor old Wheatley was grossly overweight and was wearing an ill-fitting tweed suit on his visit. He sat in an armchair opposite my mother. Adrian sat nervously in a corner of the room. It was winter and a fake fire was burning in the grate.

My mother started the conversation, not intending to overtly humiliate her guest, as he had not provoked her in any way. She intended to tease him, however. "I put *your* books on the left-hand side of the fire, and Ian Fleming's books on the right-hand side!"

It was fortunate that Dennis Wheatley had a sense of humour. Had someone spoken about my books in this manner, I would have left the room, slammed the door behind me and stormed out of the house. In fact, I would have been so incensed, that I would have written my hostess a punitive letter, and advised her to try writing a book herself!

* * *

Despite her love for getting into fiery arguments, in a naughty sort of way, my mother's outbursts of extreme jealousy and recurrent obsessive thoughts, caused her to be a troubled woman at times. The following incident proves this point.

The late Cyrus Sulzberger, an American and a prolific writer of very long books, was Marina's father. He was a gentle person who never offended anyone, although he was slightly eccentric. He once expressed a wish to take Jonathan fishing in Scotland one summer. The boy was about ten. Mr Sulzberger had not seen his grandson for about five years, and Jonathan really wanted to go fishing with him.

My mother, on the other hand, nagged Marina excessively and said how unfair it was, because it would have meant that she would not have been able to have Jonathan, and his sister, Jessica, all to herself in the villa in the south of France that summer.

The argument between my mother and Marina was tedious and continued for about twenty minutes. My mother even went so far as to tell Marina how lucky she was to have such a chivalrous husband as Adrian!

This was obviously out of order, particularly as a plan to take Jonathan fishing in Scotland, had nothing whatever to do with my brother. Also, the remark was below the belt.

Eventually, my mother showed a modicum of sense and reason, and said to Marina, "Why don't you invite your father to the villa, bringing his fishing tackle with him? That way, everyone could be together, and he and Jonathan would be able to fish in the bay of St Tropez, which is far less gloomy than Scotland?"

Ironically, like Robert Maxwell, my mother had a pathological fear of loneliness. It's almost as if they had been related, but I know they definitely had not.

My mother's possessiveness, fear of her beloved husband's demise, anger because of her lack of education as a child, and her seeming inability to write books, unlike her siblings, caused her to be a tormented spirit, although I hope her troubled state of mind does not last for the rest of eternity. Provided she has access to plenty of children, all of them blood relations, whose presence she can cherish, I cannot see her being consumed by permanent hellfire. That is, if one believes that hell exists.

* * *

Jonathan, my late brother Adrian's son, is the father of two sons and two daughters. Two of his daughters, Olivia and Charlotte, aged about six and seven at the time, repeatedly saw a dynamic-looking female figure at the end of their bedroom, at our villa in the south of France. This incident occurred at two o'clock one morning.

It has not been easy for me to interview these girls, as they have both given me conflicting views about the entity. One of them said that the vision was that of a beautiful, but much older, woman, looking benign and friendly.

The other girl said she was looking angry as well as friendly, at the same time! I dread to think how this girl would fare in a witness box! In common, though, both girls admitted to being frightened of the apparition, despite its alleged friendliness.

There is another room, in a different part of the villa, occupied by Jonathan and his wife, Aurélie. Although Jonathan has not seen anything, Aurélie has definitely seen a similar figure to that observed by her daughters. Of note is the fact that Aurélie never met my mother.

It is possible that the dead woman may have had an affinity for Jonathan's children, although she had never met them. It could well be the case that she was trying to reach out to them.

Everyone is afraid of ghosts, whether they are malignant or benign. Perhaps Jonathan's daughters will see the entity again and be comforted by it. I think the entity itself would be overjoyed by the prospect of seeing these children, without frightening them, but the overall question is: Do ghosts exist or don't they?

Leslie Smith – My Mother's Wayward Cousin

The majority of my maternal family members were respectable. I will not go into details about who they were. There was one black sheep among them, however.

A certain Leslie Smith, who was F.E. Smith's nephew and my mother's cousin, fitted into this category.

Leslie Smith was totally amoral. In fact, he asked both my father and Freddie to pay for his lavish hotel bills, including a suite at the Ritz, where he stayed for at least three weeks!

Leslie Smith's behaviour was at its worst when he visited his aunt (my maternal grandmother, that is) in her Northamptonshire house, carrying an empty plastic sack under his arm.

When his aunt's butler opened the door, he asked the butler if he could see his aunt on what he referred to as "urgent" business.

The butler explained that his boss was in the bath, but that she would be ready to see him shortly.

He ushered Smith into the drawing room, and offered him some sherry, before retiring to another room, to prepare his boss's lunch.

Smith took no chances. It did not take him long to find out where his aunt kept her silver. He seized the lot of it, shovelled it into the plastic sack, and left the premises.

He threw the sack containing the silver into the back of a van, which he had parked near his aunt's house.

Apparently, Smith was keen on horses and wished to start a riding school. He used his aunt's silver to raise money for this purpose.

Having committed the robbery, Smith approached his dumbfounded uncle, F.E. Smith, and asked him for a reference! Unfortunately, I don't know what situation Smith had been looking for.

Apparently, F.E. Smith's reply was, as always, extremely witty, but most uncomplimentary about his nephew.

"My dear fellow, if you can't make an honest man out of my nephew, I don't think anyone can!"

Joseph Severn, My Mother's Ancestor

There is a positive, rather than negative, side to my ancestry. I had a very distant ancestor called Joseph Severn. He was a dear friend of Keats, the poet, who was terminally ill for most of his adult life with tuberculosis. As there was no cure for this disease in the illustrious poet's lifetime, his death was horribly slow and painful.

Joseph Severn nursed the dying Keats throughout his prolonged illness, and not once did he leave his bedside.

He has always been regarded as a hero in my family's folklore.

My Mother and the New York Taxi Driver

In the autumn of 1968, during an American presidential campaign, my mother and I were in the back of a New York taxi. My mother told the driver that she wished to go to an art gallery. The taxi driver, a taciturn, *Midnight Cowboy* type, chewed gum rhythmically. His facial expression in the mirror was foul-tempered and bored.

"Who do you think's going to win this election?" asked my mother, her voice characteristically loud and shrill.

The driver spat his stale gum out of the window and ran his hand through his greasy, blond hair, before wiping his nose with his sleeve. "Nixon, I guess," he replied. "But I wish to hell Wallace* would win."

"Wallace? Wallace? How could you possibly want him in? I think he's to the right of Adolf Hitler!" shouted my mother.

The driver put his foot on the brake. "Aw, can it, lady!" he exclaimed. He pulled into the side of the road.

"What's going on?" asked my mother.

"I guess this is where you both get out, lady. I don't like your politics and I can't stand your clipped British rasp!"

My mother and I got out of the cab. She paid the fare, without tipping the driver. She deliberately left the back door open so that the driver would have to get out and close it.

"I don't like your manners, and I don't care for your grating, southern twang," she said.

"I'm from Brooklyn, actually, lady," replied the driver.

---

* George Wallace was the controversial, extreme right-wing governor of Alabama. He was a roguish, controversial figure, whose favourite statement was, "Come here and I'll autograph your sandals!"

My Mother Keeping a High Profile
and Attracting Attention in the Street

I was about nineteen and was preparing to go to New York on study leave. It was a fine autumn morning. I was outside my parents' house, 18 Cowley Street, and was about to get into a taxi bound for Heathrow airport.

Apart from my suitcase, I had two carrier bags with me. These were full of books. My mother came out of the house, into the street, wearing a pink bath towel dressing gown. She was frantically rubbing rejuvenating cream onto her face with a cosmetic smoothing iron.

She picked up the two carrier bags with her other hand, intending to throw them onto a skip. She also pulled out a book, which was part of J.R.R. Tolkien's trilogy, *The Lord of the Rings*.

"Tolkien? Tolkien?" she exclaimed at the top of her voice. "What does a grown girl like you want to read Tolkien for? All he ever wrote about was pixies!"

She continued to rant, her loud, carrying voice reverberating down the street, whose inhabitants pulled aside their lace curtains in abject curiosity.

"You *won't* be eccentric in America, will you darling?" boomed my mother. "Because if a girl's eccentric, the person to be blamed for her eccentricity, will be her poor, wretched mother!"

Giving Robert Maxwell a Hard-Boiled Egg

During a family get-together, Nicky asked my mother whether it would be possible to invite Robert Maxwell to lunch the following Sunday.

"I'd like to know why he wants to buy the *News of the World*," he said.

"Certainly not this Sunday," said my mother. "Adelaide Jesus has got to go to Barbados, to attend a funeral then."

"Who the hell's Adelaide Jesus?" asked Nicky.

"She's the cook. Didn't you know that?"

"No. I saw a woman in the kitchen, once, but I had no idea she had a wacky name like 'Adelaide Jesus'!" said Nicky.

"Adelaide Jesus is no stranger a name than Nicholas Berry," said my mother angrily.

"Can't we hire someone while she's away?"

"No. All we've got is Dot, a seventy-two-year-old dear, who's just about capable of boiling an egg," said my mother, adding, obscurely, "One can't give Robert Maxwell a boiled egg for lunch. He's so peculiar and sensitive, he might totally misconstrue the situation!"

To this day, no one, and I repeat, no one, can understand this remark.

The Daily Worker

My mother once saw me reading the *Daily Worker* in a smart Mayfair hairdressers which she often frequented. I was in my late teens.

"Where did you get this?" she asked.

"I bought it," I replied proudly.

"Why did you buy it?"

"Why? I like its contents, I like its editorials and I like its reasoning," I said, my voice raised.

The manager did not take kindly to what he witnessed. "I can *see* she won't be coming in here again!" he said unpleasantly.

My mother lowered her voice. "Oh, I do have an *awful* lot to put up with," she muttered.

On leaving the salon, she spoke very loudly about the perils of Stalin's collectivisation programmes.

Suddenly she said, "Lady Thornycroft, the Marchioness of Salisbury and Lady Rothermere were all in there today. You've made a laughing-stock of us both!"

Added to this, she noticed that she had a parking ticket.

Rococo Museum in Cologne

My mother and I were sightseeing in Cologne, in Germany, in 1968. She particularly wanted to see a Rococo museum, but it was shut because it was a Sunday.

"There is a lodge near the museum, occupied by the museum's caretaker," said our driver in halting English. "There is a chance that he will be able to arrange to have you let in."

My mother peered through the window of the lodge and saw a middle-aged man who was fast asleep at his desk, his head resting on his arms.

She tapped on the window. The man woke up with a start and opened the door. He automatically assumed, for some reason, that my mother was British. "What do you want?" he asked, in English.

"We have come all the way from London to see this museum. The guidebooks say it is open seven days a week," said my mother. She told the sleepy caretaker that she was a trustee of the British Museum in London, and that she intended to return to London that evening.

The caretaker rubbed his forehead with his sleeve, and reluctantly said he would do whatever he could to enable us to be shown round the museum.

He picked up his phone, dialled a number and, once his call was answered, he barked harsh, incomprehensible orders in German.

Within roughly five minutes, a young man of about eighteen walked purposefully towards the lodge. He had piercing blue eyes, was wearing lederhosen and his blond hair was cropped closely to his head, like a Nazi's. He looked pissed off.

The caretaker took a long time to unlock the door leading to the museum. He was still only half awake and was holding a considerable number of keys.

The young man, in the lederhosen, showed us into one massive, high-ceilinged room after another. The walls were richly painted and covered with ostentatious gold fretwork. The ceilings showed a bombastic display of plump, purple-buttocked cherubs, tweaking lyres against a background of fluffy white clouds.

God knows why my mother wanted to see all this!

"There is one last room for me to show you," said the young man aggressively. He took us into another immense room, which had not been maintained for many years. The fretwork on the walls was covered with dust, which caused my mother to clear her throat loudly. As she continued to clear her throat, particles of dust fell to the floor from the walls.

The windows were filthy. There was a pile of rubble on the floor in the centre of the room, and a substantial hole in the ceiling.

"I say, this beautiful Rococo room could do with a bit of restoration, what!" said my mother, her voice raised.

The young man became overtly hostile. "I am afraid it is completely beyond repair. It was bombed by the British. Isn't it a shame?"

My mother, a fervent patriot, had always despised Germans. She lost her temper. "A shame? A shame?" she bellowed. "If it hadn't been for what the British did during the war, you would now be living under Hitler's and Eva Braun's children!" She continued, "perhaps you wouldn't consider that to be such a shame, after all. What? What?"

The young German whitened dramatically. I was terrified he was going to be sick. He turned on his heels and raced out of the museum, putting as much distance between himself and my mother as he possibly could.

The Lavatory at Checkpoint Charlie

Nineteen seventy-two was a particularly happy year in my life.

I had developed bipolar disorder in the summer of 1967. Bipolar disorder is not the same as obsessive-compulsive disorder. It is also known as "manic depression," and in short, it meant that I looped up and down in spirits.

I do not intend to describe my condition in detail. I described it in my book *My Unique Relationship with Robert Maxwell – The Truth at Last*.

The melancholia gradually grew more prevalent than my elated mood. I bullied my poor GP, the late Dr Victor Ratner, and I told him I wouldn't leave him alone until he gave me some effective medicine. Robert Maxwell had told me repeatedly that if I really wanted something, I would have to bully people until I got it.

Because I had pushed Dr Ratner so hard, he eventually prescribed me with something called "lithium carbonate". This is not a liquid preparation. It comes in the form of tablets or pills. I took the pills for about five days, and I noticed a change for the better. The gloom had almost completely disappeared, and, although I felt a bit wild at times, I was back to what I had been before the summer of 1967.

July 1972 was the month and year of my recovery. I had just finished an arduous translation job in Oxford, using French and Russian. It was then that my mother and I went to Berlin.

We stayed at the Kempinski, an upmarket West German hotel, and because the Berlin Wall had always fascinated me, my mother reluctantly agreed to my request to cross the border and visit the East for a day.

We were at Checkpoint Charlie, which was drab, shabby and gloomy. I wished to use the bathroom. My mother gave me an interminable lecture about the need to avoid using too much paper. She was quite nervous and made it abundantly clear that she did not want any trouble.

Because the lithium carbonate had been so successful, I was feeling ecstatic. I went into the lavatory, which was poorly maintained. It seemed that cleaners were in short supply. A wave of extreme euphoria came over me, accompanied by an urge to grab hold of the lavatory chain, which I wrapped round my arm, and swung on it like a monkey. "Whay, Hay! Hay! Hay! Hay! Hay!" I shouted.

The plumbing was appalling. The ballcock came away in my hand and the cistern crashed to the floor.

The water level on the floor rose a few inches. At first, the door was jammed. I heard heavy footsteps walking up and down outside the lavatory. I threw my weight against the door once more. It suddenly gave way. I saw my mother outside. The heavy footsteps I had heard were hers.

"It would be you, wouldn't it?" she said mildly. "Do you realise you've been and got the man out?"

I couldn't see "the man" anywhere. We walked out to the front office. I told a bemused English-speaking guard that the cistern had accidentally come away in my hand.

"I wouldn't be surprised if the bill for the damage you did in there is going to be sent to the British government!

"Not only that, the whole episode is likely to get into the papers!" shouted my mother.

The Camera

Due to my having inherited my maternal grandmother's love for the macabre and the gory, I do not come well out of the following incident.

My mother gave me a camera for my tenth birthday. I wasn't interested in it, until she threatened to take it away from me if I failed to use up a film by the end of the day.

We were in Regent Street, London. My mother had parked her car on a yellow line. She told me to stay in the car and recite, "Sam, Sam, pick up thy musket," to the traffic wardens, to drive them away.

"Sam, Sam, pick up thy musket,
Said the sergeant major with a roar.
You knocked it down, so you'll pick it up,
Or it stays where it is on the floor…"

This bizarre ditty invariably drove most of the old biddies away.

My mother went into a shop to be fitted for some dresses. She spent nearly an hour in the shop.

On the other side of the street, a cyclist, a boy of about sixteen, was hit and killed by an oncoming bus. He lay on his back, motionless. He had been killed outright.

I crossed the road to look at him. A crowd ogled his lifeless body, preventing an ambulance from coming to his aid. Such terrible ghouls these people were, thought I.

The camera was round my neck, and I began to take photographs of the boy's body. I got at least ten close-ups of his chest. His eyes were pale-blue and were like ice. They were lifeless and staring into space.

In the meantime, my mother had got a parking ticket. She found the passenger's door of her car open. At first, she thought I had been involved in the accident. She rushed over to the other side of the street and caught me taking the photographs.

She was shocked, and dragged me away from the lifeless boy. She took me back to the car. As her shaking hand turned on the ignition, she kept repeating the words, "Oh, you wretched little brute! Oh, you morbid little monster!"

She was aware of the fact that I had inherited her mother's genes, however. The matter had been discussed at length with a paediatric psychiatrist two years earlier. Even so, she sent me to my room and made me learn a short passage from Shakespeare, on the grounds that I had been preventing ambulances, and the other helpers, from reaching the fatally injured boy.

I was not made to surrender the camera, however, because, although I had been outrageously ghoulish, I had at least shown enterprise, in my family's journalistic tradition.

My Mother and Lord Rothschild

The following story is about my mother taking up the cudgels for her great friend and possibly former lover Lord Victor Rothschild, who is now dead, alas. He was a very attractive man. Although she had faults, her behaviour on this occasion showed her intensely loyal streak towards those she cared for.

A game, well-known and feisty writer called Harriet Crawley wrote a book about a character based on Victor Rothschild. Crawley has written quite a few books but finds my books too "gruesome!"

Her book is entitled *The Goddaughter*. It came out in about 1977, and the classy Lord Weidenfeld published it. It describes the main character's love for her godfather, who is much older than she. The author expresses her extreme sadness about the fact that her godfather has become old prematurely, and adds that her heart has burst with sadness because they are not closer in age. I think Crawley has always fancied older men, on the whole.

To make matters worse, the character representing Victor staggers into his goddaughter's flat, like a dying geriatric, and bleats pathetically, "I am nothing but a ridiculous old man!" (Jesus!)

Victor had always been extremely self-conscious about his age, and Crawley was unwise enough to give him a copy of her book, and, even worse, to tell him that the ageing Sir Walter Lewis is modelled entirely on him!

Crawley is tall and very pretty. She is a good friend of mine, of my late brother Nicky's and my sister's. She once told me at dinner that although she and Victor had indulged in heavy petting, they had never had full sex. When he read *The Goddaughter*, Victor became incandescent with rage and made a livid phone call to Crawley's father, Aiden, reducing him to tears! He accused Aiden of encouraging his daughter to write the book in order to irritate him. In fact, Aiden knew nothing about the book at the time.

I'm afraid I was responsible for the following, somewhat ugly, incident: my mother was sitting by a log fire in her Buckinghamshire house, and was complaining because she had nothing to read.

I picked up a copy of *The Goddaughter* from a table near where she was sitting.

"Try this one, Mummy," I said. "You'll find it very amusing."

I was in the drawing room two days later, and I heard my mother shouting her head off on the phone in her room, which was just above the drawing room.

I wasn't fully aware who the recipient of her furious phone call was at first. It transpired that it was the wretched Aiden, whom mother had accused of encouraging his daughter to write *The Goddaughter* in a deliberate ploy to tease Victor. Poor old Aiden was ticked off twice!

My mother phoned one luckless fucker after the other. Virginia, Harriet Crawley's mother, formerly a close friend of my mother's, also got a bollocking, and was told how frightful her daughter's behaviour towards Victor had been.

Fortunately, my mother wasn't able to reach Harriet Crawley herself. When my sister, then Harriet Berry, came into the drawing room, I cleared my throat nervously and said, "Mummy is making an awful lot of noise, isn't she?"

"Yes, and you're responsible!" shouted my sister, adding, "It was really mischievous of you to have given Mummy that book!"

Harriet Crawley had once been a close friend of my sister's. My sister complained bitterly that her friendship with the talented, but controversial, writer, had never been quite the same since my mother had quarrelled so vehemently with members of the Crawley family.

After the passage of many years, however, the two Harriets are now good friends, so I am no longer guilty about my mischievousness.

My Parents' Guests
A Few of My Mother's Guests – I Have Not Listed Them All

My parents had many visitors to our Buckinghamshire house and our villa in the south of France. Kay Graham, the editor of *The Washington Post*, visited us, accompanied by her lively daughter, Lally. Lally wrote a book about American history, at a later date. She was tall, and had flicked-out, long, black hair. She had a wonderful figure and was very glamorous.

Two more guests were Lally's younger brother, Stevie, who became a New York policeman, and his unfortunate father, Phil Graham. I was about eleven at the time and I found Phil rather frightening. He suffered from bipolar disease, or manic depression, for which there was no cure at that time, but which was not uncommon, particularly among high-rising Americans. He was either very high or suicidal. He was on a high when he came to stay with us. On his return to New York, he went to the other extreme.

He was admitted to a hospital in New York, and asked his wife, Kay, to bring him his briefcase. She did so, and he opened it, pulled out a revolver and shot himself dead. I remember being very shocked by the news.

Only three weeks before his tragic death, he took us all to a performance of the musical, *Oliver* in London, during which everyone was expected to clap in time to one of the lyrics.

As I was only eleven, I felt self-conscious for some reason and refused to clap. Phil, whom I was sitting next to, put a lot of pressure on me and referred to me as a "square," whatever that was. He was so lively and boisterous that he made me feel very uncomfortable. I knew there was something wrong with him, even then, because he didn't seem normal or natural. I thought he had had too much to drink.

My judgement turned out to be monstrously unfair. I learned later that he was universally liked and that his widow, son and daughter had been more than shattered by his death. Stevie, the policeman, came to visit me in London in later years. He was exceptionally entertaining. I asked him to imitate a British accent. He had me in stitches.

The Grahams, and in particular, Kay Graham, were frequent visitors to our Buckinghamshire house after Phil's death. When, I was in my mid-teens, I heard the news that Adrian was getting married, and that he and I would be separated. I wept on Kay's shoulder. It was at that time that I had absolutely adulated Adrian. See my papers relating to Adrian.

Mad Paddy Packenham, One of Lord Longford's Sons

The following story involves my mother and the late Patrick Packenham, who was known to his friends and family as "Paddy". He was a devoted, if somewhat eccentric, friend of Nicky's and mine. One night, he met my mother in the most extraordinary circumstances.

Paddy was about sixty-eight when he died, and was one of the sons of the late Lord Longford. Although he was a manic depressive he refused to take his medicine. He preferred alcohol. Before he became ill, he was a successful barrister. It can be proved that manic depression is an extremely common condition, although it can now be easily cured, provided the patient really helps himself by bullying his doctors.

On one occasion, when he was manic, he stripped naked on a golf course, because he thought that nakedness would improve his play.

He ran to a house nearby, occupied by a vicar, shouting, "Clothes! Clothes! My need is greater than yours!"

The police inevitably arrested him, and he sang a song to the tune of "The British Grenadiers" for their benefit.

"*Some talk of Alexander and some of Hercules,*
Of Hector and Lysander and poofters such as these,
But of all the fucking pederasts, there's none that can compare,
With a bloody, effeminate copper, and a wanking, raging queer."

To add to his insane behaviour, an aunt of his left him £50,000 in her will. He threw the lot on a horse which lost!

On another occasion, he emptied a box of golf balls over his psychiatrist's head.

* * *

My cousin, the late Lord Birkenhead, (Robin) whom I will speak about later, asked my mother for permission to bring Paddy to dinner in our Buckinghamshire house. She consented and said dinner would be at eight o'clock.

Robin and Paddy travelled to the house in different cars. The former arrived just before eight o'clock, but there was still no sign of Paddy, who rang up my mother at ten o'clock, to say that he had been delayed, because there was something wrong with his car.

He finally arrived at eleven-thirty, in a lively, ebullient, mood, quite a lot the worse for wear.

Robin opened the front door and Paddy blustered in. "I say, is there anywhere here where I can empty my pisser?" he bellowed.

"Down the corridor and turn left. Another thing, keep your fucking foghorn down!"

Robin guided Paddy towards the drawing room. Paddy was unable to conceal his inebriated state.

My mother and father were waiting for him. My mother was lying on a sofa. Her dark eyes and gypsy-like features were accentuated by a glaring, angle poise lamp, near her head. She was angry and bored and was reading the *New Statesman*.

"God, Hamlet was such a maddening young man!" she muttered, half to herself and half out loud.

On entering the room, Paddy lunged against the door, knocking over a framed photograph of F.E. Smith, my mother's father.

Paddy ignored my mother and lumbered towards my dumbfounded father, who was sitting upright in an armchair, his facial expression stern, his eyebrows raised and his angry Welsh eyes questioning.

"Evening to you, Lord H,*" boomed Paddy, slapping his thigh. "Not a bad rag, *The Daily Telegraph*, what! Some of your sub-editors' wives are bloody good fucks!"

My father was struck dumb and looked as if he were about to faint. My mother, who was well-known for her caustic tongue, was also struck dumb.

"Why, in the world, were you so late?" she asked Paddy, mildly.

---

*   Lord H: Lord Hartwell.

"My car broke down, blast it! My points needed greasing."

"In that case, you should have greased your points before you set out," said my mother.

Another blistering wave of boisterousness thundered through Paddy. "Don't worry, Lady Pam, I'll grease 'em all right, and if you're a good girl, I'll take you to your bedroom, where I'll give *your* points a good old greasing, what!"

"This is hardly the kind of conversation that one expects to hear in a *William Kent* drawing room," said my mother, mildly, while my father stared transfixed, as if he had seen a vision.

"*William Kent*! William bloody *Kent*! Never 'eard of the wet fucker!" shrieked Paddy.

My father spoke for the first time since Paddy's arrival. Using extremely forceful language, he ordered his guest to leave the house.

Paddy staggered from the drawing room into the hall. My mother stormed after him, shouting angrily about his behaviour.

Paddy noticed a bright red coat, which had been draped over a chair near the front door. He was seized by yet another disinhibited gush of wild excitement. He picked up the coat, held it in front of my mother and waved it in the air, as if he were chasing a bull.

As he pursued the now-petrified woman round the hall table, he leapt from side to side, like a matador, and broke into raucous, baritone song:

"*Toreador, en garde e,*
Toreador, Toreador!"

My mother rushed into an adjoining room, and frantically locked the door behind her.

I think this was the only time in her life, in which she had feared for her safety, except for an occasion, years before, when her mad cook, fearing a burglar, had chased her down a corridor, brandishing a carving knife.

Reg Gross – Labour Party Cabinet Minister

Reg Gross (name changed), and his wife, were also regular visitors to our house in Buckinghamshire. Gross was a Labour Party cabinet minister and, for some reason best known to herself, Harriet showed him round my mother's ornately decorated bedroom.

"I really would appreciate it, if you would refrain from showing Labour Party cabinet ministers round my bedroom," said my mother mildly.

On another visit to our house, Gross got pretty inebriated, and was extremely indiscreet about some of his colleagues in the Labour Party, in particular, about Harold and Barbara (Harold Wilson, the then Prime Minister, and Barbara Castle).

This time, the Grosses had brought their fourteen-year-old son with them. A year later, the boy topped himself, but no one knows why. He constantly interrupted his father's rantings and told everyone at the table that the overly made-up Barbara Castle had always managed to "worm her way into his father's bedroom, when all that could be heard was the creaking mattress, accompanied by feminine squeals."

Gross was furious and tried to kick his precocious son's leg under the table. Instead of kicking his son, however, the drunken Labour Party cabinet minister gave my father a violent kick in the shin.

This did not prevent my father from listening to every word the dreadful boy uttered, intently but silently. He remembered his words with the speed of a fast shorthand-writer, and recorded his findings on a scrap of paper which he later put into his pocket.

The boy became even more embarrassing. After lunch, he demanded that I play a game called *Thunderbirds* with him in the nursery. He insisted that I act the part of a ghastly character called Lady Penelope. I found the whole charade bloody offensive.

After the Gross family had left, my father said he wanted to invite his sisters, Sheila and Patricia, to the house the following weekend, to make up a four of bridge, together with another guest.

Unfortunately, their visit did not go as well as my father had hoped it would. Both the sisters drank large quantities of gin and tonic and did little else. No bridge was played in the end.

"I'm not having your sisters over here again!" said my mother forcefully, adding, "All they do all day is sit around drinking great, big, brimming beakers of gin!"

Lord Boothby

My parents often invited Tory MPs to our house in Buckinghamshire for the weekend. At the time of the following incident, I was very lonely, because my siblings were away at boarding school. I was about five.

One of my parents' guests was the late Lord Boothby, who had been elected as Conservative MP for Aberdeen and Kincardine East, as far back as 1924.

Years later, he became a peer. He was said to have had a lively mind, an easy way with others and a pronounced sense of humour. Added to this, it was thought that he had had a homosexual relationship with the late Ronnie Kray, who desperately attempted to sue the *Daily Mirror*, when the newspaper tried to look into the matter in more depth.

Lord Boothby occupied the blue room in my parents' house. This had a blue four-poster bed and looked out onto the lawn.

I was bored after I had had my breakfast, and wandered round the house, intending to go to the visitors' bedrooms to chat with their occupants. This was something I wasn't supposed to do.

I went into the "blue room", which was empty. There was no lock on the door leading from the room to the bathroom, so I went straight into the bathroom. Lord Boothby was lying on his back, immersed in frothy, perfumed water. I recognised him, as I had been introduced to him the day before, and he had seemed very friendly. He did not appear to be embarrassed by my intrusion into his privacy.

"Hello. Would you like to learn to be a magician?" he asked genially.

"Yes."

"Good. I'm going to give you the power to make everything you touch, increase to three times its original size, and you can start off by touching my 'sponge'," he said vulgarly.

I did as he asked, and the object which he had referred to as his "sponge" quickly increased to at least three times its original size.

Thereafter, I assumed that all the things I touched would automatically increase to three times their original size. I touched books, ashtrays, vases, etc., but none of these things increased in size at all, let alone to three times their original sizes. I was bitterly disappointed.

When I reached my mid-teens, however, I was extremely popular with the other girls at Wycombe Abbey, mainly because I did their prep for them and made them laugh. I was always regarded as being one of the lads. Also, I love to be the centre of attention and am something of an exhibitionist. I have been that way inclined all my life.

I delighted some of the girls, by speaking with a loud, carrying voice, my words reverberating round the dining room, during lunch one day.

"When I was about five, I fondled the same cock that Ronnie Kray fondled!" I shouted.

A monitor, who lacked a sense of humour, asked me to leave the dining room and report to the housemistress for indulging in lewd and ribald conversation at the lunch table.

"I don't recall my conversation being either lewd or ribald," I said.

"That is a blatant lie!" replied the housemistress, who gave me a detention. In fact, I had more detentions than anyone else in the house. I don't deny that I was very hard-working and always got good grades, however.

I refrained from telling my parents about the erring Lord, because I had been forbidden to go to his bedroom and bathroom, as well as other visitors' bedrooms.

Sir Laurence and Lady Olivier

The late Sir Laurence and Lady Olivier were frequent visitors to my parents' Buckinghamshire house. Lady Olivier was known as Vivien Leigh before her name was changed. She was a friend of my mother's.

On this occasion, I was about six and my sister, Harriet, was about eleven. Nicky and Adrian were at boarding school.

After lunch one day, Lady Olivier lay down on a *chaise longue* on the lawn and chain-smoked nonchalantly through a cigarette-holder. She set fire to the *chaise longue,* and the fire brigade were called out.

"That woman nearly set us all on fire!" I said precociously to my father, in Lady Olivier's hearing.

"Kindly do not refer to her as 'that woman'. She is a distinguished lady!" my father retorted.

It is known that the late Lady Olivier was somewhat eccentric. She suffered from bipolar disease, like dozens of others, but failed to take her medicines for the then easily cured condition. When she was high, she could be outrageously promiscuous and undiscerning about her male partners. On coming home late at night, she often tormented her sleeping husband by lashing him across the face with a wet towel!

She died of tuberculosis before the appropriate antibiotics had come onto the market.

Despite her occasional sexual foibles, she was a unique and highly professional actress. Her performance in *Gone with the Wind* was more than legendary. So were the films and plays of her husband, Sir Laurence Olivier, who was bisexual.

During his stay in our house, Sir Laurence was unnecessarily rude to Harriet, and asked her whether she was from Leicestershire, of all places! He was critical of her accent and vowel sounds, and told her she was in urgent need of elocution lessons.

Lady Olivier, divorced him after a short period of time. They had not really been meant for each other, it seemed.

Robin Day

Robin Day, the television interviewer, and his wife, whose name I can't remember, came to lunch at the villa in the south of France on many occasions, accompanied by two rather sweet, well-behaved boys, aged about eight and nine.

One of the boys had had an accident of some kind, and his parents had been told that he wouldn't be likely to reach adulthood.

Despite his misfortune, I disliked Robin Day from the start. He was extremely rude and aggressive towards everybody, as if he were interviewing them on the television. He appeared to be permanently drunk, from soup to nuts, and he demanded more and more Claret.

As Day continued to knock back the Claret, his conversation became increasingly ribald.

My mother turned to the butler. "Please don't pour anymore wine into Mr Day's glass!" she said irritably. I struggled to keep a straight face.

Day's behaviour continued to be unacceptable. He told an absolutely disgusting story in the hearing of my nephew, Jonathan, who was only six.

Someone at the table told Day an anecdote about me, which, I'm bound to say, was not all that interesting.

"Who the hell's Eleanor?" shouted Day.

I was sitting next to him, and I introduced myself.

"Why the hell aren't you married?" he demanded.

"Because I've been waiting for your proposal all these years," I replied, after a long silence. There was another silence. We left the table, to have coffee.

My mother took Day aside, and I could hear every word she uttered to him. Although she meant to speak to him in a whisper, her voice was characteristically loud. "If you're not careful, you will get out of bed one morning, and will find a note on your dressing table from your wife.

"The note might easily say that she intends to leave you, because of your drinking problem, and your failure to do anything about it!"

I was unable to hear Day's muffled reply. It could easily have been, "Mind your own business!"

At about three-thirty, Day's wife led him, by the hand, while he staggered towards their car. The boys got into the back of the car. I really didn't think Day was setting a particularly good example to them.

My mother continued to invite this frightful man to lunch at the villa. My father put up with him patiently. The next time he visited, he bought a bloody guitar with him, sat with his sons on either side of him, on the lawn after lunch, and sang country and western songs, which I can't abide, although they were preferable to his dreadful conversation.

I haven't got much more to say about this man, other than that he is dead now, thank God!

Eleanor after graduation from University

Eleanor's father, Michael, who later
became the Editor-in-Chief of
The Daily Telegraph.
Sadly, he sold *The Daily Telegraph*
and *The Sunday Telegraph* to a
certain Conrad Black who later
served a custodial sentence!

Eleanor's mother, "Pam" who died
of breast cancer in January 1982 –
just before the Falklands War.

F.E. Smith, Eleanor's maternal grandfather. F.E. became the Earl of Birkenhead and Lord Chancellor, which was his boyhood wish. He died in 1930 at the age of 58.

Margaret, Eleanor's maternal grandmother, from whom Eleanor inherits her taste for the gruesome, the macabre and black comedy. She attended the trial of Dr Crippen when pieces of his wife's body were passed round the jury box. Eleanor also attends gruesome and macabre court cases and watches films of the same. Margaret died in 1968 aged 90.

Eleanor's paternal grandfather, William Ewart Berry, newspaper proprietor. Born in Merthyr Tydfil, South Wales on 23rd June 1879 and died on 15th June 1954.
Became Editor-in-Chief of *The Daily Telegraph* and *The Morning Post*, et alia in 1927.

Eleanor's paternal grandmother, Mary Agnes Corns. "Agnes" is Eleanor's middle name. This lady often gave Eleanor "Rupert" books.

Robert Maxwell and Eleanor's father, Michael, at Headington Hill Hall, Oxford (Maxwell's House). The two newspaper proprietors were somewhat jealous concerning Eleanor.

Dr Carl Heinz Goldman, one of Eleanor's favourite doctors, to whose wife she said, "God that man is attractive! He must come like the Volga!" She was 16 at the time. His wife was furious. Her father ticked her off, and said her behaviour was as "fast as that of Stirling Moss!"

Eleanor's elder brother, Adrian. Her favourite photograph of him. He was not modest and put a notice on his bathroom door, saying, "I've got a damned good figure and am devilishly handsome!"

Eleanor and her elder sister, Harriet, after Eleanor had made a long speech about Robert Maxwell.

Eleanor disguised as a 12-year-old boy, with intent to get into White's All Male Club, as a bet for £100. She won. The year was 1973.

Lady Rothermere

Lady Rothermere and her ageing husband often visited my parents in the south of France. She also gave my mother a lot of pleasure in a London hairdresser's, by dictating, in a very eccentric manner, to her secretary. Both women were under the dryers. My mother was surreptitiously leaning towards Lady Rothermere's dryer so as not to miss a word she was saying.

Lady Rothermere's nickname was "Bubbles". She was visited at her opulent London home by one of her many hairdressers, who said she kept endless bottles of pills in her bedroom, which had all passed their sell-by-date! She also kept a large supply of electric vibrators in her room, together with a vast collection of red wigs in different styles.

"What's her own hair like?" I asked one of her hairdressers, who was doing my hair at the time.

"Her W-H-A-T?"

"Well, her hair?"

"Her hair? She hasn't got any of the bloomin' stuff!" the hairdresser exclaimed.

Bubbles was really dotty, until the day she died of an apparently accidental drugs overdose. Her very distressed son, Lord Rothermere was apparently in her bedroom at the time. Incidentally, he was quite rude to Robert Maxwell, whom he referred to as a "pompous ass".

She always carried a bottle of champagne in a plastic bag, whenever she went out to dinner. This was accompanied by an empty, pint-sized beer glass. She asked the puzzled butlers of her hosts to pour the champagne into the beer glasses, and drank the lot in one gulp.

Bubbles was dictating at length to her secretary, who was sitting beside my mother. Some of her dictation was in the form of lengthy letters, mainly of complaint. The rest of her dictation consisted of orders about the payment, or non-payment, of bills. "Pay that ASAP. No, no, don't pay that! My dentist and psychiatrist will have to wait…" Bubbles failed to realise that my mother was listening to her words from over her shoulder, and that a grossly exaggerated account of her intimate business would soon be circulated at dinner tables all over London.

In short, one newspaper proprietor's wife had been spying on another's and she had no idea that her words had been overheard.

Bubbles was said, by one of her hairdressers, to have interviewed her many gardeners, wearing an open bath towel dressing gown with nothing on underneath it. The gardeners must have been scared out of their wits, or embarrassed beyond belief.

Bubbles and her geriatric husband, Lord Rothermere Senior, sometimes visited my parents in the south of France. Bubbles looked very pretty on these occasions. She often wore a turquoise jumpsuit and a curly red wig. She startled my nephew, Jonathan, then aged two, by picking him up and talking to him as if he were a dog. "Who's a pretty boy, then? Who's a pretty, pretty boy, eh?"

Apart from Bubbles' strange approach towards Jonathan, neither of my parents' guests that day were scintillating conversationalists, and Lord Rothermere Senior looked as if he were on his way out.

Sir Charles Forte, Sir Cecil Parkinson and Joan Collins

Another very brief visitor to the villa in the south of France was Sir Charles Forte. He rang the bell at the back of the house. I answered it.

"Can I help you?" I asked him.

"I'm Sir Charles Forte." Apparently, this gentleman had some connection or other with the catering industry.

"Have you got any evidence on your person to prove that you are Sir Charles Forte?" I asked him.

I can't remember a great deal after my stern manner of interviewing the gentleman. My mother wasn't very pleased.

Sir Cecil Parkinson, a Tory cabinet minister, visited the villa at a later date. As soon as the minister arrived, my parents retired to their rooms.

Parkinson was as high as a kite, possibly on amphetamines, possibly on cocaine. He chased me round the terrace in circles and kept taking my hat off and throwing it about.

"Do you do that to the Prime Minister's hats?" I asked him. (Lady Thatcher's hats.)

"She never wears hats," Parkinson replied. This statement was inaccurate. I had often seen photographs of the Prime Minister wearing a hat.

The actress, Joan Collins also visited the villa. She planted herself on a *chaise longue* and made sure she was surrounded by every man on the premises. She liked to poach other people's men and was an awful bore.

She was wearing embroidered, thigh-high white leather boots, which left parts of her thighs uncovered. (In those days, I invariably wore boots myself.)

I was staring admiringly at her boots and Adrian's eyes were parked on her thighs.

On leaving the villa, she shook my hand. "Gee, what a horrible, greasy handshake you've got!" she said rudely.

I paused so that I could find time to reply to her appallingly insolent remark. "Halts the ageing process, lady!" I remarked eventually.

Jeremy Thorpe

Jeremy Thorpe, whom I considered to be a perfect gentleman, often came to the villa, although my parents ceased to invite him, after the details of the Norman Scott affair had hit the headlines.

My parents lent the villa to Mr Thorpe and his wife, Marion. I answered the phone at 18 Cowley Street one day. Mr Thorpe was on the line, and he was calling from the villa. He was very upset because he had inadvertently broken a china vase belonging to my mother.

I tried to calm him down and told him I would pass the message on. I also told him, lamely, that, as it had been an accident, I was sure he would be forgiven.

I left my mother a brusque message which read, "Jeremy Thorpe broke one of your vases in the south of France. E."

Mr Thorpe was not entirely homosexual. He was bisexual. Caroline, his first wife, had been approached by the infamous Norman Scott, who had informed her that he had been Thorpe's lover.

As a result, Caroline was exceptionally distressed and suffered from nightmares until the end of her short life. She was killed in a road accident and was alone in the car. It was not unlikely that her unbalanced state of mind had caused her demise.

Mr Thorpe wrote a very distressing letter to my mother, ending with the words, "Oh, God, I miss her so!"

Thankfully, his son Rupert was not in the car at the time of the accident, although apparently he suffered from epileptic fits for quite a while during his childhood.

Unbelievably, Scott had also written an interminable letter to Mr Thorpe's mother about his affair with her son!

Mr Thorpe was alleged to have conspired to have Scott murdered. It would appear that the conspiracy, so called, had been in the form of schoolboy-ish, light-hearted banter only.

In fact, Mr Thorpe had been very indiscreet, while stating his wishes, fantasies or whatever they were, when walking up and down staircases at the House of Commons, shouting his head off, addressing the conspirators, so called! His behaviour might have seemed, in the eyes of staggered witnesses, to be no more than a black humoured joke.

I attended parts of the trial. Mr Thorpe sat in the dock, accompanied by his comrades. He rubbed a gold pen against the back of his ear throughout the trial, but apart from that, he sat motionless.

When he was found not guilty, he showed little emotion other than throwing his supporting cushion into the air and smiling broadly.

Norman Scott owned a Great Dane, to which he was apparently very attached, and which played a large but very comical part in Mr Thorpe's trial. The dog was also involved with a proverbially stupid airline pilot, called Andrew Newton.

Newton had the face of a fool and the mannerisms of a fool, to boot. He invited Scott into his tattered, old car, one rainy night, took the wheel, but suddenly said he was "exhausted". He asked his puzzled passenger to take the wheel for him instead, and to bring his dog into the car as well. This was a difficult operation, given the dog's enormous size. He then appeared to be afraid of the dog and spontaneously shot it dead! He turned the gun onto Scott, but found he had run out of ammunition. Oh, how I love black comedy!

He drove off leaving Scott and the dead dog in the middle of the road. Nobody knows what happened after that. Had an accomplice of Thorpe's gone out of his way to hire a dickhead like Newton to shoot Scott himself, rather than his massive dog?

The whole business had been organised so incompetently that I really can't imagine someone of Mr Thorpe's extraordinary brain and insight, trying to pull off such a crass, infantile stunt. In any event, the Judge, whoever he may have been, was vehemently on Mr Thorpe's side and was militantly biased against the desperately sordid Scott, throughout the trial.

"The bugger's as guilty as sin!" stated Robert Maxwell forcefully, when I spoke to him about the case. Bob was a fanatical homophobe.

Poor old Jeremy Thorpe! Despite his foibles, I was really sorry for him. After he had got into trouble, he led a very short and uneventful life.

I found it impossible not to like him and sympathise with him. Despite his eccentric dalliances, the word "gentleman" seemed to be written from one part of his forehead to the other, in my eyes.

Whenever he visited my parents' villa, he dressed impeccably, in a pale blue tropical suit and a navy blue tie, regardless of the fact that his companions may have been wearing more beach-like clothes, depending on the weather.

He made everyone around him feel comfortable, blended into the conversation, made suitable jokes when necessary, and spoke liberally to children of all ages, joking with them whenever they craved entertainment and humour.

In fact, he turned out to be the most welcome of all the guests on the premises. I regretted it profoundly when my parents never invited him to the villa again, after the Scott scandal.

He died of Parkinson's disease, and I felt very sad on reading about his death in the newspapers.

My parents did not appear to be intolerant of gay people, provided they behaved themselves and kept a low profile.

My father had been a friend of Guy Burgess's for many years, and not once had they fallen out, until Burgess's sudden and unexpected disappearance. I find it extraordinary that my father had failed to notice that his friend was as queer as a nine-bob knock.

Also, Sir Cecil Beaton, who was hardly a heterosexual, to say the least, was chosen, by my mother, to be my godfather.

She was friendly with two clock-makers, known as "Tick" and "Tock", as well. Both men lived and operated in a small shop, in the south of France, quite near my parents' villa.

The walls of their shop were covered from top to bottom with loudly ticking clocks which, on some occasions, were actually deafening. I found these men paralysing bores, but my mother invited them to the villa for drinks, on one occasion. They were not invited to dinner, however.

Once the pair were off their territory, where they wore conventional clothes, they came to the villa, dressed in shocking pink, flowing, silk garments, wore wigs of outrageous and unnatural colours, and bright gold flashy earrings. These were accompanied by more bulky rings on each finger like a couple of common didicoys, attending their first wedding.

Their expensive perfume travelled from one end of the villa to the other. Although my mother was amused by them, at first, in a strictly perverse way, another part of her was repulsed by their flamboyant, inappropriate mien, and the deliberately high profile which they affected.

When she had visited their shop, however, she had once been fascinated by their clocks and had even bought one from their collection.

They were not welcome to the villa after that.

My Father

My father's original name was Michael Berry. My mother addressed him as "Mike". Everyone else called him "Michael".

He was born on 18th of May, 1911 and was given a life peerage in 1968 by a Labour government, headed by Harold Wilson. He became Lord Hartwell, and his wife, Pam, became Lady Hartwell.

My father was the former editor-in-chief of *The Daily Telegraph* and *The Sunday Telegraph*. As I mentioned earlier, he sold both these papers in 1985, to an ex-con called Conrad Black. This was not a long time after my mother's death. It is thought by many that he would not have sold the papers had she been alive.

My late brother, Nicky advised my father not to sell the papers, but to no avail. Robert Maxwell also tried to persuade my father not to sell them. Although I don't know the true reason for the tragedy, I think my father lacked appropriate advisors.

Unfortunately, the transaction was made awkward by Nicky's aggressive behaviour towards Conrad Black's lawyers. Nicky thought that Black had actually stolen the newspapers from my father. I had not been reading my father's newspapers at the time, as I had been busy working at the Royal Free Hospital, but I soon learned the sad news from some of the other newspapers.

I was very upset. How do you think I felt on seeing the front pages of other newspapers, which were splashed with headlines such as "The Fall of the House of Berry" – when my father had once been so powerful, not to mention brilliant?

I do not wish to go into further details about this painful subject, other than to say that my late brother Adrian really wanted to be editor-in-chief of *The Daily Telegraph*.

My paternal grandfather, William Ewart Berry, whom my father adulated, was Welsh, and hailed from Merthyr Ttdfil. He died at the age of seventy-four, when I was four. He had retained his strong Welsh accent throughout his life.

Following the sale of *The Daily Telegraph* and *The Sunday Telegraph*, my father wrote an extremely lucid biography of his father. His prose is stark and simple throughout the book, and his paragraphs are redeemingly short. I have always thought that he would have been a superb writer, rather than a newspaper proprietor.

* * *

My father inherited from his father, both a strong belief in the work ethic and a fascination for the publication of newspapers. He (my father, that is) attended Eton and graduated from Oxford, with a BA Hons degree in Politics, Philosophy and Economics. He also distinguished himself as a colonel in World War II.

He worked with his father on *The Daily Telegraph*, until the latter died in 1954. My father then became the newspaper's editor-in-chief.

As of 1961, *The Sunday Telegraph* came into existence, which made it necessary for my father to work twice as hard. He came home late every Saturday evening. My mother and I, and sometimes other members of the family, waited up for him. He threw a rolled-up copy of the following day's *Sunday Telegraph* into the keen arms of my mother, and a rolled-up copy of *The News of the World* at me. Before he did this, he insisted on my encircling every article which interested me, so that he could understand exactly what my interest in the paper entailed. When I encircled such articles as *Mr Harold Wilson* plays golf yet again, he stopped giving me the paper, but I was more than persistent and insisted that he give it to me. In the end, my father did so.

* * *

My parents got married in 1936. They had met at an Oxford lunch party. My mother lit my father's cigarettes before they were married and, although she hated doing so, she frequently accompanied him onto the shooting fields and picked up his pheasants, with extreme reluctance.

My father, though very kind, was both stern and strict, as well as funny. There were two things which he wouldn't allow in the house, however. One was *ouija* boards, which he said, caused their operators' lives to end in tears. The other was violins, particularly when someone was learning to play them. His younger sister, Sheila, had been determined to learn the violin. My father said the noise she made sounded like "a cacophony of incarcerated mice".

When my father was about twenty, he went to a hostel in Paris, to pick Sheila up and take her out to lunch. He rang the doorbell and waited for the concierge to answer. "*Je cherche une femme**," began my father in hesitant French. The concierge chased him down the street, and, quite unnecessarily, called the *gendarmerie*.

When I was a small child, my father intrigued me by saying that our Buckinghamshire house was haunted by a character known as "the man with the brown beard".

I was terrified of the man. My father said jokingly that he would set him onto me if I was naughty. On one occasion, when we were walking down the corridor, he said the man was hiding in his bedroom. (My parents slept in separate rooms at this stage of their lives, because of their different habits.)

I wanted to see the man with the brown beard, but I was afraid of going into my father's room with the lights turned off. My father said he was frightened as well.

"*You* go first," he said. I always enjoyed his sense of humour, which lasted all his life. The stories which he told us, particularly when he was older, always had a black-humoured edge to them. We were having lunch at the villa in the south of France, and my father told us about Beria's execution. Beria had been Stalin's right-hand man, and was head of the dreaded NKFD, his secret police. He was a bad chap.

According to my father, the following incident occurred just after Beria's execution. The Russian delegation was sitting on one side of the conference table, and the French delegation was sitting on the other side. A ripple of laughter passed from one Russian to another. The head of the French delegation asked the Russians to share the joke with them.

"You are sitting in exactly the same seat that Beria was sitting in when we sentenced him to death!" came the reply.

This was one of my father's more popular lunchtime stories.

---

*   I'm looking for a woman

He told us yet another story, which, like the first one, contained magnificent black humour, (which I think I may have inherited).

Stalin had three children, two sons and a well-known daughter, Svetlana. She was the youngest, and his favourite child. He was fond of one of his sons, but far less fond of his other son. Svetlana addressed Beria as "Uncle Lara"!

The son Stalin was less fond of tried to commit suicide by slashing one of his wrists with a mere paper-knife! The boy ended up in hospital. The first person he saw was his cynical-looking father, who was leaning over his bed.

"You couldn't even get that right!" remarked Stalin in a caustic tone of voice.

The stories which my father told over the lunch table were not only brilliant but legion. Sometimes, he got cross when I referred to Beria as "Bright Button Berrywinkle". Beria liked to pick up girls in the street in his tinted limousine. He favoured twelve-year-old girls and took them to his flat. He played the first movement of Rachmaninoff's Second Piano Concerto in C minor to them and told them that he sometimes cried when he listened to this piece on his own. He raped one of these girls and confessed to someone that he had been *obliged* to put a cushion over her mouth, to stifle her screams. I particularly liked the word *"obliged"*, as opposed to "had to", etc.

* * *

I am deliberately refraining from telling stories about my father in consecutive order. Not only would this be boring; it would cause my prose to be unreadable.

My next story goes way back in time to the days when I was fourteen. During the summer of 1964, I read in *The Daily Mirror* that the actor Peter O'Toole had had to abandon a play in London's West End, simply because he had a sore throat! At the time, I had a *penchant* for this actor.

Due to my phobia about other people being ill, which I inherit from my mother, I assumed, in my characteristically obsessive way, that he had cancer of the throat, and that I should meet him on his deathbed to say how much I had enjoyed his films and also to ask him for "other favours". I was extremely precocious for a fourteen-year-old girl. I had frequently given hand-jobs to my father's chauffeur's son in the bushes, and my brothers had often taken me to see adult films.

I worked out a complicated strategy to gain access to this unfortunate man's hospital bed. I decided I would ring him up and say that I was David Lean's* secretary, and that my boss was in possession of a film script about Christ, in which he had chosen Peter O'Toole to play the leading part. I made up my mind that I would tell the ailing actor that I would be coming to his private room, script in hand. On entering his room, I planned to say, "I'm not leaving your room, until I've had my way with you!"

The next stage of my plan was by far the most difficult. I assumed that the actor would be in a private hospital, rather than a National Health hospital.

I got hold of a copy of the *Yellow Pages* and settled down in one of the spare bedrooms in my parents' house. There was a phone in the room with two lines. One line was an ordinary line. The other line enabled callers to get straight through to *The Daily Telegraph's* switchboard.

I made a list of all the private hospitals in and near London, and in order to speed things up, I used the *Telegraph* line. My parents were out for the day and would therefore not be using it.

Unfortunately, I overlooked the fact that reporters needed to use the *Telegraph* line to phone through their "copy" for the following day's edition.

There are legions of private hospitals in and near London. I rang up each one, got through to "Admissions" on all occasions, said I was David Lean's secretary and that I needed to speak to Peter O'Toole urgently. No one knew who he was, however.

On one occasion, I rang up Queen Charlotte's hospital, not knowing it was a maternity home.

I used the phone from ten o'clock in the morning until almost one o'clock. After lunch, I continued to do my work until at least six o'clock in the evening. Soldier on, girl! "Dogged does it," has always been my motto!

It was at about six o'clock that my parents returned to the house. A call was put through to my father, informing him that the *Telegraph* line had been jammed throughout the day and that none of the reporters had been able to phone the paper to submit their copy.

My father thought originally that the printers had been playing up again. Not so. Unfortunately, an employee on *The Daily Telegraph* switchboard recognised my voice and the subject of some of my calls. He told my father

---

* The late David Lean: a famous film director.

that, "Miss Eleanor has been making an enormous quantity of calls to the London area to ascertain the whereabouts of the actor, Peter O'Toole."

To say that my poor father was livid would be an understatement. So furious was he that he was unable to speak and shook from head to foot.

He allocated the chastisement process to my mother.

"What in the world were you doing?" she asked mildly.

"A schoolfriend of mine is dying of leukaemia, and I was trying to find out where she was, so that I could visit her," I lied.

My mother flew into a towering rage, partly because she had been lied to, but mainly because of the enormity of the offence I had committed.

My parents were particularly angry, yet again, the following morning, because *The Daily Telegraph* had appeared with a blank front page.

As a punishment, my mother confined me to the library, and made me learn lines and lines of Shakespeare by heart, just as all my siblings had to, when they were naughty.

As a further punishment, I was made to forgo a holiday in Scotland, with one of my school-friends.

I didn't get back onto "speakers" with my parents for at least two weeks.

I am going forward in time. We were staying in the villa in the south of France, and we had a full house. My mother had been dead for some years. My cousin, the late Juliet Townsend, her charming husband, John, and their three noisy, precocious daughters, Eleanor, Alice and Melissa (name changed), were also there. Harriet and her two sons were there too.

We were having lunch on the terrace facing the sea. It was intolerably hot. I was waiting impatiently for the dishes to be passed round, as I, too, was terribly hot. Lunch never seemed to end. Suddenly, my father fainted. I had failed to take into account the fact that he suffered from habitual fainting attacks. His head hit the flag stones, making a horrible, cracking noise. Then his face turned black and his eyes became glacial. I thought for one terrible moment that he had died.

I got up, held on to my chair, had a shaking fit and couldn't speak for a while. Harriet, by far the most practical member of the family, rushed indoors and phoned for a doctor.

My late cousin, Juliet, had always had a calming effect on me, when my nerves were shattered, and she read a section from *Brideshead Revisited** aloud to me, as if I were a child, while we waited for the doctor to arrive.

Juliet's youngest daughter, Melissa (name changed), who was somewhere in her teens, was obsessed by men at the time and gazed lecherously at the doctor on his arrival. He came by motorbike. This excited her even more.

She continued to stare at the doctor while he took my father's blood pressure and pulse and listened to his heart. "God, isn't he sexy!" she kept

---

*   The late Evelyn Waugh, the author of *Brideshead Revisited*, was far from being decent. On one occasion, he sat up for half the night, debating whether or not the Berrys were Jews.

In his tawdry memoires, he was also very rude about Adrian, Nicky and Harriet, whom he referred to as "shifty urchins".

Finally, when my mother had been indisposed and unable to see him, he referred to our nanny as a "boring old woman who never had any money".

Apart from the delivery of most of these insults, Waugh was unbelievably ugly.

repeating. The doctor asked her to get out of the way, as she was interfering with his work.

He had a gap between his front teeth, like the Yorkshire Ripper. Melissa once had a fetish about men with gaps between their front teeth. My father was rather embarrassed by the lewd advances which she kept making towards the doctor.

The episode continued to have a devastating effect on me, and I suffered from "post-traumatic stress" for weeks afterwards.

* * *

Melissa was very naughty, and enjoyed drinking. Mercifully, she had not been particularly upset by my father's fainting attack.

This time, she drank a fair amount of vodka, because she had been extremely upset on reading my novel *The Rendon Boy to the Grave Is Gone*, which has a few pornographic scenes in it, not to mention a tragic ending.

Melissa left the villa and staggered into a nearby restaurant, where she was sick into a Frenchman's lunch.

"*C'est n'est pas vrai!*" the Frenchman shouted. Unbeknown to Melissa, he followed her back to the villa, where he found my father alone on the terrace, eating a *piperade*.

The Frenchman needed a scapegoat. He shouted at my father, waving his arms theatrically in the air, like a swimmer calling for help. My father did not speak a word of French. "Who is this man?" he shouted. "Does he want any money?"

For some reason, Melissa described the contents of my book, detailed a few of the sex scenes and told my father what had happened at the end of the book, which had upset her so much.

"Oh, I do wish Eleanor would stop writing these disgusting books!" said my father obscurely.

The Frenchman continued his Gallic tirade, and my father took out his hearing aid. This enabled him to be completely deaf. (He had lost the hearing in one ear when he was a baby.) The Frenchman continued to shout, but to deaf ears.

My father asked me about the book which had had such a negative effect on Melissa, and I told him that it was going to be republished under the title *Stop the Car, Mr Becket!*.

He was anxious to read the manuscript, because he didn't want to suffer any further embarrassment, caused by the ribald episodes in the books which Adrian and I were persistently writing.

I was flattered by the fact that he had taken an interest in my book, but because he was quite elderly, and therefore likely to be sensitive to risqué material, I asked my secretary to type two manuscripts, one wholesome and the other unwholesome.

There is a description towards the end of the book, of the death of a man suffering from lung cancer in the Royal Free Hospital, London. The man, Ian Rosen, is a publisher of very raunchy books, and he is obsessed by sex, particularly when it is delivered to him by his obliging wife. A short passage in the real version reads as follows:

"Take my cock," said Rosen, adding, "When it's hard, try to get it into your mouth. Oh, Christ, this is nectar! Get your head up quick before I come down your throat and choke you!"

The version I showed to my father was totally different:

"Take my hand," Rosen says. "When it's warm, press it against your cheek."

Everything proceeded well, until my father's secretary went out and bought him the original copy of the book. My father referred to Ian Rosen's words.

"Oh, him?" I said casually. "He was the man who died in the Royal Free Hospital, wasn't he?"

"I'm not interested in the name of the hospital he died in," said my father. "All I'm concerned about is the filthy, disgusting language he used, just *before* he died!"

* * *

For a change, I took up temporary medical secretarial work once more in the autumn. I was given a job in the chest department of the Whittington Hospital in Highgate. I was intrigued by the work. The secretaries were often visited by loud-mouthed prisoners in handcuffs. They screamed and shouted obscenely as they were dragged along the linoleum corridors to see their consultants.

The staff members were sympathetic, and the food in the canteen was really good, unlike that in the canteens in many other London hospitals. I went out of my way to tell the head of the kitchen staff how good I thought the food was, and I also gave these people my name.

I deliberately refrained from giving the number of the chest department to any of my relatives, as I wanted to be free from distressing phone calls.

I was reasonably contented for a few months, until I went home early one day, and found a note from Harriet in my letterbox.

In it, she said she had tried to contact me by ringing almost every employment agency in London, but she failed to say what the matter was. All I knew was the fact that she wished to speak to me urgently.

I poured myself a stiff gin and tonic, and dialled Harriet's number. It was engaged. It continued to be engaged for at least half an hour or more. I poured myself another gin and tonic. Finally, I bit the bullet, if the reader will pardon the cliché, and rang my father's offices. I asked to be put through to him.

"Hello, Murray here," said someone I did not know. The man I spoke to had a very agitated manner and a southern Irish accent.

"May I speak to my father, please?" I said.

"Do you mean to tell me you haven't heard the tragic news?" asked Murray.

"What tragic news?" I shouted.

"I really can't believe you haven't heard the tragic news," repeated Murray.

I have no idea what I said, or indeed what kind of language I used. Murray hung up in disgust. I had obviously taught him a few new words.

I rang back. To my horror, Murray answered the phone once more.

"Who the hell's died?" I shouted.

It was only then that Murray told me that my uncle Seymour had sadly died. He was my father's favourite brother, who had got on so badly with my mother.

During my first phone call to Murray, I had automatically feared that my father had died. Worse was to come. Shortly after speaking to me, Murray suffered from a fatal heart attack and fell dead on top of his desk.

Someone in the offices had tried to tell my father roughly what I had said to Murray, including the singularly inappropriate language I had used in desperation. I will never know to this day what my father had heard, or whether or not he had been wearing his hearing aid at the time.

"I understand you spoke to Mr Murray, just before he died," he said mildly.

My uncle's funeral took place at the Golders Green Crematorium on a dour February afternoon. Everyone there looked tired and grey. My obsession about my father's health had returned and multiplied. My traumatic stress disorder was still very much in evidence.

The late Sir Jack Profumo was there. I had met him several times in Seymour's house. He was standing near my father outside the church. I suddenly noticed how short he was. My father was looking downcast, like the weather.

I approached Sir Jack, and, as I knew him, I began to question him obsessively. "Do you think my father is going to faint or be taken ill?"

"He's not ill," Sir Jack replied. Because I was ill, myself, I questioned him over and over again.

"I think this has become a somewhat repetitive conversation," he replied mildly.

He had made me laugh, although he had not intended to be humorous. He told someone else at the gathering that I was an "amiable crank".

Ever since my uncle's funeral, I rang my father's butler up every morning at eight-fifteen, to find out whether his boss was all right. On each occasion, I was travelling to the Whittington Hospital by minicab. It had once become necessary for me to ask one of the minicab drivers to stop, so that I could get out and find a better signal for my mobile phone. Signals were poor in those days.

I explained to the driver what I was intending to do, and he very rudely called me a "certified raving basket case".

I rang my father, repeatedly, say several times a week, and cross-examined him about his health. I have suffered from obsessive-compulsive disorder all my life, and as I said before, I inherit this trait from my mother.

"Don't keep worrying about me. I'm always all right," said my father kindly on one of these occasions.

So frightened was I of his demise, that I also rang him while he was having lunch on Sundays. I took advantage of the fact that he kept a phone on the lunch table.

On one occasion, I went over the top and referred to Dostoevsky at length. First, I spoke about *Crime and Punishment*. Then I moved on to *The Brothers Karamazov*. I said, "I've just read this book and I think Dostoevsky has bitten off far more than he can chew. Instead of describing three brothers, why couldn't Dostoevsky have settled on one, with three different personalities?"

"Oh, buzz off!" said my father. That really made me laugh and helped to diminish the obsession somewhat.

As for the major obsession itself, it died at the time of my father's death, on 3rd of April 2001. I had finished all my grieving before his death. He died of a heart attack at the age of eighty-nine. He had a good innings.

* * *

My beloved Peachey, the love of my life, whom I will write about later on in this book, had sensed my continuing concern about my father's health and my fear of his demise. He suggested that he accompany me to his Buckinghamshire house for Christmas one year.

He and my father hit it off straight away. Peachey approached my father's armchair, and the older man said, "Do you mind if I don't get up?"

My father was delighted when Peachey addressed him as "Michael". He treated him like a son and left money to him in his will.

My father had been particularly preoccupied with a statue of Einstein and Bohr, which he wanted placed between two hedges in his garden. Peachey helped him in this regard, although I don't know the details of the help he gave him. My father wanted the statue to be erected on his ninetieth birthday, but he sadly died just before he had reached this golden age.

Peachey also smoothed over the uncomfortable feelings which my father suffered from about Robert Maxwell's relationship with me. During my younger years, I had been pulled in different directions, like a ragdoll, by the two obsessively jealous newspaper proprietors, one right-wing, the other left-wing.

I have covered this matter in my book *My Unique Relationship with Robert Maxwell: The Truth at Last*.

I went to see Ratty (Dr Ratner) just before my father's death. Fortunately, Ratty knew me intimately but not physically, of course, and was also familiar with the jealousy between the two men.

"Write your father a letter," he advised, "and tell him how much happier your life has been with him as your father, and not Robert Maxwell."

I wrote the letter and my father really appreciated it. Unfortunately, I failed to keep his reply.

Later on, my father visited me in London and noticed David's painting of Marat after being murdered in his bath. The painting is on my bathroom wall.

"You really are a *mawkish* woman!" commented my father. I very much enjoyed his remark.

* * *

When I was younger, my father was, as always, a really good sport. He found out that I had joined the Communist Party. Instead of resenting my action, from the point of view of a Tory press baron, his face lit up.

"I say, have you got a card?" he asked.

I showed him my card.

"Let the mother see it first," pleaded my mother wistfully.

My father was also a man of great humility. Although he admired Sir Winston Churchill, he was slightly in awe of him. He was sitting next to him at a lunch party.

He had been trying to make conversation to Sir Winston. He passed a remark, to which the older man put his hand to his ear and replied, "W-H-A-T?"

My father was not one to give up easily. He tried again, but he received the same crusty response: "W-H-A-T?"

After my father had tried a third time, Sir Winston, with his head almost in his soup plate, replied, "Oh."

* * *

We once had a golden retriever, a really randy dog called Rex. My mother adored him.

Rex liked to bugger off for dirty weekends; that is to say, he chased bitches. On each occasion, a search party was sent out and my mother would sink into a mood of uncontrollable gloom.

My father was at the helm of one of the search parties. He found a golden retriever in a country lane. He took off his tie and attached it to the dog's collar. He bought the dog home and everyone, including my mother, was euphoric. She caressed the dog warmly and got straight on the phone to Mr Taylor, who was very fond of Rex, and who looked after him when my parents were away. She invited him into the house.

Mr Taylor seldom minced his words, and didn't mince them on this occasion, either. "That's not Rex. That's a bitch!" he exclaimed.

My mother looked crestfallen. She said that it was my father who had found the dog.

"Mr Berry may have a lot of talents, but where telling the difference between a dog and a bitch is concerned, they lie elsewhere," said Mr Taylor dryly. My father was very embarrassed.

* * *

Most of the time, my mother wore the trousers in her marriage to my father. She often wrote very abusive letters to luckless individuals, a few of whom had written critical articles about my father. Some of these letters had been written about other subjects, however. She paid me to type them. I found this task very amusing.

One particular letter was written to the local master of hounds, Dorian Williams. She was very angry because his hounds had stampeded across her lawn, terrifying her dogs. She complained that the huntsmen had resembled the marauding hordes of Genghis Khan and laced her prose with exceptionally virulent language. Unfortunately, she addressed Dorian Williams as "Dorian Gray", which cast a somewhat effeminate shadow on the macho-man's image.

Further, my father insisted on her showing him her punitive letters before posting them.

I, personally, thought my mother was in the right for a change, but she showed the "Dorian Gray" letter to my father, who said it was inappropriate because it antagonised quite a few of the county's inhabitants.

My late brother, Nicky had a most unusual encounter with Dorian Williams. He rode to hounds unhatted and wearing a black rubber mackintosh, which was two sizes too small for him.

He barged through a gate in front of Williams, who shouted, "Back, sir!"

"It's alright," said Nicky casually.

"Why on earth do you bother to come out hunting at all?" demanded Williams.

"To get fresh air and exercise," Nicky replied.

"If you want fresh air and exercise, you should bugger yourself with a pair of bellows!" shouted Williams.

Politeness had never been Dorian Williams's forte.

My father, who liked to maintain a low profile, heard about the incident and was extremely embarrassed. He even went so far as to threaten to cut Nicky out of his will, due to his singularly inappropriate clothing and bizarre behaviour. He would never have done so, of course.

* * *

My father suffered from a few minor medical issues. One of his doctors was a very fiery individual called Dr Carl Heinz Goldman, a Jewish refugee who spoke with a guttural Leipzig accent. Dr Goldman had rooms in Harley Street.

Dr Goldman was a manic depressive, as I think I said earlier. Sometimes, he was fantastically high. Other times, he went to the other extreme and sat gloomily behind his desk staring into space.

Occasionally, my father saw a less qualified doctor than he, called Dr John Crieghtmore, whom Dr Goldman disdainfully referred to as "your locum". Dr Crieghtmore was as queer as a nine-bob note and had a *penchant* for very young men with inky-black hair. He liked to take these men to smart restaurants and show them off to the shocked waiters and diners.

* * *

On one occasion my father was in hospital, with a king-sized bottle of whisky on his bedside table.

Dr Goldman and Dr Crieghtmore came into his room simultaneously. Dr Goldman's wife had refused him sex for a week, and as he was dependent on sex, he was in a furious temper. When he was in such moods, he could be violent, particularly towards other male doctors.

He seized the king-sized bottle of whisky from my father's bedside table with one hand and gave Dr Crieghtmore a resounding slap on the ear with the other.

"How dare you allow him this, you brainless nincompoop, when I've just saved his liver!" he shouted.

"Oh, do please give that back to me," pleaded my father. His pathetic request fell on deaf ears.

Dr Goldman had a very colourful personality, despite his outbursts of temper. Sometimes, he was considered to be quite a rake about town. He was married to a humourless woman called Berthe, with whom he lived in Hampstead, and who had no interest in sexual matters. Dr Goldman had endless love affairs. One of his mistresses was Mia Farrow, the American actress. I gained this information from his former partner, Dr Victor Ratner, whom I have mentioned.

Mrs Goldman apparently left her husband twice, because of his promiscuity. He went berserk, searching for her, and forced Dr Ratner to see all his patients.

My parents liked Dr Goldman very much and I idolised him, on account of his sexually attractive looks and his seductive foreign accent.

Unfortunately, my parents were having a lot of trouble on the domestic front. A temperamental cook called Anne constantly fought with an equally temperamental parlour maid called Marie.

Both these women were French and they fought in the kitchen, which had a very thin wall. Acoustics were poor and even the sound of a mouse could be heard in the room next door. This was my father's study, in which he scoured all the newspapers each morning.

The noise the two women made when they quarrelled, was earth-shattering. My mother was extremely worried because she thought they were interfering with my father's work, whether he was wearing a hearing aid or not.

Worse was to come.

Anne and Marie were no longer content to fight in the kitchen. They took a black cab to Fleet Street and stormed into the lobby of *The Daily Telegraph*'s offices. One of them kicked the other in the shin with one of her high-heeled shoes, producing a pool of blood. The police were called and spectators, working for the newspaper, left their desks and swarmed into the lobby to watch the women fighting. The scene was not dissimilar to an overcrowded bullfight.

My mother was overtly distressed on hearing about the commotion, but she insisted that Anne and Marie go to see Dr Goldman.

Both women were menopausal. Dr Goldman, who had been low in spirits, because he had not had sex for several days, suddenly began to rub his hands together with glee, when I went to see him later that day for a flu injection. He was giggling like a hyena, and rocking backwards and forwards in his chair.

"There seems to be a great deal of disagreement among Lord Hartwell's servants!" he said, his strong Leipzig accent even more pronounced than ever.

* * *

It was not difficult to reduce Dr Goldman to paroxysms of giggles. My father saw him shortly after the doctor's encounter with his fiery servants. Dr Goldman came into his waiting room, where he saw my father perched on one end of an uncomfortable-looking sofa and Lord Rothermere Senior also perched, just as precariously, on the other end. Neither my father, nor Lord Rothermere Senior, had very much to say to each other, apparently. Both appeared shy of each other.

Dr Goldman was tickled pink. He was laughing so much that he could hardly stand up. My father saw the funny side of the situation, but Lord Rothermere, then in his nineties, did not.

To return to the legendary Dr Goldman, I was really keen on him during my teens. His gynaecological examinations were to die for. I made appointments for him to examine me every week, to "determine whether or not I could have children". I was not keen to have children, only to write books, however. His internal touch was such that he could just as well have been having sex with the women he was examining.

He asked me why I requested examinations on a weekly basis, and I told him that I suffered from obsessive-compulsive disorder. He continued to grant my requests and sent the bills to my father, as before. In the end, my father asked him why I was having all these tests.

"Eleanor wants to have children," lied Goldman.

I really blotted my copybook again on the following occasion: I saw another receptionist in Dr Goldman's rooms. I hadn't seen her before.

I was in a disinhibited mood and approached the woman, who was somewhere in her fifties.

"My God, that man, Dr Goldman, is attractive. He must come like the Volga!" I shouted.

"Go and sit in the waiting room, and keep your opinions to yourself, if you don't mind!" she replied.

I asked Dr Goldman's secretary who this rude woman was and whether she was an agency temp.

"No," said the secretary. "She's Dr Goldman's wife!"

Somehow, news of the incident got back to my father, through an inebriated guest sitting next to him at White's. He was deeply shocked and complained that my conduct had been "faster than that of Stirling Moss!"

* * *

Despite the repetition of one printers' strike after another on two of my father's papers and my mother's hysteria, my father managed to keep his sense of humour, even during his darkest hours.

At other times, he sat gloomily in the corner of the drawing room, at 18 Cowley Street, with his head bowed, as if all his relatives had been run over by a bus.

I tried to humour him whenever I found him in this state, but I got nowhere. Harriet, too, tried to humour him, but to no avail. My mother sometimes went to her bedroom in tears. Adrian was no longer staying in the house. He couldn't bear the haunted mood which prevailed throughout its walls.

The sad atmosphere was invariably lightened when Nicky came to dinner. He invariably made light weight of the crippling printers' strikes, which certainly shortened my father's life. Despite his troubles, I occasionally got a laugh out of him. I was having dinner with him one evening, and he offered me some wine.

"No, thank you," I said. "I don't drink on Tuesdays."

"Why not?" he asked.

"Because, I give my liver the day off on Tuesdays."

"Oh? Do you dress it up in its best clothes and send it to the seaside with a bucket and spade?" he asked.

Throughout his troubles, my father was very witty on yet another occasion. I was in bed with a cold. I was wrapped up in towels and was making heavy weather of my complaint.

My father came into the room. "Do you want me to send for a priest?" he asked.

My father was immensely brave, whatever his dire circumstances were. Even when my mother was dying of breast cancer, he was capable of cracking the odd joke in front of Harriet and me.

For some reason during her final illness, my mother asked my father to go to a chemist in search of suppositories. He winced and told Harriet and me that he had deliberately put them in the boot of the car, rather than on the passenger's seat.

That evening, I poured myself a treble gin and tonic. He said, "You've just poured yourself an *enormous* gin and tonic." (He didn't approve of my drinking gin.)

"Oh, no," I replied. "It was just tonic. There wasn't any gin in it."

He took off my voice. "There wasn't any gin! There wasn't any gin!" He reduced Harriet and me to giggles.

One afternoon, my father rushed downstairs and urgently called Harriet and me upstairs to my mother's room.

Harriet rushed into the room first and I followed behind her. My father was sitting on a chair next to the bed.

"I wish I was dead!" said my mother. "It's so awful for poor Daddy!"

Harriet, as always, knew what to say. I did not, however. "Look at him. He's alright!" she said. My father forced himself to smile.

"What is so awful is my having to lose all of you!" said my mother.

"You're not going to lose anybody!" said my father. "Tomorrow, you'll be going to London for a scan. Then, you'll be coming back here."

"Am I going to have another operation?" asked my mother hysterically.

"No, no, just a scan," said my father.

"I know the scan will show the end!" said my mother.

While the unpleasantness was continuing, I found relief in Nicky's company, as I always did, particularly during printers' strikes and other gloom-inspiring events.

Despite the snow, I motored over to the house in Charlton where Nicky was staying. My maternal grandmother had lived there in the past, after F.E. Smith had died. Nicky and I went for a short walk along the icy roads.

An American service man came up to Nicky and asked him, very aggressively, whether he had a spade with him.

"I don't normally carry a spade when I'm going for a walk," Nicky replied tersely.

I managed to persuade Nicky to drive me to our Buckinghamshire house, to cheer my father up. Nicky reluctantly agreed, and my father told him how nice it was of us both to come over.

My mother died in the Westminster Hospital at six o'clock the following morning. When she died, the curtains at 18 Cowley Street were drawn. My father and the rest of us had a post-cremation lunch. For some reason, the table was uncharacteristically small. It was Marina (Adrian's wife, that is) who held the grim conversation together, and just about kept my father's head above water.

* * *

Because of the snow and ice on the roads, Harriet had a dispute with Kenyons, the funeral directors. She complained that they were unacceptably sarcastic and that they persisted on making inappropriate references to the weather. Incidentally, Kenyons are notoriously rude. They were also pretty rude at Reggie Kray's funeral, some years later, and they refused to provide me with a hymn sheet.

Harriet told them that next time she had to arrange for a funeral to take place, she would take her custom elsewhere. Her feisty words brought a degree of comic relief to us all.

We went to our family's Buckinghamshire house later that day and tried to cheer my father up every weekend thereafter. When the snow remained on the ground, particularly in the afternoons, my father gazed sadly out of the French windows onto the lawn.

Harriet often rang Adrian up and asked him to come to see my father alone, some weekends, to take the weight off the rest of us. Adrian couldn't take it, because of his complicated relationship with my father. Whenever Harriet rang his number in London, he told Marina angrily to say he was out.

"Come on, Harriet's your kid sister!" Marina retorted on one occasion.

"I'm not taking this call!" Adrian protested. Harriet gave up on him in the end.

We continued to stay with my father at weekends. He came to the table late one evening, because of a complication with a machine on *The Sunday Telegraph*. In the meantime, I cracked a joke and everyone laughed. I was describing a funny incident in the film *Taras Bulba*, when a character cries passionately, *"Papa, I'm a good Cossack and I love the Steppes!"* This character speaks with a heavy American accent.

"I thought I heard someone being very funny!" said my father, on entering the room. I repeated the joke. He thought it was amusing, and it took him out of his misery, if only for a short time.

Harriet's first son, Miguel, was born on 2nd March, 1982.

"Will everyone please stop being so nice to me! I'm sure you've all got your own lives to lead," said my father suddenly, just before dinner, although he had been comforted when Miguel was born.

After Miguel's birth, the atmosphere in the house gradually improved. My father began to laugh at our jokes. He was sometimes a bit irritable with Adrian, however. There was poor brain chemistry between my father and Adrian, as is often the case between fathers and sons. Also, Adrian took umbrage because my father didn't like his books! They are scientific books, some of which are futuristic.

My father didn't like my books either, but I didn't give a fuck, particularly as I wrote them in order to shock him, whereas Adrian wrote his books to please him. My books are grisly and gruesome in places, and come under the category of black comedy, as I have said before.

Adrian and I spent hours in the library at our Buckinghamshire house, writing our books. Whenever my father expressed dislike for one of Adrian's books, Adrian, though a grown man, rose to his feet, went over to a pane glass window and sobbed loudly.

Although my books are shocking, I was grateful to my father, as he helped me to write some of them.

"I say, this book contains some pretty grisly humour!" he said, referring to one of my books, entitled *The House of the Mad Doctors*.

In essence, my father had a tendency to bully Adrian and spoil me. He always sent me a crate of champagne for Christmas and my birthday.

Although Adrian and I had a lot in common, we bickered about our books and their superiority over each other. On one very tearful occasion, when Adrian told me that my father disliked all his books, I replied, "At least he didn't kick any of your books round the room. He kicked my *Never Alone with Rex Malone** round the room!" There was much sibling rivalry between Adrian and me because of my father's reactions to our books.

My nephew Jonathan told me that Adrian had been severely depressed *after* his father's death, for some time. The two men definitely did not get on, as I have stated. On one occasion, the bone of contention was someone's gun! My father kept telling Adrian to return the gun to its previous owner. For some reason, Adrian failed to do so. His motive could possibly have been obstinacy. They often argued about this matter. I found the argument boring.

---

*   As stated before, the Malone book is a eulogy of Robert Maxwell, and it aroused my father's jealousy.

On another occasion, when my father and I were alone, I asked my father whose books he would have chosen, if he were wrecked on a desert island, Adrian's or mine?

"Neither!" replied my father assertively. I told Adrian this, to humour him, and he said he would rather not discuss the matter.

Adrian's depression following my father's death, could have been brought on by the simple axiom which I wrote myself: "It is more painful to hate the dead, than it is to love them."

Jonathan told me an amusing story, about an incident when the three were eating scrambled eggs and smoked salmon at 18 Cowley Street. Adrian had a passion for salt, which my father said he didn't need. He and my father fought viciously over the salt container and upset the salt all over the table. The situation became ugly and Adrian stormed out of the house, slamming the door.

In the end, Adrian died of pancreatic cancer not long after my father's death. He never made peace with my father. Whenever I went to see him, his appearance was horrific and he no longer had his thick black hair. He was completely bald and had almost wasted away. He rang me up almost every day and told me not to worry about him.

It wasn't until after his death that one of his friends told me how much he had loved me. As he had such a stiff upper lip, I wasn't able to recognise the extremity of his love for me during his lifetime. He said I was his favourite sibling, apparently.

Nicky died in Paris shortly after Adrian had died and had told everyone not to tell me he had been ill. I had no idea until the day before he died, that his time was up.

My beloved Peachey died very shortly after that. He was lying on his back and I was sitting on a chair by his bed, holding his hand. A nurse told me it was time for me to leave the ward. "Don't worry, Peachey's not going anywhere," he said. "He'll be here for you tomorrow morning."

The following morning, he was dead, and I was shown his body.

I have told the whole story about my loss of Peachey later on.

Encounter with a Gypsy

My father always thought I was something of a "sucker", because of my tendency to believe everything I am told, and, in particular, due to my superstitious beliefs in the words of gypsies.

I believe implicitly in their alleged power to bring either good luck or bad luck. I was strongly influenced by a story I heard not so long ago. A loving couple had just moved into an idyllic country cottage. The lady's husband was out and a gypsy knocked at her door. She turned the gypsy away.

"When you came to live here, you were very happy. When you leave in two weeks' time, you will be very sad!" Two weeks later, her husband died unexpectedly of a heart attack.

My father's opinion that I was a "sucker" is shown in my encounter with a gypsy. It was a cold afternoon in early 1982. My mother had died in January of that year, and my father was gutted.

I was out of work, was feeling very sorry for my father and was below par generally. I was walking down Oxford Street towards Marble Arch.

A gypsy woman, aged about fifty and wearing the livery of her occupation, blocked my path, startling me.

"Have you got some money for the gypsy?" she asked, adding, "I can see you've recently had a sad loss."

I wondered how she knew my business. In a moment of crass stupidity and vulnerability, I believed that my parting with money could possibly bring me some luck and help me to find a job. My situation was not helped by the fact that I was hypnotised by the woman.

I placed a ten-pound note into her palm. Somehow, I felt she had already sussed that I was a "sucker", to quote my father's words.

"You've got more money on you than that. Any money that you hold back will only bring you more bad luck than you've had already. You've only given me a brown.* Give me a few more browns," she demanded.

So hypnotic was her stare, and so low were my spirits, that I weakened. I confess that my conduct was not very Maxwellian. I gave the gypsy eighty pounds in all.

"Is it by any chance alright if I keep fifty pence, for my bus fare to the nearest bank?" I ventured meekly.

"I think I'll allow you that," the gypsy replied.

"That really is *awfully* generous of you," I said.

"I can see that this is going to be your lucky day," she commented.

It certainly was her lucky day, if not mine. When I told my father the story, about my having parted with eighty pounds, he was furious at first, but he laughed heartily when I said that I had asked the gypsy if it was alright for me to keep fifty pence for my bus fare to the nearest bank!

---

* A brown: a ten-pound note.

Lord Astor
(Quite a Long Anecdote)

To go back in time, it was Boxing Day in 1963. Both Harriet and Nicky had planned to go hunting. There was a meet near our house in Buckinghamshire. Nicky was dressed in his characteristically unsuitable clothing, which embarrassed my grandmother so much that she couldn't bear to look at him. He was looking like a member of the Gestapo, wearing a coat two sizes too small for him.

My grandmother always came to stay with us during the Christmas break, and was delighted on seeing most of her grandchildren performing.

Nicky disgraced himself a second time. He simply couldn't control his horse. It kept rearing up in front of someone's Rolls Royce and finally smashed the wretched owner's windscreen!

Nicky had nervous, hysterical giggles. "I'm so sorry, I just can't control my horse!" he kept repeating helplessly. My grandmother flushed and stared at the ground in shame.

Harriet, on the other hand, was impeccably dressed. My grandmother gazed at her proudly.

The whole incident was made more comical by the presence of a certain Lord Astor, who was among the spectators at the meet. He had joined the crowd who were waiting for the huntsmen to ride off.

Before I describe the conversation between my father and Lord Astor, I will have to explain who the latter was and how he became involved in the notorious Profumo Affair of 1963. I will be as brief as possible. I will try to be brief, but I'm afraid that this certainly won't be easy!

Lord Astor was considered to have been rather a "rogue". He lived in a smart stately home known as "Cliveden" and had rented an idyllic cottage on his estate to a rather indiscreet, reckless and, dare I say it, a bit mischievous osteopath called Dr Stephen Ward. It was impossible not to like Ward, apparently, even though I had never met him. Despite his faults, I felt really sorry for him: he was a brilliant osteopath.

Everyone knows about him and his tragic fall from grace, ending in his suicide. Ward was a martyr in his own world. First, he was accused of spying for the Russians. When that failed, he was accused of living off the immoral earnings of prostitutes. Fucking, bloody bollocks!

He lived in a flat with Christine Keeler, a somewhat promiscuous woman. The flat was in the West End of London. She was glamorous and had done modelling work on arriving in London. She originally lived in Slough. She had started to work in a nightclub called "Murrays", where she had met Ward, who took a shine to her. No one could have described her as being a particularly industrious woman, however.

I met her once, years after poor Ward's suicide. She was launching one of her books and was dressed up to the nines. She had taken enormous trouble with her appearance, which I really respected her for.

I feel very guilty following my encounter with her. I'm afraid I reduced her to tears, when she had done nothing whatever to provoke me. Usually I only attack those who provoke me first. I regret my behaviour to this day.

I started the conversation by saying, "In one of your earlier books, *Nothing But*, you boasted about your having broken some unfortunate man's heart seventeen times. You went on to say that, on the seventeenth occasion, the wretched man found you in bed with Ringo Starr." I added, "Did Ringo Starr give you his permission to say that you had been to bed with him?"

The poor woman didn't reply. Tears poured down her cheeks.

"Do you think it's attractive to break a man's heart seventeen times? Just because he's a man, does that mean to say he doesn't have feelings?"

Christine must have felt guilty. I said I was very sorry for humiliating her and bought two copies of her book.

* * *

One hot Saturday evening, in 1963, Christine travelled to Ward's cottage on Lord Astor's estate, and, because of the heat, she swam in his swimming pool. Ward kept daring her to take off her bathing suit. No more than a hard-working man's liking for a bit of hanky panky. It is to be noted that at that time, the cottage was technically speaking on Ward's land and he was entitled to do what he wanted on it, within reason, of course.

It was on that evening that she met the late Sir Jack Profumo, Minister for War, who was enchanted by her. They had an affair. I have mentioned Sir Jack Profumo earlier. He was at my uncle's funeral.

Ward had also introduced Christine to a naval attaché from the Soviet embassy, called Eugene Ivanov. She had an affair with him as well. Although he was thought to be a communist spy, there was absolutely no evidence that this was so!

It was a wild weekend. On the Sunday, Lord Astor's guests, as well as Ward, Christine, Profumo and Ivanov, spent a lot of time frolicking about in Lord Astor's swimming pool.

Because Profumo was Minister for War, and Eugene Ivanov was connected with the Soviet embassy, the entire episode absurdly was regarded as a security risk. Lord Astor himself was involved, because all the fun and games had taken place on his soil.

My second axiom - security risk: "Not on your life," say I. A storm in a teacup much more likely! Just because a woman has sex with two men, no matter who they are, the chances of politics being discussed, is 1 out of 30!

I was thirteen while this was going on. Later on in my life, I thought the whole business was no more than a vicar's tea party. My father, however, who was extremely conservative, as well as being very cautious, thought that Lord Astor had behaved, to quote his own words, "disgracefully".

Ward was, quite wrongfully, in my opinion, suspected of being a spy. Because the police were unable to pin that extraordinary label onto him, he was accused, wrongfully in my view, of living off the immoral earnings of prostitutes! I do not believe this accusation to be true. In England, one is innocent until proven guilty. Ward was made a cruel scapegoat of. In other words he was stitched up.

Although Ward was fascinated by vice, a pimp he certainly was not. Dozens of women wept after he had killed himself, towards the end of what had been referred to as "the trial of the century". It was better known as "the trial of Stephen Ward," or, more fairly, the hideous injustice befalling Anne Boleyn.

To return to the conversation between my father and Lord Astor at the hunt meet, Lord Astor sidled up to my father through the crowds. Eventually, the two men met.

"Hullo, Michael, old chap!" boomed Lord Astor, desperately trying to suck up to my father.

"Hullo," replied my father curtly.

"I say, Michael, old chap, have you got any progeny out today?"

My father glared at him, his brown, Welsh eyes glacial. "Yes!" he barked.

"Who have you got out, old chap?"

"One of my daughters!" snapped my father.

There was a short silence.

"You don't like me very much, do you, Michael?" ventured Lord Astor.

"Nope!"

Later, I asked my father who he had been speaking to, in this hostile way.

"Oh, just someone whose behaviour was nothing short of disgraceful!" replied my father vaguely.

"In what way?" I persisted. "What had the man done to you to make you so angry?"

"It doesn't matter," said my father. He changed the subject and asked me why I hated riding so much.

"Because horses are bigger than I am!" I replied.

* * *

Lord Astor's behaviour towards Ward was cowardly beyond belief. There is only one thing I can't stand and that is a coward. Astor had turned the poor, defenceless wretch off his land when things were getting too hot, and although the two had been good friends, Lord Astor virtually disowned him to save his skin. What was even more underhanded was the fact that Lord Astor indiscreetly asked his former tenant to put the keys of the cottage he had rented into an envelope and leave the envelope somewhere where it could be collected.

Not only had Ward been a reliable and punctilious tenant at all times, he had also been a remarkable and wonderful osteopath, who had healed Lord Astor's many back pains, every time he had suffered, and had charged nothing.

* * *

I remember Stephen Ward's trial well. My mother prevented me from reading the papers, for fear of corrupting me at the age of thirteen! She had also forbidden Adrian to speak to me about the affair.

Before I knew anything about it, I questioned Adrian and told him I wanted to hear the facts. He displayed his quirky sense of humour: "All I'm able to tell you is that the word 'Cliveden' is a swear word. Hence, if you drop something, be it an ashtray or even a box of matches, you just say, 'Oh, Cliveden!'"

"That doesn't tell me very much," I said.

"Well, that's all I'm able to tell you," he replied.

I was determined to find out what was going on, so I raided the dustbins, and became quite an authority on the Profumo Affair and Stephen Ward.

Fights between Adrian, Nicky and Harriet took place regularly in the dining room at breakfast, when the newspapers were laid out on the table.

On one occasion, Adrian inadvertently cut Harriet with a bread knife, just below her hairline, because she had seized the *News of the World* from his hand. There was a headline covering the top page of the paper, which read, "*My Men by Christine*".

When I came down to breakfast, about half an hour later, I found there was blood in the butter.

My maternal grandmother loved the press coverage about the trial. She was hard of hearing, so Adrian used to sing the news to her. She responded to his singing, but not so much to the spoken word.

Harriet queued up outside the Old Bailey for two nights in a row to witness part of the trial. She was wearing a blonde wig to avoid being recognised by my mother, who was wearing a red wig. This, she wore so as not to be recognised by her daughter.

They both wished to hear the evidence given by Christine and her flatmate, Mandy Rice-Davies, but were unsuccessful.

Instead, they were only able to hear Stephen Ward giving evidence, and, because they had waited for two nights in the street, they were knackered and repeatedly fell asleep in the visitors' gallery.

All Ward could say was, "Yes, sir," and, "No, sir." Because members of the vicious, ignorant crowds had spat at him in the streets as he walked to and from the Old Bailey each day, he could take no more. He consumed a bottle of Nembutal and washed the pills down with whisky while he was staying in the house of one of the few friends he had left.

On hearing the news, Harriet was very upset. "Ward's dead," she announced sadly.

Adrian sang to my grandmother, in a sepulchral chant, "I am very sorry indeed to have to tell you that Stephen Ward has died. When the judge heard the news, he said, 'Oh dear!'"

My grandmother, whose black sense of humour was accompanied by a very dry sense of humour, was amused by the judge's monosyllabic reaction to the news.

What made the coverage of the trial particularly tragic, from a different point of view, was the fact that the printers on *The Daily Telegraph* decided to stage yet another strike. They really were such bastards! Over the years, they crucified my father, little by little.

This meant that the newspaper came to a standstill once more and was unable to publish any information about Ward's trial, suicide, and the subsequent reactions of the women who had known him as friends.

Naturally, my father was devastated. *The Times*, *The Guardian* and all the other newspapers were covered with the story from beginning to end. I've never understood why *The Times* and *The Guardian*'s printers seldom had strikes on their hands.

My mother was hysterical, as she always was, whenever there was a printers' strike on one of our family papers. She actually believed, quite erroneously, that we would have to beg for bread in the streets, if the strikes continued for much longer.

Because I was only thirteen, I believed her, like the sucker my father said I was. I dreaded sitting pathetically in doorways, with my hands extended, palms upwards, begging for bread.

"Pay no attention to that kind of talk, old bean," Nicky assured me when I repeated my mother's words to him. He often used to say, "I'm very fond of my sister". It was always Nicky who picked me up when I was down, and who rescued me when I was in trouble. He was always by my side, and I knew he would stand by me whenever there was a crisis. That is why his totally unexpected death was such a dreadful shock.

Often, I would say to him, "Will I get over it?" and he would invariably reply, "Yes, you'll get over it, immediately old bean!"

I went to Wycombe Abbey, instead of having to beg for bread in the streets! I will cover my career at Wycombe Abbey later on.

Writs That I Served

I'm going forward in time now. This time I was in trouble with my father, although the nature of the trouble was not my fault. Nicky came to the fore once more and turned the matter into a joke, thus comforting me. I served writs on a couple of fuckers in 1994. The first one I served on Mrs Gida Ratner, the widow of the late Dr Victor Ratner, who had been my GP and close friend at one time. He was known as the royal doctor, because he had treated some members of the royal family. I had accused Gida of robbing me of £16,000, but she was discharged, although I got some of my money back.

I served a writ on her, because she had handed my medical records to her lawyers without my consent. It goes without saying that the records were strictly confidential.

The second person I served a writ on was a certain Dr Gordon Kells (now dead thank God). He had unofficially taken over Dr Ratner's practice, and Gida had insisted on handing the records over to him. The two had become lovers, and she had told him that it was absolutely imperative that the notes be passed over, "in order to get me to back off".

This is a complicated matter. Please see "Eleanor in Court" for further details.

Very regrettably, *The Evening Standard* ran a story about the case in the "Londoner's Diary" column, and the headline was worded in a most unfortunate manner.

My photograph appeared in the newspaper next to the article. The newspaper only stated that I had served a writ on Gida Ratner. It said nothing about Dr Gordon Kells.

Sadly, *The Evening Standard's* headline was worded in such a way that my family, in particular my father, suffered severe humiliation and embarrassment.

"Maxwell's Girl Sues Royal Doctor's Widow," said the headline.

My father had always felt a certain amount of animosity towards Robert Maxwell, whom he regarded as a "crook" and a "baby snatcher". Maxwell did not reciprocate my father's hostility, however, and had always done his utmost to get on with him.

"What does Michael think of me? Does Michael like me?" Bob asked me earnestly on several occasions. He even went so far as to say that if my father, had served as such a father-figure towards his daughter, Isabel, and had pampered her in the way he had pampered me, he would have approached my father aggressively. Oh, how I liked that!

I have referred to this lamentable matter in my book, *My Unique Relationship with Robert Maxwell: The Truth at Last*.

My father was enraged by the headline in *The Evening Standard*, because it had implied that Robert Maxwell had been my natural father and not he. So furious was my father that I feared for one moment that he intended to cut me out of his will.

This serious misunderstanding was not my fault, however. I have never had any connection with *The Evening Standard*'s choice of headlines.

My father was livid on another occasion, apart from when *The Daily Telegraph* came out with a blank front page. This particular incident was witnessed by Adrian, who happened to be outside the door of my father's office, late one afternoon.

He was speaking to the crime correspondent whom he had summoned to his office, intending to complain about the persistent lateness of his handing in his "copy".

The crime correspondent lurched forwards and burped.

"You're drunk!" said my father angrily.

"Yes, of course I'm drunk!" replied the crime correspondent aggressively. "And if your wife had been sleeping with a different man every night of the week, you'd be pretty drunk, sir!"

The wind was taken out of my father's sails. There was a long silence. Finally, he rang a bell to summon his secretary, whose name was Mrs Larby (name changed). She had worked for my father for at least twenty years and was very loyal to him, even though she was hostile and jealous towards other secretaries, sometimes causing them to have nervous breakdowns.

Mrs Larby, who was wearing a neat, tweed suit, topped by starched white collar, scurried into my father's office, holding her notepad and pen.

She sat on a stiff, upright chair and crossed her legs, showing a pair of conventional, black shoes. "What can I do for you, Lord Hartwell?" she ventured.

My father did not give her any dictation, as she had expected. He looked at the red-faced crime correspondent in disgust.

"This gentleman wishes to be driven home. He is somewhat the worse for wear. Please arrange a car for him."

My father turned to the crime correspondent.

"Your services will no longer be required," he said mildly.

* * *

My father, though an exceptionally kind man, was not without a temper. For some reason, he vehemently disapproved of Princess Diana, despite her uniquely charitable works. When she was pregnant with her son, William, she recklessly rolled down a steep flight of stairs at Buckingham Palace, thus seriously endangering the foetus. The Queen was very shocked, and commented mildly, "Diana has been acting strangely!!"

My father, on watching *Panorama*, heard Diana being interviewed and saying "There are three people in my marriage". Indeed, there were, due to Camilla's open affair with Charles.

I've no idea why my father was so angry. It's possible that he didn't approve of anyone, particularly royalty, washing their dirty linen in public.

He stormed out of the house, got into his navy blue Ford Fiesta, reached about seventy-five m.p.h on a country road, swerved off the road and deliberately drove into a tree. It was fortunate that he was wearing a seat belt.

After the accident, he remained in a state of shock, however, and was ambulanced off to Stoke Mandeville Hospital. He was still not quite right, and he stayed there for about a week.

Summary of My Father's Personality

Overall, my father was modest, generous, charitable and exceptionally hard-working. He hated being given presents for Christmas or birthdays. His modesty could be seen in his request that his ashes be thrown into a dustbin! Mercifully, Harriet had them interned with a headstone, accompanied by a grave in the churchyard near his house in Buckinghamshire. My mother's grave lies by my father's.

My father's selfless generosity can be seen in his behaviour towards a lunch guest who had expressed an interest in making crab-apple jam. It was a Sunday, just before the tragic sale of his newspapers.

There was a crab-apple tree in his garden. He spent the whole afternoon shaking crab-apples from the tree and collecting them in a basket.

He worked on Sunday afternoons as a rule but sacrificed two or three hours of his time to enable his guest to have a decent supply of crab-apples to take home.

My father resented ostentation of any kind. He insisted on driving a Ford Escort and despised the behaviour of members of his family who drove sports-cars, Rolls Royces, Bentleys, etc.

Despite his loathing for ostentation, my father generously gave me a crate of champagne for my birthday and for Christmas. He always referred to it as, "You know what!"

He was quite exceptional.

I could go on but won't, other than to say that I was really lucky to have had him as a father.

The Most Tragic Event in My Life:
The Loss of My Beloved Peachey
My Beloved Peachey – Part I

When I'm faced with horror or tragedy, the only way I can cope is through wallowing in black humour.

My beloved common-law husband, Harry Hobbs, nicknamed Peachey, because he reminded me of a peach, died on 21st March, 2017. He had just turned seventy-five. He was resistant to all antibiotics. He had suffered from grade IV emphysema since 2003. The immediate cause of his death was pneumonia in both his lungs.

He and I had a perfect relationship and we had been together since 1977. He was a saint and did not have a single bad bone in his body. At Christmas, he handed out cards to all the residents in the street where he lived, even if he wasn't feeling very well. He also knocked on the doors of old ladies' houses and offered to do their shopping. On Robert Maxwell's birthday (10th June), he wore his best clothes in order to please me. That hit me harder than anything else in the world, particularly as he had sometimes been jealous of Robert Maxwell. Added to these favours, he once changed the wheel of a freemason's fancy car, when it was the freemason's job to do so. The freemason didn't even thank him. I was with Peachey at the time. "Thank you, is the word I think you're groping for," I shouted.

He died in a National Health hospital and asked all the patients on his ward if there was anything he could do for them or get for them, despite the fact that he was dying.

Once, when he was having a "good day", he went to the paediatric ward and danced in order to amuse the children.

He was kind to everyone he met and never delivered a cruel word to anyone in his life. One of his mottos was, "Never make an enemy, if you can possibly make a friend." Another was, "It costs nothing to show consideration towards another human being."

I keep the urn containing Peachey's ashes in my flat in London, as well as several photographs of him, which comfort me at times. I miss him more than I can say in words.

We first met in a hotel in Brighton. I was reading English at Sussex University. A man was due to have dinner with me, but he got cold feet at the last minute, for some reason. He rang Peachey up and said, "I'm afraid I've got to meet a woman for dinner tonight, but she scares me stiff, and I haven't got the nerve to face her alone. Will you come and give me moral support?"

Peachey obliged. He brought me some flowers.

Peachey was beautiful. He had light brown hair and big blue eyes. We never quarrelled. He took me to every place I wanted to go to, including Marseille, my favourite place, where I used to swim backwards and forwards across the harbour, much to his consternation. When I die, I will have my ashes scattered there.

Peachey was a Cornishman and was proud of it, and he had a strong Cornish accent. He was born in Looe. He was a keen sailor. One thing which I will always remember about him was his extraordinary ability to make me laugh.

When he was on holiday, during his degree course, he took a job as a gravedigger in Cornwall and told me that a clergyman had given himself a heroin injection by the graveside. This anecdote had me in stitches. In fact, I continued to laugh for days on end.

He refurbished several Cornish luggers singlehanded, one of which he sold and another which crossed the Atlantic. He called it the *Eleanor B.*

Peachey lived in a cottage in Bristol, which he had refurbished himself and built from practically nothing. He did the same thing to several cottages in Bristol. This was his passion, as well as boat-building.

Before he moved to Bristol, he lived in Brighton, where he took an honours degree in Fine Arts. After that, he worked for an antiques dealer, as an artist, designer and craftsman.

Due to my love for the macabre (inherited from my maternal grandmother) I bought him a second-hand Austin hearse to carry his things in. I preferred driving the hearse myself and reached speeds of 110mph in it. Much earlier in his life, Peachey served in the navy, due to his love for the sea. I'm afraid that I don't know the exact details regarding his service. His other loves, apart from the sea, were Mozart, champagne and me.

When Peachey was living in Bristol, I experienced the happiest period of my life. I stayed with him for long weekends, where I did most of my writing, played the piano and watched my favourite videos. I got to know Peachey's son, Gareth, who moved into a house near his father's house after a horribly abusive childhood.

Peachey's ex-wife, Mildred, left Peachey when Gareth was eighteen months old. Gareth was raised by Mildred and his sadistic stepfather, whose name was Martin Jones (name changed). They lived in Cornwall. Jones, a Scotsman, was nearly always drunk, was very cruel to Gareth and beat him savagely, even when he did not deserve it.

I can name one occasion when the almost permanently drunken Jones treated Gareth with particular cruelty. The boy was about eleven, when boys start to wet beds, apparently. He had wet the bed. Jones ripped off his stepson's bedclothes, dragged him out of bed and threw him into a bath of freezing cold water. If Gareth had told me about this during Peachey's lifetime, Peachey would have gone to Cornwall and beaten the bastard up!

Shortly after that incident, Gareth, still aged about eleven, travelled with some friends to meet Peachey and me in the Lord Elliot Hotel in Cornwall. There were tears in the boy's eyes. I put my arm round him and asked him what the matter was.

"Nothing," he replied.

"That bastard, Jones, has been roughing you about, hasn't he? I'm going to tell your father how unhappy he is making you," I said, adding, "Then, hopefully, your father might take you away from Jones and have you to stay in his own house with me. Would you like that?"

Gareth was frightened. "I don't know," he ventured.

Peachey had a younger brother called Ivor, who was really wild. When Ivor stayed in Peachey's house in Bristol one winter, he wrenched down a door to convert it to firewood. Peachey and I were furious.

Ivor's Cornish accent was far stronger than Peachey's, and when we went to pubs, he kept a higher profile than can be accounted for in words.

He had once been a merchant navy chef but had been thrown out because he was always getting into fights with knives. When in pubs in civvy street, he cracked a cacophony of ultra-crude merchant navy jokes, mainly about prostitutes catering for deformed clients. He upset the punters visiting the pubs to such as extent that we were frequently thrown out. In the end, we were banned from almost all the pubs in Bristol.

Ivor knew that I had a *penchant* for taking a lot of pills, which were mainly vitamins. When we went into yet another pub, he became legless, banged his fist on the counter, and bellowed: "You'm don't need to take all them tablets and mablets. Twenty press-ups a day is all you need!" As he spoke, he knocked a few glasses off the counter.

Peachey took his brother gently by the arm. "Ivor," he said quietly. "I think you ought to apologise. Then we will have to leave."

Although Ivor's behaviour was absolutely outrageous, he never failed to make me laugh.

* * *

I have finally tracked down the evil Martin Jones and written him one of my punitive letters. That is to say a punitive letter in the first degree. He hasn't made much of his life, although he "worked" in a mortuary once and only stayed there for about a month, for inappropriate behaviour! Shortly after that, he worked as a swimming pool attendant. He nearly drowned a ten-year-old boy in a fit of impatience. He lasted for three days! He has spent the rest of his tawdry life on the dole, and goes round dressed as a tramp. I have found out where he drinks. Not only have I sent him one of my punitive letters I have also sent a copy of my letter to his landlord, in the hope that he will be banned from drinking under his roof.

I have a final word to say about boys wetting beds. An Irish psychiatrist once said to a friend of mine in a thick Irish accent, "Wetting the bed, to be sure, is a question of getting yer peein' muddled up with yer fockin'!" (See my book *Your Father had to Swing, You Little Bastard!*)

Letter to Martin Jones

Eleanor Berry
London
My ref: EB/rm/fab1

Martin Michael Jones
c/o The Landlord
The Royal Standard
Launceston
Cornwall

20th May 2018

c.c. to The Landlord

Dear Sir,

It has been brought to my attention that you drink at the The Royal Standard in Launceston, Cornwall, and that you have two natural children, Corinne and Mary Francis.

I am also informed that your wife, Mildred, is deceased, and that you used to beat her up.

Finally, I am informed that you have a pronounced drinking problem, and that you were exceptionally cruel to your stepson, Gareth Lyndey Hobbs, the natural son of Harry Lyndey Hobbs, who is now deceased.

To give an example of your unforgivable cruelty towards this boy, when you were clearly under the influence, you plunged him into a bath, which was filled with freezing water, in a very small, poorly heated house, on a cold winter's day.

He was then about eleven or twelve years old, and his sole provocation was that of having wet the bed, which, as you must know, boys of approximately that age do, as a matter of course. Your behaviour in this regard shows that you are not a gentleman and never have been. Even worse than that, you are a despicable, not to mention, horrible cad.

I have informed the landlord of the pub, in which you drink for such long periods of time every day, about the deplorable conduct which you exhibited when you were younger. This certainly has not improved over the years, apparently.

Although the offence towards your poor, innocent stepson was committed a long time ago, you are by no means exempt from the revenge which I intend to take against you. I may choose to attack you within a month's time. On the other hand,

I may choose to do so at a later date. My attack will not be mild, Jones. It will be unpleasant.

You committed the unforgivable crime of abducting this boy, and taking him away from his natural father, when he was a baby. You went out of your way to raise him, with a more than inappropriately iron hand, and you broke his poor natural father's heart, and left him heartbroken for the remainder of his short life.

Your behaviour towards Mr Hobbs and his son was evil beyond belief, and it is on behalf of Mr Hobbs, God rest his soul, that I will not rest until you are properly punished.

By the word "punished", I do not mean the light administration of a rap on the knuckles. I mean the kind of torture towards lost souls, witnessed in the darker panels in the paintings of Hieronymus Bosch.

Your stepson's natural father was a hundred thousand times the man that you are, or were, or ever could be. It makes me incandescent with rage, knowing that he is dead, when a vicious, befuddled, and dare I say, ugly tramp, like yourself is still alive. If prisons did not exist, I would kill you with my own bare hands, using a weapon inflicting such indescribable pain that you will never forget, until you are laid in earth.

I know where you live and where you drink. I was born under the sign of the Bull. Be warned, Jones, you will meet me in the flesh, not a long time hence. I will not come alone either, and my visit will certainly not be friendly.

Yours faithfully,
Eleanor Berry
BA Hons (English) – author of twenty-six books

* * *

Let us come to Peachey's heart-breaking end. He was in hospital since 4th October 2016 and stayed in hospital until 21st March 2017, when he died. He had been in a private hospital, but when his insurance ran out, he was transferred to a National Health hospital. Both hospitals are in London.

His lungs got weaker and weaker until his body could take no more. The last time I saw him alive, a nurse told me it was time for me to go home, and Peachey said he would still be there the following morning. When I returned, he was dead. I think I mentioned this earlier.

Now, we come to the comic part of this horrible story. The shock, due to his death, had not yet registered with me. I was asked to see him in the mortuary of the hospital in which he had died. His beautiful face had been transformed into a vile and hideous mask. His head was thrown backwards as if he had broken his neck. His big blue eyes and mouth were wide open, and his skin was yellowish.

I screamed and screamed and went on screaming. Harriet was with me. She was very distressed. I shouted, "Get me tea!" to the mortuary attendant, who was a walking, proverbial dickhead.

"Get me tea, *please!*" corrected Harriet. She tried to close Peachey's mouth.

After I had had some very weak tea, I lost my temper with the mortuary attendant.

"Do you think this is an appropriate manner in which to present a dead body?" I asked him angrily. Harriet tried to calm me down but without success.

"I was only doing my best," replied the mortuary attendant.

I said, "I'm not interested in your blasted, bloody best, when your best clearly isn't good enough!"

"There's no need to be rude," said Harriet.

The mortuary attendant gaped at me like an owl waiting to be fed. He had foul breath, was unshaven and spoke with a hideous Nottinghamshire accent.

I took him by the scruff of the neck and dragged him to an unoccupied slab.

"Bend over the slab, boy!" I shouted. I beat him savagely with my walking stick. Harriet was very embarrassed and shook me off him.

"I've never met anyone quite like you before," said the mortuary attendant.

"Don't worry, boy. I'll be back!" I replied.

It is ironical that Peachey used to say, "Mortuaries are places to be spoken about with *fucking* reverence!"

I know he had been watching the scene from above, and was laughing his head off, God bless him!

I might just mention that, towards the end of Peachey's life, I received a phone call from one of the nurses in the hospital where he had been incarcerated, saying that he was "dying". It was early on a Tuesday morning.

I rang up Harriet, having sent for a minicab, which was driven by an idiot who drove unnecessarily slowly all the way, and who slowed down even more at green lights.

"If you dare to slow down at one more green light, I'll seize your licence and I'll take you off the road. I've got the authority to do that. I am a magistrate!" I shouted. The man burst into tears.

"She is not a magistrate," corrected Harriet, adding, "she has not got the authority to take you off the road."

Long before his death, Peachey was in my flat in London and was deteriorating. He intended to be admitted to a private hospital and was struggling to make a phone call to his insurance company. He wanted to know whether he could be admitted see the Princess Grace Hospital, his chosen hospital. He was speaking to a woman and it was clear that she was very stupid and was making his task particularly difficult. I could tell that she was really upsetting him. I thought she was cowardly and was taking advantage of a sick person.

I must have seen red. I snatched the receiver from Peachey's hand and shouted, "Why are you persecuting a dying man, you fucking prostitute?" The woman put the phone down, but I felt much better. Fortunately, Harriet was not there on this occasion.

Also, an agency nurse had been making mockery of Peachey when he was critically ill. She was a sadist, and she asked him in my hearing, "What does it feel like to be dying?" He was in the Princess Grace Hospital at the time.

I punched her in the jaw, just like a man.

Towards the end of Peachey's incarceration at the Princess Grace Hospital, some of the nurses addressed me as "the Fuhrer".

My Beloved Peachey – Part II

After Peachey died, I was demented with grief. His funeral took place on 6th of April, 2017 in the Kensal Green crematorium. Harriet and I invited a lot of people to say "goodbye" to him. Predictably, I was sitting in the front row between Harriet and little Jonathan. I always insist on sitting next to little Jonathan, whatever the occasion.

Harriet read a moving address which she had written herself, and which I know Peachey would have liked. When the curtains closed behind the coffin, I rushed forward and tried to open them. Harriet and little Jonathan grabbed my arms and held me.

The visitors assembled in an anteroom where there was an abundance of flowers. I sat down on a seat and wept. My nephews gathered round me and comforted me, as did many other friends, including my great friend Ian Maxwell, one of Bob's sons.

When I woke up the following morning, having consumed a few gin and tonics to lull me to sleep the night before, I thought that Peachey was lying beside me and was about to make me tea.

It did not take me long to realise that he was no longer with me and that I would never see him again.

I felt as if I were falling to the bottom of a dark, damp well, unable to get out. The loneliness I felt was far more than loneliness. So horrific was it that I could not describe it in words.

I lay on my back and was unwilling to get out of bed. I stayed in the same position for about two hours, my mood becoming blacker and blacker. I was absolutely gutted. It was then that I decided to take an overdose.

I had told my housekeeper, Mary, that I planned to visit some friends in Golders Green that day, to get her out of the way. I took a vast quantity of

Diazepam (10mg) and another entire bottle of pills, *Clomipramine* (50mg), for obsessive-compulsive disorder. I poured the whole contents of each bottle down my throat, and washed everything down with plenty of milk.

I decided that in no circumstances could I go on living without Peachey. I wished to die and hopefully to join him in death. I am not a depressive person by nature, but Peachey's death was so ghastly and so traumatising that I had irretrievably broken down.

After I had swallowed the pills, and the milk, I lay on my back once more, waiting for the Reaper to take me to Peachey. I had left a copy of my will on the bed for all to see. I felt very sleepy and therefore happier. Peachey's and my souls were about to be united.

I don't know what happened next. I had sunk into a deep sleep. I didn't feel anything, except darkness. A lot of people say that a person committing suicide experiences a "near-death" feeling, which is "very unpleasant". This did not affect me at all. Mary, my housekeeper, sussed that I was not going anywhere near Golders Green, and suspected that I had taken an overdose. The woman was right. She had a sixth sense. This was not surprising as she was Irish. She came into my room at about midday and found that I was unconscious and breathing in spasms. Instead of dialling 999, she rang Harriet up.

Harriet came round as quickly as possible. She felt my pulse, which didn't appear to be working. She put her ear to my chest and was unable to hear my heart beating. She did everything in her power to restart my heart, by banging my chest. While she was struggling to bring me back to life, Mary, who was in a state of severe shock, shouted, "Dial 999!"

"I'm trying to restart her fucking heart! I've only got one miserable pair of hands. You dial 999!" Harriet replied.

Mary dialled 999 and also phoned my GP, Dr Guy Staight, who was admitted to the building by the hall porter. The doctor came into my room, where he apparently gave orders. He accompanied Harriet and me to St Thomas's Hospital in an ambulance. Apparently, he said to Harriet, "It doesn't look as if she's going to make it."

First, I was taken to intensive care, where I stayed for about ten days. I was in a coma and hovered between life and death. My nephew, Alexander Berry (Nicky's youngest son), apparently sat with me, holding my hand for several hours. When I finally came out of the coma, I was put onto a ward with a lot of other fuckers. I had terrible hallucinations on the ward. They were in the form of imaginary voices, coming at me from all directions. I thought that they were real.

A patient by the window had visitors sitting with her in her cubicle. I was convinced that she and her visitors were talking about me. First, they called my name, over and over again. I ignored them. I heard hostile voices from one hour to the next, as a paranoid schizophrenic does. I heard the same woman shouting disdainfully about my book *Help Me, Help Me, It's Red*. It is a raunchy book, and one of my favourites. She seemed to say, "How can that woman lie on her back like that, like the bloody Queen of Sheba, after writing such obscenities?"

According to a doctor, working on my case, the hallucinations were related to the massive overdose I had taken. The only reason I had survived is that I have a fantastically strong heart. Berry hearts are like cricket balls. No member of my family has ever suffered from a heart-related illness, although there has been a lot of liver damage in my family. Liver damage is known as "the Berry disease".

The hallucinations continued.

A male charge nurse, who said his name was Peter, suggested that I accompany him to an empty room. At first, I thought he had done so to save me from further distress, but I was wrong.

I was convinced that he had said, "If you don't stop crying, I'll tie you up and set fire to you, you fucking whore!"

Naturally, I thought he was a threat. I waited for him to look the other way, rushed back onto the ward, and got into bed with an elderly woman who was dying. There was blood on her chin and she was breathing in gasps, like a poor soul facing the flag of death.

The charge nurse ripped back her bedclothes and wrenched me out of her bed. "Get out of there, you fucking whore!" I heard him shout.

* * *

The auditory hallucinations changed to visual ones. I thought that an epidemic of bubonic plague had broken out on the ward, so I locked myself in a lavatory, to avoid being infected by it. I stayed there for four hours, until Peter, the charge nurse, broke the door down. He was quite extraordinarily rude and abusive.

As was stated in the diaries of Samuel Pepys, the plague that I had witnessed in my mind turned to fire. I opened the curtains surrounding my bed and imagined that I had seen flames licking the curtains of other beds. I reached for my mobile phone and called the fire brigade.

Within about ten minutes, firemen stormed on to the ward, their hoses ready. When they found that there was no fire, they were just as rude as the charge nurse had been. I have always thought that there is something awfully endearing about firemen, with their earnest faces and their sweet little yellow hats.

I continued to cry, and the woman in the bed next to mine said, "Shut up your stupid blubbing!"

"I've just lost two brothers and my common-law husband, in close succession."

"Oh, well, we all have our crosses to bear," she said.

"I'll be the first to spit on your fucking husband's grave!"

I had yet another hallucination. I was certain that the woman occupying the bed opposite mine had died. It seemed that her body had completely sunk, making a deep dent in her bed, like a ditch. I called one of the nurses and told her that the woman had died, and that her body should be taken to the mortuary before it decomposed.

Fortunately, my nephew, Miguel, Harriet's eldest son, was visiting me at the time. He spoke good, sound sense. "If that woman's dead, I'm the king of Siam!" he said, his voice raised.

As for the woman, she appeared to recover and made several phone calls.

I saw a man kneeling over one of the beds. It was that of the dying woman, into whose bed I had scrambled the night before.

I tapped the man on the shoulder, thinking that he was someone who had come to make the bed. "Sorry to interrupt you, boss. Could you please come over and fix my television?" I said.

"Not now, I can't. I'm giving last rites to a patient," he replied.

"I don't care what you're doing!" I said. "I don't want to miss *Holby City*!"

Yet another nurse descended on me. "Kindly leave that gentleman alone. Can't you see he's a priest!" she shouted, adding, "How on earth do you think he'd be capable of fixing your bloody television?"

* * *

The majority of the nurses working at St Thomas's Hospital were, at that particular time, foul-mannered, unsympathetic and aggressive. This surprises me, since most of the windows have a wonderful view of the Houses of Parliament and the Thames. Peter, the charge nurse, shook my hand as I was leaving the hospital. Harriet was with me.

"I hope I won't be seeing you again," he said.

"I hope I won't be seeing you again, either, or indeed, any of the poor sods who replace you, when you're relieved of your responsibilities," I replied.

"There's no need to be so rude," said Harriet.

However, at the time of the coronavirus pandemic, the work done by the nurses at St Thomas's Hospital was truly exemplary, apparently. Indeed, they saved the life of the Prime Minister, Boris Johnson, together with a lot of other patients' lives.

They worked tirelessly. It shows that when such people are really pushed to the limit, they are prepared to work like pit ponies.

Mercifully, I have recovered from most of my grief, following Peachey's tragic death.

A dear friend, called Sally Grylls, has very kindly allowed me to rent a house next door to hers on the Isle of Wight. It's such a lovely place. I go there every weekend to write my books. I used to go to Peachey's house in Bristol every weekend to do the same, before his demise. Sally is Harriet's best friend.

The Following Still Relates to Peachey's Death

This is a different matter, which I feel I ought to mention to get it off my chest. I won't give the name of the woman who offended me. I will refer to her as "Jenny". In my opinion, she behaved unacceptably on more than one occasion.

Just after I had heard about Peachey's death, of which she was aware, she rang me up and shouted at me, telling me who I was to invite to my birthday party, as if it were any of her business. I was seething with rage and I shouted back, "Don't you dare attack someone when they're on the ground. Only a fucking coward does that!"

This is not the only time that Jenny stood out of line, just after Peachey's death. Harriet had been very upset and told her how traumatised she had been, when I had screamed and screamed on seeing Peachey dead.

"You really shouldn't have screamed like that, when other people were coming to see their dead," said Jenny, in a horribly bossy tone of voice.

On another occasion, she came onto the ward, on which I was grieving, and said, "I hope you realise that Cynthia [her friend, name changed] is much more unfortunate than you are."

Just after that, she said to Mingo, Harriet's youngest son, who was very kindly coming upstairs to visit me, "I warn you. Your aunt is in a foul mood!" What sort of mood did she expect me to be in, when I had just lost Peachey? Did she think I'd be swinging from a chandelier? Not only that, Mingo is a very sensitive boy who is easily hurt. He dotes on me and felt absolutely wretched on hearing Jenny's cruel words. I might add that, when I told Jenny I had lost two brothers as well as Peachey in close succession, she replied, "That's not my fault, is it?"

I am still angry to this day. Apart from the loss of a brother whom she barely ever saw, Jenny has never had a real bereavement in her life, let alone the loss of her nearest and dearest.

"Cynthia" had always been a friend of Jenny's and had once been a friend of mine as well. I was on my own in my flat in London, just after Peachey's death. All my friends were out of town. The only person in town was Cynthia.

I was so desperate and so lonely that I rang her up and confirmed that Peachey had just died. I asked her whether I could come to her house for tea sometime during the weekend, at a time of her own choosing.

"No," she said. I pleaded with her once more and she still said, "No." It wasn't as if I had said anything to offend her either.

Apparently, this woman feels she has lost me as a friend! If the reader feels any sympathy for her, he/she would be mindful of the following incident:

I do not think that Cynthia is totally malignant, but she can be rather foolish and has absolutely no idea how to control her men.

Her volatile lover, in a thunderous rage, once emptied all her cupboards and threw her dresses over the bannisters into the hallway of her house.

What was the first thing that Cynthia did? She got straight on the phone to me, at a grossly inconvenient hour of the night, told me what her predicament was and begged me for moral support. I never let friends down without provocation. I got dressed, called a minicab and went to her house. Why? She was a friend who needed my help and I was decent enough to be there for her. It goes without saying that the incident regarding her dresses was not in any way as horrible as the loss of my beloved Peachey and my subsequent loneliness.

Was she there for me when I had just been bereaved, was totally alone and only wanted a cup of tea? No, she wasn't. Why? Because it would appear that she thinks only of herself. She told others that she suspected I didn't like her two sons. Balderdash! I get on very well with both of them.

I did actually try to meet Cynthia for dinner to sort out my grievance. Firstly, I wrote her a letter, suggesting that we meet, but she failed to reply and certainly didn't turn up either. I suggested we meet on a second occasion, in the presence of another friend of mine who acted as a witness.

I told her exactly what I thought of her abysmal and disloyal behaviour towards me. She stared into space and failed to answer. I surmised that she felt too guilty to speak.

Finally, she said "sorry" to my witness, without saying "sorry" to me. I simply cannot comment. She then slid a five pound note to me across the table!!

After a long pause, she bleated the words, "I did go to his funeral".

"No you didn't," I replied, "your name wasn't on the list. You're a bloody liar!"

I parted company with her after that. I just wonder whether she fails to enjoy decent hearing and didn't hear a word I said to her when I complained about her behaviour.

I don't intend to see her ever again, and I told her so.

A man, by and large, would have behaved in a much more decent manner than the way these two women had behaved towards me. No man would have inflicted so much pain on me, as they did, when I was suffering so much.

Adrian and Jonathan – My Late Brother and My Nephew Adrian

I hero-worshipped my late brother Adrian when I was a child, because he always gave me an audience. I worshipped anyone who gave me an audience, particularly Adrian, because of his good looks. He had thick, black hair and large brown eyes.

He was very good-looking and knew it. I believed everything he told me and he used my gullibility to his advantage. He was eighteen and I was much younger; he wanted me to run errands for him. He made me interested in his "plan" by telling me what he referred to as a "vital secret" which only he knew about, and which concerned the "safety of the City of London".

"Now that I'm eighteen, I have a considerable influence over many heads of state, and I advise them regularly on the phone," he stated.

I believed him. How could I not believe such a handsome brother? "What's your secret?" I asked.

Adrian spoke in a hushed tone of voice. "I am bribing Khrushchev,* with seven and six a week, not to drop a hydrogen bomb on London. If I don't pay him regularly, he will do so, and we will all be wiped out."

I was terrified. "How long have you been paying him for?" I asked.

"For six months, but he has ordered me to alter the arrangement. He has told me that my act of paying him deserves a reward, and that he will launch his missiles within two hours if he finds out that I have not been rewarded," said Adrian.

"How does he want you to be rewarded?"

---

* Nikita Khrushchev became president of the Soviet Union after Stalin's death. He scared everybody in the world to death during the Cuban Missile Crisis of 1962.

"Ah! That's where we come to the point. He feels most strongly that you should run errands for me, whenever I ask you to do so, generally fetch and carry for me, wash my socks and put toothpaste onto my toothbrush."

"How will he find out if I refuse to do what you want?" I asked.

"He'll find out very quickly. Do you remember when some men came to the house last week, dressed as workmen?"

"Yes? What about them?"

"They weren't really workmen. They were Soviet, that is to say, Russian, agents disguised as workmen. They have bugged the house by putting microphones behind the walls of every room in the house to make sure you run errands for me.

"If you fail to do so, the whole of London, and indeed, a good part of England, will be reduced to rubble. We will all lose our lives."

"Is this really true?" I asked.

"I'm afraid it is. Every word of it."

"In that case, I'll do everything you ask me to do."

"That's my girl!"

I ran errands for Adrian for about a month, revelling in his good looks. Then I asked him how he managed to send the seven and six a week to Khrushchev.

"Oh, that's easy. I just write out a cheque for seven and six, once a week, put it into an envelope, marked, 'Urgent Life-Saving Powders'. I address the envelope to President Khrushchev, c/o The Kremlin, USSR, and post it.

"May I post the envelopes for you every week myself?" I asked.

"Oh, no! Khrushchev says I've got to do this myself, without anyone seeing me doing it."

Finally, I became suspicious. My brother and I were sitting outside, under the trees.

"Could you please go up to my room and bring me a paperback book entitled *No Orchids for Miss Blandish* by James Hadley Chase," he asked.

"No, I don't think I will," I replied.

"Have you no compassion for us, poor, poor Londoners?" asked Adrian. "Aren't you terrified of everybody being blown up?"

* * *

The following incident occurred when I was about eight or nine. Adrian and I were in a hired speedboat, near Cannes, in the south of France. I looked out to sea and expressed an interest in some islands on the horizon. I asked Adrian to take me to the islands, but he was unwilling to do so, because the sun had got to his head that day and had exhausted him. He wanted to go home, to the villa we had rented, and lie down.

"*Please*, take me to the islands," I pleaded.

"It's not a good idea," he replied. "They are occupied by really fierce Indians who don't like their islands to be visited. Every time strangers come anywhere near their islands, they get into their canoes and shower the intruders with poisoned bows and arrows."

"Are you telling me the truth?" I asked.

"Of course, I'm telling you the truth! When would I ever lie to you?" asked Adrian.

* * *

Sometimes, before I turned my light out at night, Adrian came into my room and sang Frank Crumit's song "*Abdul Abulbul Amir*", a rambling but very catchy song about two nuts who fought to the death because one had trodden on the other's toe.

I loved the song and asked Adrian to sing it to me over and over again. Eventually, he bought me the record.

There was only one negative incident regarding my relationship with Adrian. We were in my parents' Buckinghamshire house. I was about seven. He came into my room, carrying a toboggan. The ground was covered with thick snow.

"Eat your breakfast, little sister, and I will give you the time of your life," he said.

He walked me through the snowy fields until we came to a steep slope. He got onto the toboggan and told me to hold on to him. I thought we were going too fast.

I was a bit alarmed and dug my heels into the ground, causing the toboggan to slow down.

Adrian was furious. "You've spoiled our ride!" he shouted. "Go home. I don't play games with cowards!"

My immediate reaction was to take the toboggan to the top of the slope and descend once more without digging my heels into the ground. I was gutted because he had called me a "coward", the most insulting word in the English language.

"Look at me! I'm not a coward anymore," I shouted, once I had reached the bottom of the slope. "I didn't dig my heels into the ground, did I?"

"So I see, little sister, you're getting much braver. I'm very proud of you."

I was delighted by his words, but I was still rather embarrassed. I feared being regarded as a coward for the rest of my life.

* * *

Where his career was concerned, Adrian started off at the bottom. No strings were pulled. His first job was that of a cub reporter on the *Walsall Observer*, where he worked for several years.

He lived in New York for a while and worked on *Time* magazine. He chose to live in very humble circumstances to enable him to save enough money to hire a Cadillac and drive the whole way across the United States in it. God only knows why he wanted to do this!

He lived in a terrible place, namely West 90th Street. I think I'm right in saying that this is in Harlem.

My mother, who was staying in New York, hired a taxi to visit Adrian one afternoon, having told the taxi driver that she wished to see her son, who was living at West 90th Street. At first, the taxi driver was unwilling to take her to such an insalubrious address, but in the end, he did so with extreme reluctance. The taxi approached the property.

"Lady, get that kid out of there!" he said forcefully.

My mother was only two pleased when "that kid" came back to London.

My father was more cynical, however. "You went to America common, and you came back vulgar!" he exclaimed. He was referring to Adrian's two very racy books, *The Fourth Reich* and *The Empire in Arumac*, which he wrote under the name of Martin Hale. Both these books contained a lot of sexually explicit passages.

Adrian became the lobby correspondent on *The Daily Telegraph*. He wanted to become science correspondent and achieved his wish in the end. This post gave him inspiration to write his other books, all of which were written under his own name.

I once wrote to Adrian complaining profusely about an unnecessarily strict secretarial college which I had been attending at the time. Foolishly, I got carried away in my letter and likened the college to Caligula's Rome. I have kept his reply.

Dear Eleanor,

I am sorry to hear that your secretarial college is as bad as Caligula's Rome.

According to I Claudius, the novel by Robert Graves, at a banquet, Caligula suddenly burst into a most extraordinary howl of laughter. Nobody knew what the joke was. The two consoles, who sat next to him, asked him whether they might be graciously permitted to share the joke.

At this, Caligula laughed even louder, the tears smarting in his eyes. He said, "It's a joke you wouldn't think at all funny. I was just laughing to think that with one nod of my head, I could have both of your throats cut on the spot."

He then did so.

If anything like this has been going on at your secretarial college, please let me know. The editor always pays well for a good story.

Love,
Adrian

I was most irritated by Adrian's reply, although, later on, I thought it was quite witty. Adrian and I once made a pact that, when we died, we would both be as famous as the Brontë sisters. We shared a passion for writing. There are many writers in our family whom I have mentioned already.

When I was in my early teens, I wrote a book about some young East Germans who escaped from East Berlin to West Berlin, in the early 1960s. I was very ignorant in those days. The hero of my book, an East German postman, with the extraordinary name, Andy Slapstick, bathes in a huge, sunken bath, filled to the brim with perfumed asses' milk!

"Do you really think that an East German postman, living in the early 1960s, would have been able to bathe in a sunken bath, filled to the brim, with perfumed asses' milk?" asked my father in a baffled tone of voice.

* * *

Adrian helped me to write the book, and even suggested that I put in some sex. A bond developed between us. I fell madly in love with him and I wanted to elope with him. I was about fifteen at the time.

The next year, he got married to a girl called Marina. Adrian and Marina had a daughter called Jessica.

Jonathan

Marina wife gave birth to a second child, a boy, two years after Jessica was born. His name is Jonathan, that is to say, Jonathan William, the "William" coming after "William Ewart Berry".

I am absolutely devoted to Jonathan and am his godmother. He has a really deep voice. It gives me great pleasure to take him out to dinner at the Ritz, about once a month. The Ritz is his favourite place. Only the Ritz is good enough for him.

When Jonathan was about two, he contracted septicaemia. No one in the family knew how he had picked this up.

He was rushed to the Great Ormond St Hospital (in London). This hospital specialises in the care of sick children. He was incarcerated for a considerably long time and hovered between life and death for several weeks.

His parents sat by his bedside all day, in desperation. Initially he showed no signs of improvement. My mother even thought of making funeral arrangements.

The year was 1971. My parents had arranged for me to throw a twenty-first birthday party in a fancy Arab restaurant in London.

"Why are Adrian and Marina not here?" I asked Nicky. I knew Nicky would give me a calming reply.

Although he had been sworn to silence, he said that Jonathan was very seriously ill. Naturally, I couldn't enjoy the remainder of my twenty-first.

In the end, Jonathan turned the corner. A phone call came through to our Buckinghamshire house.

"Is he going to be alright?" I shouted hysterically.

"Yes!" said Nicky. He was smiling reassuringly, as he frequently did.

Ever since Jonathan's near-fatal illness I have had a particular love for him.

When he was three, I was walking with him in the south of France, near batty Bridget Bardot's house.

Three of her Baskerville-fanged curs charged towards us. Bardot hadn't even bothered to put them on leads. Jonathan burst into tears and leapt into my protective arms.

The old harridan made no effort to control her dogs and stared vacantly at us.

"*Oh, madame, que vous étiez belle, quand vous étiez jeune!*"* I said.

As a coincidence, I had a passionate love for Beethoven's ninth Symphony, and in particular the "Ode to Joy" in C major, occupying the composer's fourth movement. How dearly I love the "Ode to Joy"! What moved me particularly was Beethoven's passionate love for his nephew, Carl. To me, Carl was Jonathan.

When Jonathan was seven, a lady knocked on the front door carrying a *bouquet* of flowers for his mother. We were staying in the villa in the south of France. The lady handed the flowers to Jonathan and asked him when his mother would be returning to the villa. Jonathan lowered his head, and when he spoke, his voice was two octaves lower than normal.

"When will they die?" he asked.

I can remember another incident: Jonathan was about eight and I was taking him for a walk along the Brighton seafront. We came to a shop which sold seashells.

"Aren't they pretty?" he said.

"Yes, they are. Would you like me to buy you some?"

Jonathan thought for a while before saying, "I'd rather we left them where they are so that everyone can look at them."

Jonathan has not changed. In adulthood, he is still as engaging and original as he had been as a child. I address him as "my boy", and sometimes as "my lovely boy".

When he was about twelve, he had a crush on the late Marilyn Monroe. His thirteenth birthday was coming up. It gave me enormous pleasure to walk round London looking for biographies of the woman and videos of her films.

---

*   Oh, Madam, you were so beautiful when you were young!

I bought at least three books about her. Among them were the memoirs of one of her cooks, an Italian woman called Lena Pepatone.

This is a rather saucy book which implies, in places, that Monroe had a lesbian relationship with her cook!

Jonathan was thrilled with his presents. I was so pleased to see the smile on his face.

* * *

When he was in his early teens, Jonathan's confirmation took place in Eton's over-heated, claustrophobic chapel. As I am his godmother, I had to attend it. I accompanied Adrian and, Marina, neither of whom were devout. Nor, for that matter, am I.

I wore kinky, black, patent, thigh-high boots, which even my unconventional brother complained about.

"Oh, fuck off!" I said. That made him laugh. Besides, I couldn't find any other boots in my cupboard, and I had dressed in a hurry.

The chapel was packed and the overpowering heat was unendurable.

The boys, their parents, godparents and relatives, went to the front of the chapel to take Holy Communion, which I had never taken before. I went along with the throng, not really knowing what I was supposed to do.

A bishop was providing wafers and wine from a chalice. I was struck by the phenomenal lack of hygiene in the procedure. The bishop held the chalice to my lips.

"I won't, thank you very much," I said. "We are slap in the middle of a flu epidemic, and if everyone drinks from the same receptacle, germs are going to spread." I added, "May I make a suggestion: why can't you pour the wine into a series of beakers, and give one beaker to each communicant?"

The bishop looked perplexed and laid a wafer in the palm of my hand. "The body and blood of Christ," he muttered.

"What do I do with this?" I asked.

"Eat it, you fool!" said a woman who was kneeling next to me.

To my great embarrassment, news about this incident travelled round Eton, almost at the speed of light.

"I say, Berry's got a pretty eccentric aunt!" commented a few of the boys, some of whom were friends of Jonathan's. He was given film-star status for a while.

A very starched, judgemental acquaintance of mine was shocked and horrified by my story, which I told her in order to shock her. Her name was Miranda Brown (name changed).

"What do you think the significance of Holy Communion actually is?" she asked me officiously.

I bitterly resented her tone of voice. "Holy Communion is holding Robert Maxwell's hand and telling him how much I like reading *The Daily Mirror*," I replied, in a deep, reverent tone of voice. She didn't boss me around after that, although she never stopped giving orders to others and upsetting them. She had a son aged about eleven, who ran all over Seymour's house in muddy Wellington boots and ruined his carpets. Seymour, who was very sensitive, needed tranquilisers afterwards. As for the boy's mother, she failed to apologise!

* * *

At the time of a different incident, Jonathan was about eight and I offered to accompany him on a train from Marylebone Station in London to Aylesbury in Buckinghamshire. We were sitting opposite each other. The compartment was crowded. We were travelling on one of those old-fashioned trains with seats facing each other.

A suspicious-looking man near us, with "paedophile" written all over his face, tried to chat Jonathan up. The boy was intrigued by the older man. He smiled at him and asked him questions. There was a strong hint of impropriety in the man, particularly about his eyes, which were small, piercing and bloodshot.

He was about fifty and had greasy, crinkly, blondish hair, which was parted at the side, causing his head to look like a corrugated iron roof. He was wearing a grey, leather raincoat, which was similar to those worn by members of the *Gestapo*.

I tapped the man on the shoulder. "Out into the corridor!" I commanded. Surprisingly he followed me.

"If you say one more word to this boy, with intent to chat him up, I'll twist your fucking cock off!" I said.

The man looked terrified. He went back into the carriage, ignored Jonathan, who was playing with his Action Man, picked up his briefcase and shuffled into another carriage.

Lord Longford

I was having dinner in Adrian's and Marina's house in London. I sat next to the late Lord Longford and spoke to him at length. During the conversation, I expressed my strong view that Myra Hindley should not be given parole.

"Are you completely without sin?" replied the potty peer.

"I may not be completely without sin, but at least I've never murdered any children. How would you have liked it if that woman had murdered any of your children?" I said.

The old fruitcake told my father that I had been "velly, velly wude" to him. My father was most embarrassed. I thought Lord Longford was a terrible old sneak.

On another occasion, he cycled to 18 Cowley Street, and told my mother I needed "psychiatric treatment", because I had written to him, asking him to arrange for me to interview the Cambridge Rapist. I had told him that I was working on a thesis on the Marquis de Sade and on his influence on contemporary sado-masochism.

My mother, too, was particularly embarrassed. She spoke about the matter, in a terrifyingly loud voice, in Locketts, a sedate restaurant in Westminster. It has since been closed down. My mother was having lunch with Harriet and was complaining bitterly about the frightful embarrassment which I had caused her.

"Lord Longford really was looking *awfully*, *awfully* ill," my mother kept repeating, sounding like a foghorn, as startled waiters tried desperately not to drop piles of plates.

There are still a lot of maniacs and paedophiles about, however. Had I not accompanied Jonathan on the train that day, he might easily have suffered the same fate as Myra Hindley's victims.

* * *

Once Adrian and I had grown up and become serious writers, we bickered like cats and dogs.

"I won't read your *The Rendon Boy to the Grave Is Gone* unless you read my *Koyama's Diamond* first!" he said on frequent occasions.

Adrian was particularly proud of his character Simon Farr, who was the main protagonist in his novels *The Fourth Reich* and *The Empire in Arumac* (both written under the name of Martin Hale, as I have mentioned earlier).

I, too, was very proud of my creation of a crooked funeral director called Natalie Klein, one of the main characters in *Never Alone with Rex Malone*, a book which left Robert Maxwell "absolutely flabbergasted".

"Natalie Klein's a bore!" said Adrian assertively.

"Well, Nicky said Simon Farr is a fantastic oik!" I retorted.

When I read *Koyama's Diamond*, I was irritated by the fact that I was not represented in it.

The relationship between Adrian and myself was pretty reasonable on the whole, however.

"I'll tell you what!" said Adrian. "I can invent a very eccentric character called 'Groshka', who wears leopard skin, is always shouting at the top of her voice and stabbing the air with her index finger, in *Koyama's Diamond*."

"Thanks a heap!" I said. Incidentally, Adrian was furious because I had called him "Ethelred" Klein in my *Malone* book. He complained bitterly because Ethelred was always late.

* * *

I have another Adrian story.

He had appointed himself as skipper of a rather small sailing boat, known as the HMS *Hysteria*. We were in the south of France, where we invariably went on holiday.

Adrian and I were on the boat, which had been left on a beach. We were accompanied by my father; Jonathan, aged seven, and a frisky Alsatian dog called "Vichy". Vichy had a *penchant* for large quantities of gin and tonic, and liked to run round the lunch table, barking his head off. Once, he had consumed so much gin that he jumped onto the table and knocked plates and glasses onto the floor.

On this occasion, a mistral had started. Adrian managed to turn the boat

150

round and point it out to sea. A sudden gust of wind blew it round in a circle, however. Yet another gust pushed it violently up the beach, crashing it into a restaurant full of furious French diners.

My father, in the meantime, who was wearing a green bath towel dressing gown, was sitting on the edge of the boat reading *The Daily Telegraph*, which was flapping in the wind. Adrian shouted at the top of his voice, above the sound of the wind, while a cynical French crowd giggled and made jokes about the eccentricity of the English.

"As you can see, we are in a crisis, so I'm going to appoint you all as officers," began Adrian.

He pointed at me: "You are officer-in-charge of the front, right-hand rope."

"It's actually called the starboard jib sheet," said my father irritably.

Adrian pointed to Jonathan: "You are officer-in-charge of that big piece of wood, swinging backwards and forwards, hitting everyone on the bloody head."

He turned to my father: "Hey, you there, crewmember!"

"How dare you address me as crewmember, boy!"

Adrian ignored my father's rebuke and continued, "You are officer-in-charge of the tiller."

My father got quite cross. "I do wish you'd stop talking all this rubbish about officers, and concentrate on what's going on in the water," he said mildly.

"What water?" asked Jonathan. Although he was only seven, he was the only sensible person on board. He was staring vacantly at the sand which stretched around us.

Vichy, in the meantime, was licking two naked lesbians' bottoms.

* * *

As I stated before, we were made to learn passages from Shakespeare's plays as children, whenever we were naughty. Adrian and I often took it in turns to recite Shakespearean speeches and ask each other to identify the plays from which they came.

He specialised in speeches from the Wars of the Roses plays, with which I was less familiar than he. My mother had taught him extracts from these plays when he was little. I specialised in speeches from such plays as *Julius Caesar* (my favourite), *Hamlet* and *King Lear*.

Together we made an awful lot of noise and were told to shut up by anyone unfortunate enough to listen to us.

Peachey was hilarious whenever he teased Adrian and me about our bickerings, and on witnessing our complaints because we hadn't read each other's books.

Peachey imitated a couple of lifeboat boys obsessed by each other's prowess during a violent storm:

"If you don't watch me throwing *my* lifeboat out, I won't watch you throwing *your* lifeboat out!" said one to the other.

While this was going on, people were drowning in rough seas.

Peachey was so funny. Sometimes he had me in stitches for hours. He and Adrian got on very well together.

* * *

Adrian was seventy-eight when he died, in the Charing Cross Hospital, in London. He had pancreatic cancer for a considerably long time. He had lost all his thick, black hair and was wasting away, as I stated earlier. Pancreatic cancer is the deadliest of all cancers.

Marina spent a lot of time with him every day. She stayed with him from ten o'clock in the morning until four o'clock in the afternoon. She read his favourite books to him most of the time.

It was late on a Tuesday morning when he passed away. Marina, Harriet, Jessica and Jonathan were by his bedside.

Harriet tried to ring me repeatedly but couldn't get through. I wish I had been present.

At the cremation service, I stood next to Jonathan's and comforted him when the coffin was brought in. I kept saying, "Be brave, my boy, be brave," and held him round the waist.

He was particularly upset when the curtains closed behind the coffin. "It's alright, my boy. It's alright. It will soon be over."

The more I see Jonathan, the more closely he resembles his father. He inherits his father's mischievous wit and wicked sense of humour. Sometimes, I tell others that he is my son.

Anecdotes
A Visit to the Grand Hotel in Brighton

It was my last year at Sussex University where I had read English. I had just completed my finals. It was a pleasant, sunny evening, so I drove towards the Grand Hotel in Brighton, having watched the sun setting over the piers and beaches. I went into the hotel, which was very crowded.

I planned to have a double gin and tonic, so I went to the bar and placed my order. One of the barmen gave me a glass containing gin and ice, as well as a small bottle of tonic water. I poured the tonic water into the glass and asked the barman for the bill.

Suddenly, I noticed a middle-aged, purple-faced man, standing beside me. His eyes were tiny and red. His cheeks were covered with sweat and he looked extremely unhealthy all round.

For some reason, he was trying to interrupt the transaction between the barman and myself. The barman told me what I owed him, and I handed him some coins. I drank the gin and tonic in one go. It was very hot and I was thirsty.

"Women who drink alone do so in order to solicit," said the stranger unpleasantly. I was outraged and gave him a thunderous slap on the ear.

I later found out that his name was Oswell, that he had a pronounced drinking problem and that he was actually the hotel manager! On this occasion, he was proverbially drunk. He grabbed me by the shoulders and tried to steer me towards the door.

I took advantage of the fact that the hotel was crowded, and that he could ill afford to have a major scene on his hands, particularly if a woman were involved.

"Get your slimy hands off my tits, you filthy, old man!" I shouted as loudly as I could.

Several disapproving customers rose to their feet and left the hotel.

"Sorry about your dwindling clientele," I remarked sarcastically to Oswell.

Once I was outside the hotel, I called the police. Oswell, coward that he was, had temporarily found somewhere to hide, namely behind the bar.

Two officers tracked him down. I told them that Oswell had been paralytically drunk when on duty, and that he had also sexually assaulted me in a public place. The stench of alcohol on his breath confirmed his drunken state.

The once-crowded hotel was almost empty by this time.

"What a shame about your reduction in trade!" I called out to him as the cuffs were being put onto his wrists. "I do hope you will be happier in a police cell."

The two officers marched Oswell out of the hotel. Respect for me grew, due to the fact that he had a reputation for being rude and insulting towards women.

I waited for the panda car to leave the promenade, before I got behind the wheel, as I didn't wish to be done for drink-driving. I drove back to the university campus and parked my Ford Focus. As for Oswell, I heard a rumour that he had been admitted to some kind of clinic.

Dinner at Barbara Cartland's

It was mid-summer and I was about twenty-one.

I had received an invitation from Barbara Cartland, the author of 325 books, with recorded overall sales of between five hundred and six hundred million copies.

She had invited me to dine at her Hertfordshire house one Friday evening, and I came by taxi. Naturally, I thought I had been expected to stay for the whole weekend. I was carrying two suitcases, one containing my clothes and the other, my medicines.

The front door was opened by Barbara Cartland herself. She was dressed from head to toe in brightly coloured fluff, which comprised her trademark. The expression on her face, framed by a shock of candyfloss-like hair, was unwelcoming.

I introduced myself.

"Do you usually carry two suitcases when you have only been invited for dinner?" she asked confrontationally.

"I assumed you had invited me for the whole weekend," I replied. "Your house is a long way from London, and it's not really the done thing to expect a young woman to travel across the country at dangerously late hours of the night."

Due to the fact that her tone had been hostile throughout our exchange, I, too, was hostile.

I added, "I'm sure you wouldn't allow any of the heroines in your books to be turned away from country houses late at night, particularly when they don't know their way back to London!"

There was a silence.

"Did you say your name was Eleanor Berry?" she asked.

"Yes."

"And you're from London?"

"Yes," I said rather angrily. I was fed up with being made to stand in her doorway, like a bored soldier on parade. "I've had enough of this, Miss Cartland," I said. "Do you want me to enter your house, or would you prefer it if I sent for another taxi and returned to London?"

She reluctantly ushered me into her house and asked her butler to take me to a room where I could change for dinner.

The room was almost as uninviting as my hostess. The curtains were drawn, and the bed and chairs on either side of it were covered with dustsheets.

I went to the nearest bathroom, bathed and changed. I noticed a wall-to-wall bookshelf in the bedroom. This only contained Barbara Cartland's books.

I looked briefly at two titles. They were *The Wings of Ecstasy* and *The Proud Princess*.

I looked at another title and removed the book from the shelf, although I can't remember what the book was called.

I found a passage in it which struck me as being almost as raving as its author:

"A woman wants to fantasise about meeting a tall, dark, brooding man, who crushes her like a flower to the medals on his chest."

I sat next to the prolific novelist at dinner. "I'm an admirer of your books, Miss Cartland," I lied.

"Which ones?"

"*The Wings of Ecstasy* and *The Proud Princess*. I was struck by your vision of love in its purest form, rather than the tarnished and tacky infatuation, which, in this perilous, modern world, is often mistaken for love."

The writer fixed me with a curious stare. She may possibly have been put off by my academic language, which I had used without thinking.

She became more friendly towards me, however, no doubt because I had lied to her about my alleged appreciation of her books. I couldn't help admiring her, due to the enormous number of books which she had written.

Also, I later learned that she had virtually risen from rags to riches, and had done a lot of charity work, including tireless campaigning for gypsies' rights. This reminded me of my late aunt Eleanor Smith, whom I had never met, and who had a fixation for gypsies. She, too, had campaigned for their rights.

I found out that Miss Cartland was the daughter of a Birmingham businessman who had died penniless. She had started her career by selling articles to gossip columns, before writing romantic fiction.

In other words, she was quite a woman!

Mayhem on the 8.15

At the time of the following incident, I was four, Harriet was nine, Nicky was eleven and Adrian was about seventeen.

We were travelling from Aylesbury to London in a single railway carriage, on the crowded 8:15am train. We had ensured that we kept the carriage to ourselves.

This was easy to do. Adrian, who had always been somewhat eccentric, lay on his stomach on the luggage rack and read aloud the striking opening paragraph from *The Fall of the House of Usher* in a loud, menacing monotone. Nicky tunelessly sang, *"Everything's Up to Date in Kansas City"*. I waved a rattle in the air, and Harriet, some would say the most sensible of the four of us, shouted at us and told us to shut up.

The noise we made had the desired effect. No one came near our carriage, or indeed the corridor it occupied.

A guard, who knew my father well, told him about the disturbance we had caused. My father was particularly angry with Adrian, the eldest of us.

"A seventeen-year-old boy, who lies in a luggage rack on a train, reading Edgar Allan Poe aloud, in a savage monotone, is *mentally* ill," said my father to Adrian assertively.

Laugh Not, Sweet Sister, When a Hearse Goes By

I had always been morbidly inclined when I was a child. I read in *The Bucks Herald* whenever funerals were going to take place locally. Every time this happened, I attended them, accompanied by my father's gardener's daughter, Ruth Swithenbank. I had always been enthralled by the sight of the coffins being lowered into the graves. It seemed like a glorious work of art, or even theatre.

"Isn't it wonderful, Ruth?" I said to her, as we stood by the grave on this occasion.

I noticed tears on her cheeks. This encouraged me, as I felt I had found something in common with her.

She failed to look at the grave, however, and stared vacantly into space.

"Are you ok?" I asked.

"Isn't it sad about the poor, little princes who were murdered in the tower?" she remarked obscurely.

My mother found out about my hobby and was not very pleased. "Every time you go to a funeral, I will give you a French lesson," she threatened.

This worked. I hated French lessons at the time. As for my father, he said I was a "morbid little brat".

My Encounter With The Writer Piers Paul Read

This anecdote, or article, is lengthy, I fear. I have felt the need to make a strong point, however.

The following describes my encounter with the staunch Roman Catholic writer Piers Paul Read. He is well known throughout London, and indeed throughout England.

I have been brought up to despise anti-Semitism, as I may have said earlier. When we were children and passed any anti-Semitic remarks, we were sent to bed.

I'm sorry to say that there is a lot of anti-Semitism in some of Piers Paul Read's books. I can't understand how his publishers have allowed him to get away with this.

I can give an example of his most extreme anti-Semitic outburst, although it pains me to do so. In one of his earlier books (*The Junkers*) a character says, "The trouble with Jewish girls is that they have black hairs growing out of their tits."

Mr Read also wrote a novel entitled *Polonaise*, which describes a family of Polish aristocrats, who are deprived of their riches and who are forced to live in poverty in a Warsaw slum. For some reason, most of these unfortunates become card-carrying members of the Communist Party! Khrystina, the mother figure in the family, works for a Jewish gentleman, who owns a jeweller's shop. This gentleman is shown to be greedy, money-grabbing and conniving, as well as having other unattractive faults.

On leaving the jeweller's shop after work every evening, Khrystina stands in an endless queue to buy food and walks up about five flights of stairs, to a tiny flat inhabited by her members of her family. She prepares the food and serves it. Mr Read goes into extraordinary detail about how she does this:

laying the table, washing her hands, peeling potatoes and carrots, arranging pieces of meat, and God knows what else! Quite unnecessary anti-Semitic remarks frequently drift into the family's dinner table conversations.

Khrystina, a pious, humourless young woman, has a brother called Stephen. They are the novel's main protagonists. Stephen is a writer whose prose is laced with bizarrely sadistic overtones. He marries a wealthy Jewish girl called Rachel, who, for some unknown reason, keeps repeating the words, "I want to work in a factory and live in a slum!" (Are you feeling all right, Mr Read?) Although her parents are well off, Rachel is ashamed of her riches and wishes to give them away. She too, becomes a commie. Jesus!

When Rachel has children, Mr Read states how embarrassed Stephen is about their "Jewish" features. It's almost as if he thinks the reader is so stupid that he/she and needs to be told this over and over again. Also, although not relevant to my anecdote/article, Stephen refers incessantly to the nape of Rachel's neck. This is an awful bore. Why does he not dwell on her earlobes instead?

Anti-Semitic sentiments are expressed regularly throughout this novel and are deeply offensive. I once attended a cocktail party in London, hosted by a cousin of mine, and I was told that Piers Paul Read would be among the guests. I approached him and did not pull my punches.

"Mr Read, there is a lot of anti-Semitism in some of your books," I began, my voice raised.

He looked both baffled and dumbfounded, as if he had returned to his house and been surprised by a burglar.

"I am a rabbi in civilian clothing, and my name is Sadie Klein," I continued. "I am also a high court Judge, and as such, I have the power to have all your books shredded." I admit I had gone a bit over the top at this point. I was a trifle inebriated.

Mr Read continued to look dumbfounded. No doubt, he couldn't remember anti-Semitic tones in his books. He blushed and smiled at me vacantly. Then he leant over one of the tables, displaying mountains of food.

"Do you like quail's eggs?" he asked, as if he were saying, "Do you like Mozart?"

"Yes. I like them very much indeed," I replied. I was rather taken aback.

Apparently, he complained about me to my cousin. I was surprised he knew my name.

"Eleanor's just attacked me!" he said. "I can't understand why. I've never attacked her. Not only that, she told me she was a rabbi in civilian clothing called Sadie Klein, as well as a high court Judge, who had the power to have all my books shredded."

"I wouldn't worry about that. Eleanor has always been a bit eccentric!" said my cousin. I resented her disloyalty.

Piers Paul Read's novels almost always follow the same pattern. They describe spoiled, rich protagonists, who are so ashamed of their wealth, that they give all their riches away, and become copper-bottomed left-wingers to boot.

Mr Read's novel *The Professor's Daughter*, set in Boston, is an example of this trend, although I am happy to say that there is no anti-Semitism in this novel.

Louisa, a spoiled nymphomaniac, and the daughter of a spineless professor with oodles of money, is the novel's main protagonist. She has a *penchant* for chasing shady-looking men, provided they are complete strangers, as well as being very dirty. Her younger sister, who is equally as spoiled, is heavily into drugs. Both sisters somehow manage to persuade their idiotic father to give away every cent he has. Very bizarrely, he does just that!

The authorial presentation of this book, is absolutely potty, but both its prose and its dialogue are unique.

I will not describe any other novels written by this man, and I hope he will eventually grow out of his anti-Semitism. I will not deny, for one moment, that he is a talented and intuitive writer, however.

Harriet met him in Munich on one occasion. When she asked about his plans for the future, he told her assertively that he intended to become a "great writer". Although I don't care for some of the material in his novels, I can at least respect him for being a man of his word.

I Knelt Down on Soft, Wet Earth...

When Robert Maxwell died, I contacted several psychiatrists. One of them was an American living in London. His name was Dr Mortimer Schatzman, and he spoke with a soft, Eastern Seaboard accent. He was very slim, had moist lips and a long, red beard. He is still alive, but I don't consult him anymore because he keeps interrupting me.

When I asked him why he had chosen to become a psychiatrist, he told me that he had had a difficult and unreasonable mother, who had insisted on addressing him as "Hitler" when he was a boy. He said she looked like Norman Bates's mother from behind, and that she used to sit on a rocking chair all day, reading the Bible aloud to him. He was an only child and never got on with her even when he had come of age. His father had been killed in World War II.

I always cross-examine psychiatrists about their relationships with their mothers. Sometimes, I get answers. Sometimes, I don't, and, very rarely, I get extremely abusive answers.

I spoke to Dr Schatzman, my voice lowered, because my spirits were low, following Robert Maxwell's death. I described my drive to Headington Hill Hall, which was untidy and uninhabited within. There were stacked-up piles of chairs, all over the place, particularly in the dining room.

"It was pouring with rain," I said. "I drove down the drive, towards the house. The circular swimming pool had been filled in with grass, which was a horrible yellow colour." Schatzman remained silent. I continued, my voice still lowered, "I walked onto the lawn. I knelt down on the wet earth, and I recited *The Raven.*

I was suddenly interrupted by the American's uncharacteristically loud voice. "So what?" he shouted.

I had hysterical giggles, and went on laughing, before having hiccups. The American had certainly washed away my gloom.

He sent me a large bill, however. I wrote back to him, and said that I was only prepared to pay half the desired sum, because during a good part of the consultation, he had spoken to me about his relationship with his mother.

"You sure do drive a hard bargain!" he commented.

As for his having made me laugh, I continued to laugh for about three weeks, in restaurants, in pubs, in dentist's chairs and even when I was walking down the street. On these occasions, I made no effort to control my laughter, irrespective of the stares of passers-by.

Elizabeth Taylor

I used to have a GP whose name was Dr Victor Ratner. I have mentioned his name on several occasions. He was a Harley boy. That is to say, he had consulting rooms in Harley Street. I worked for him as a debt collector for just over a year. He offered me the post because he thought I had the right tone of voice for the job. He also asked me to do some secretarial work for him.

Very sadly, he died in suspicious circumstances, in August, 1993.

He also treated Elizabeth Taylor, the actress. Sometimes, she travelled all the way to London to seek his services. We both called him "Ratty".

"Miss Taylor, you are my second most difficult patient," said Ratty to her, on one occasion.

"You mean there is someone more difficult than me? I can't support this rivalry!" said Miss Taylor, in her adopted American accent. "Oh, Ratty, when am I gonna *meet* this person?"

Ratty told me that Miss Taylor would be visiting his Harley Street consulting room, one sunny summer's afternoon. Her chauffeur drove her from the Dorchester Hotel to her destination.

Ratty had organised a snack, consisting of cucumber sandwiches and china tea. Miss Taylor, who was grossly overweight and who was wearing a flamboyant, silk maternity gown, wolfed down almost all the sandwiches, as if she had never eaten anything in her life before. Ratty ate nothing and sipped the china tea.

He introduced us. I shook hands with Miss Taylor and was struck by her alarmingly strong handshake.

"I understand you are Ratty's second most difficult patient," I ventured. I added, "I am his first most difficult patient."

Miss Taylor struck me as being extremely unfriendly and devoid of a sense of humour.

"Is that so now?" she muttered eventually, in an indifferent tone of voice.

Sock It to Me, Miss!

Elizabeth Taylor reminded me of the few visits I had made to the States. I went to New York, Washington, Chicago, Boston and Miami.

I did not enjoy my visits to the States, because I was very lonely and also because I don't like American accents.

Harriet had just got over an attack of glandular fever, and my mother had arranged for her to stay with some friends of hers, called the Reitsmans. I'm not sure how this name is spelt.

I stayed in a motel in Miami for a few days, and because there was no one with me, I hailed a taxi and went to the cinema in the afternoons, without doing any research about the films I would be seeing.

I sat down near the back row of the cinema, but failed to realise that I would be watching a pornographic film. There was hardly anyone in the cinema.

Suddenly, I heard a voice saying, "Miss?"

It was a man's voice and he sounded hysterical. He was sitting behind me, and I turned my head. I saw a man who had obviously come straight from a golf course. Apart from clean white slacks, he had on an equally clean, white baseball cap, with white hair protruding from underneath it. He looked about seventy.

"Sock it to me, Miss!" he kept repeating urgently.

I spoke to him with an exaggerated English accent. "What exactly do you want me to sock to you?" I asked.

The man looked slightly embarrassed. "Are you British?" he asked eventually.

"Yes, I am," I replied confrontationally. I was irritated by the fact that the cinema was showing a pornographic film.

"I thought so. I can tell by your accent," he said aggressively, adding, obscurely, "I don't think you guys distinguished yourselves too well in World War II!"

I paused, in an attempt to find the appropriate words. I found the man totally out of order.

"You lot are fine ones to talk. You were all a bunch of useless Johnny-come-latelies", I said in the end.

"What do you mean lady?"

"It's perfectly obvious what I mean. You all failed to come downstairs until long after the bell had been ringing!"

I wasn't all that satisfied with my words, but the weird man in white buggered off all the same.

The Van Praagh Brothers

This story also goes back in time, but it relates to an important period of my life. I was about twelve. I was staying in Rebecca's parents' house once more. There were two boys staying in the house as well. One was called Peter Van Praagh, who was about the same age as Rebecca and me.

The other boy, Charles Van Praagh, was two years older than his brother.

Both boys had had a bereavement. Their father had just died. Peter was more grief-stricken than his brother was. Their mother could not cope with her sons being in her house all the time, so she asked Mrs Roberts (Rebecca's mother) if she would take them off her hands for a few days.

Mrs Roberts, a very kindly hostess, took us all to the cinema in Guildford. She left us outside the cinema as she did not wish to see the film. She bought tickets for Peter, Charles, Rebecca and me.

The film *Taras Bulba* made a great impression on me, because there was a reference in it to one of the characters, a Cossack, living in seventeenth-century Ukraine, who had been called a "coward".

Although Adrian had finally been very impressed and had told me how brave I was when I had taken the toboggan up the slope, and come down a second time without digging my heels into the snow, I was embarrassed by the fact that I had appeared "cowardly" in his eyes the first time. I had adulated him at the time and was determined to impress him. I have always considered the word "coward" to be the most insulting word in the English language. My attitude was part of my obsessive-compulsive disorder.

I ignored complaints from other members of the audience, who hissed for silence. I talked to Peter and said how terrible it must be to be considered a "coward".

There was an interval. A middle-aged woman was selling ice-creams in the aisle.

"I'll give you a chance to prove you're not a coward," said Peter.

"Oh, yes?"

"I dare you to go up to the ice-cream vendor, and say, 'There's a very good-looking boy in the cinema who'll fuck you for a shilling,'" he said.

I did as I was told.

"Tell your friend, he's going to have to offer me a darn sight more than just one shilling!" said the ice-cream vendor angrily.

I repeated her words to Peter.

"Tell her she's only worth a shilling," he said.

I passed Peter's second message to the woman.

"'Ere! Get out of it, and don't be so bloomin' cheeky!" she shouted.

After the film was over, the four of us played on a building site on the outskirts of Guildford. Peter handed me a brick and dared me to throw it at a fancy-looking sports car, which had stopped at a red light.

"I'd better not do that," I said.

"You wouldn't want me to think you were a coward, would you?" said Peter mischievously.

I didn't think twice. I hurled the brick at the sports-car and made a dent in its paintwork.

The driver got out and went straight for Charles, the biggest of us. "Is this little brat your sister?" he demanded.

Charles opened and closed his mouth, like a goldfish biting the dust.

"N-no, sir!" he eventually managed to splutter.

Thereafter, I was known throughout Rebecca's parents' neighbourhood as "that maniac".

My parents were also told about the incident. They made me learn *"The Charge of the Light Brigade"*, but because of the way in which the poem rhymed, I didn't find this too difficult a task. Strangely, my father was more incensed than my mother. However, it was she who suggested that I recite the poem to the sports-car driver as well.

"I think that would be unjustifiably hard on the sports-car driver, given what he's been through already," commented my father mildly.

Gaining Comeuppance at the Royal Free Hospital

Like the Piers Paul Read anecdote, this anecdote is quite long, unfortunately, but it is particularly mindful of my view of the difference between right and wrong.

The Royal Free Hospital is in Hampstead, North London. I can't remember the date of my employment there. Nor can I give any names, or indeed the name of the department I worked in, due to the libel laws. I was working for an agency as a temporary medical secretary. This requires a lot of skill but does not carry much rank.

A temporary medical secretary earns more than a permanent medical secretary, but she is often double-booked and can be sacked at a moment's notice. I have explained this before.

This does not prevent permanent medical secretaries from resenting the presence of "temps" in the workplace, and from treating them with disdain.

My job at the Royal Free Hospital was to type long letters from the consultant to general practitioners, as well as the senior registrar's letters. I also had to type letters dictated by SHOs (an SHO is a euphemism for a junior doctor).

I was given at least ten discharge summaries to type every week. These were on average about six hundred words long. They described the circumstances leading to a patient's admission to hospital, details of his/her stay on the ward, results of blood tests, details of operations, biopsies and X-rays etc. which had been performed. There is frequently a long list of medications prescribed for the patient on discharge.

Discharge summaries are fiddly and quite difficult to type. They have to be completed as a priority before letters to general practitioners.

I was working under a consultant and a PA, or personal assistant to the consultant. The PA was three years my senior.

"My office!" she said to me peremptorily one morning, for no apparent reason.

"What about your bloody office?" I replied.

The PA had jet-black hair which was cropped close to her head. Her face was heavily made-up and she wore an exaggerated amount of crude green eyeshadow, making her look extremely common. She always wore a black suede miniskirt, an array of tight-fitting, different-coloured T-shirts and black criss-cross tights. Her shoes were equally as punky as her clothing, and she spoke with a strong Liverpool accent, which was very hard to decipher.

She had less typing to do than an average medical secretary, be she temporary or permanent. Some of her duties were to book air flights and rooms in five-star hotels for the consultant, who travelled abroad a lot to give lectures.

This did not take the PA very long. She also had to type letters relating to her boss's private – that is to say – Harley Street practice.

Although the consultant did not have a Harley Street secretary at the time, the PA did not have to do much typing, because the consultant had so few private patients. The PA's duties were therefore minimal, so she spent almost all her time making personal phone calls when the consultant was out of the room.

The first incident I am about to describe occurred late on a Friday afternoon.

I was taking dictation from the consultant, whose office was thronged with clinic clerks. A clinic clerk is lower in rank than a medical secretary, and her job is to sift through results contained in a cardboard box. It was almost time to leave for the weekend. I had worked hard throughout the week; my desk was practically clear and I was looking forward to five o'clock.

The PA, whose name I cannot give, as I've said earlier, suddenly blustered into the consultant's office, startling the clinic clerks. She was holding a small piece of paper, on which a result had been printed. The document stated that a man suffered from terminal lung cancer.

Because of my huge workload, I could not possibly have been expected to notice the document, which had been put into the cardboard box, among a large pile of other documents, stating patients' results. Unfortunately, the man suffering from terminal lung cancer had died that morning. Because the

PA bitterly resented the fact that I was earning more than she, she shouted at me, so that the consultant and clinic clerks would be able to hear her words.

She continued to bellow viciously and accused me of having caused the lung cancer patient's death. "That gentleman is dead because of your negligence! He would never have died if you had done your job properly. You are no more than a common murderer."

I was incensed, particularly as she had passed this offensive and untrue remark in front of an audience. Besides, it was the job of the clinic clerks to sift through the results contained in the cardboard box.

I shouted at the PA, using the first words which came into my head. I no longer cared whether I would be sacked or not. "What the hell do you expect me to do about it? Bowl over to the mortuary and cross his fucking hands?"

The consultant had a very black sense of humour, and laughed out loud. The PA had lost the first round.

She was determined to get rid of me all the same. She overlooked the fact that I could easily be out of work for the whole of the following week. Fortunately, the consultant admitted in front of the PA that I was a very hard worker, and that I had a huge workload each day, whereas the PA had been spending sixty per cent of her time making personal phone calls. Another member of staff had grassed on her.

The PA continued to do everything in her power to get rid of me, but I refused to surrender. In situations of this nature, I fight to the death, and I play as filthy as I can. I always hear the speeches of Sir Winston Churchill in my head.

The PA approached me the following Friday afternoon. She knocked on the door of my office at four-thirty. This time she was without an audience. She was carrying a light brown velvet blazer.

"What do you want?" I asked her in a hostile tone of voice.

"I'd like you to take my blazer to the cleaners, sometime during the weekend."

Using very offensive language, I pointed out to her that it was not my job to take other people's blazers to the cleaners.

I also threatened to report her to the consultant, due to her persistent harassment. I added, "I am a distinguished woman of letters, with a number of published books behind me, two of which have been translated into Russian, and are studied by Russian children.

"I am sick of your squalid, cowardly bullying, not to mention your common personal appearance. No one dares to ask someone like Eleanor Berry to take their blazers to the cleaners!"

Strangely, she backed down, and left the room. She and I arrived at the workplace at about nine o'clock on Monday morning.

She knocked on the door of my office and was unusually civil. "You speak Russian, don't you?" she asked, in an uncharacteristically genial tone of voice.

"Yes!" I snapped.

"Perhaps I went a bit too far on Friday afternoon," she said.

"You did! You're so right!" I replied.

"I wonder if you could possibly do me a favour?" she ventured.

"As long as you don't treat me like a lackey and ask me to run errands for you."

"No. My husband and I have got a new *au pair*. She's Russian and she doesn't speak a word of English."

"So what? I suggest you hire an interpreter."

"There's no need to. I've got you, haven't I?" she said, almost kindly, adding, "Incidentally, what is the Russian for, 'Hullo, you are most welcome'?"

I didn't reply straight away. I couldn't forgive this woman for accusing me of murder, at the top of her voice, in a room full of clinic clerks, as well as the consultant.

The more I searched for words, the more I loathed the PA to distraction. I hated her to such an extent that I was even prepared to kill her by pushing her under an underground train. I might indeed have done so, had it not been for my fear of going to prison.

"Well, what's the answer to my question, then, or has your Russian got so rusty that you can't remember?" she demanded unpleasantly.

I gave her the Russian for, "Have you got a big cunt?"

The following morning, she came to work with most of her teeth missing. "I just don't understand what happened!" she said mildly, adding, "I repeated your words."

I struggled to keep a straight face.

"Well, you know how you are!" I replied.

She was fired within a few days. One of the reasons for her dismissal was that she had cheekily demanded three months off, just to get a new set of dentures fitted.

I also told the consultant that the P.A. had been making anti-Semitic remarks on the phone. I had overheard her speaking to her husband and telling him that she didn't want any Jewish cleaners in her house. This helped my case most of all. The consultant was Jewish. The P.A. only lasted for another week

Ian Fleming

I was about eight at the time of the following incident. My parents had taken me to a house owned by the spy writer Ian Fleming, in London. He had been to Eton, the same school as my father.

I can hardly remember speaking to our hostess, Ann Fleming. I learnt later that she was very tough and liked to wear the trousers during her marriage. I also learned that she liked her husband to whip her before sex.

Someone told me that she had once read aloud a passage from one of her husband's books in front of her friends. Apparently, he had been humiliated by her behaviour.

The Fleming's had an only child, a boy called Caspar, who was about my age. He got into serious trouble with firearms and heroin in early adulthood, and committed suicide. I only knew him when we were children.

The adults were having pre-lunch drinks. Caspar asked me to accompany him to the attic, although I soon realised that this was a bad idea. He was extremely rough and was much stronger than I was. He produced a heavy, blunt object, possibly a poker, and dared me to break some of the windows in the attic.

I never say "no" to a dare, so I broke the windows. I can't deny that I was stimulated by the sound of smashing glass.

The door leading to the attic suddenly swung open. I dropped the blunt object and turned round. I saw an intensely angry-looking man who was staring me straight in the face. It was Ian Fleming. I had never liked the man because he wasn't very friendly. He and Ann came to our house in Buckinghamshire a lot. He smoked through a cigarette-holder and always swaggered about, with a sly, contemptuous grin on his face.

Caspar was very rough, even then. He pushed me violently under a bed. I had to scream for help.

"Who broke these windows?" shouted his father.

"She did, Daddy," said Caspar.

"That's not how it happened," I said. "Caspar dared me to break them. It wasn't my fault."

"Rubbish!" exclaimed Fleming. "Get out of here and go downstairs."

Ann Fleming, whom I saw in the drawing room, gave me a filthy look.

As a punishment, my parents made me learn the first six verses of Elizabeth Barrett Browning's poem, beginning with the words, *"What was he doing, the great God, Pan/Down in the reeds by the River?"* I didn't like the poem at all, and I found it extremely difficult to memorise the verses.

I later learned that Ian Fleming suffered from severe depression, and that he had sado-masochistic tendencies. One of his sado-masochistic victims was Sonia Quennell, whom my sister, Harriet, had half-heartedly intended to take the place of my mother after her death. My father had bitterly disapproved of her plan.

"No, Ian, I simply can't take this!" Sonia had complained to the melancholic writer, who had tried to jab a fork into her shin under someone's dinner table.

Fleming was obsessed by sex. He was once dining at my parents' house in London and was sitting next to a woman who had taken his fancy.

He put his hand under her dress and began to stroke her thigh, causing her to let out a sharp scream.

"What the hell's going on, Ian?" my father called across the table.

"Oh, sorry, Michael," ventured Fleming. "I was just offering this lady some toast, and my hand must have inadvertently brushed against her leg."

My father refused to accept his guest's feeble excuse. He threw him out of the house.

Fleming suffered from heart trouble. He was also a heavy drinker as well as a chain-smoker. One of his doctors advised him to reduce his alcohol and tobacco intake, which the doctor said would be likely to damage his heart even more.

"I couldn't give a fuck!" his rebellious patient replied. He had always had a death wish. According to several biographies of him, he had an unusually difficult mother.

A Séance in Paris

When I was staying in Paris once, I was in someone's bedroom, with various people whom I barely knew. There were about six of us. There was also a phone in a corner of the room, whose owner had gone away for the weekend.

One of the occupants of the room suggested that we hold a séance, using a table which covered a good part of the room.

I concurred, and so did all the other fuckers. We laid our hands palms downwards on the table.

The man who had taken charge, but whose name I can't remember, got up and dimmed the lights. He returned to the table, and asked a few questions, about the death of a jilted girl who had hanged herself in the room we were sitting in.

Everyone eased their hands backwards and forwards across the table.

"Are you resting in peace? Knock the table once if your answer is no," said the man running the séance.

I had to make a lot of phone calls to London. There was a payphone in the hall of the lodgings I was staying in, but it was out of order. I had no choice but to use the phone by the bedside of the person who had gone away for the weekend.

I kicked the table from underneath, once. The dickheads participating in the séance were scared shitless and left the room, screaming.

I made at least nine phone calls to London. I was decent enough to leave some money for the absent person to pick up on his/her return, as well as an explanatory note in French. As for the others, they rushed out of the building, terrified and huddled in a group on the pavement.

Eleanor's favourite brother, Nicky, with whom she lived in London for about ten years.

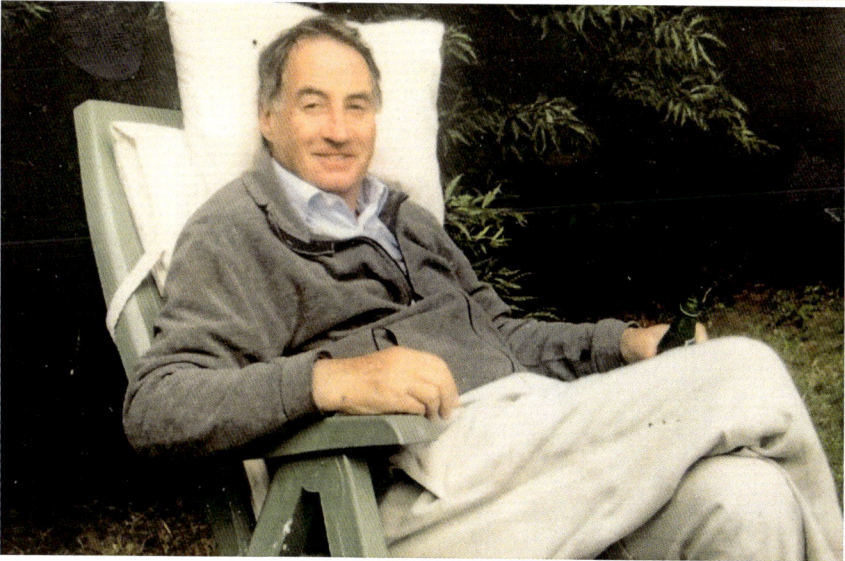

Another photograph of Eleanor's favourite brother, Nicky.

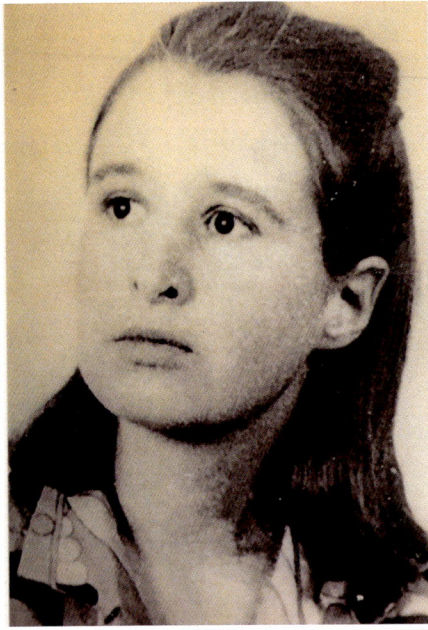

Eleanor
aged sxteeen.

Eleanor's beloved nephew,
Jonathan.

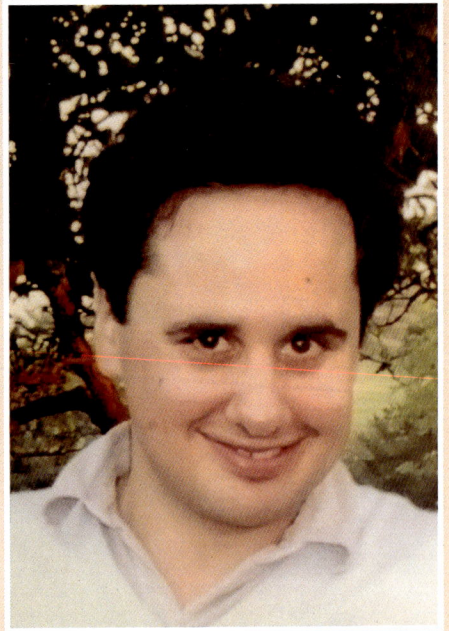

Eleanor visiting Robert Maxwell's grave. This was a proud moment.

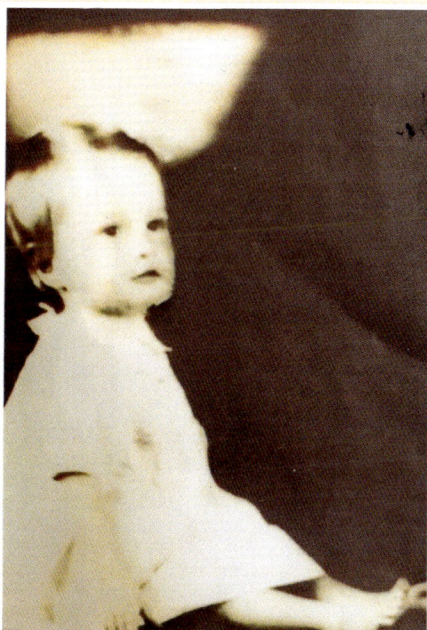

Eleanor as a baby.

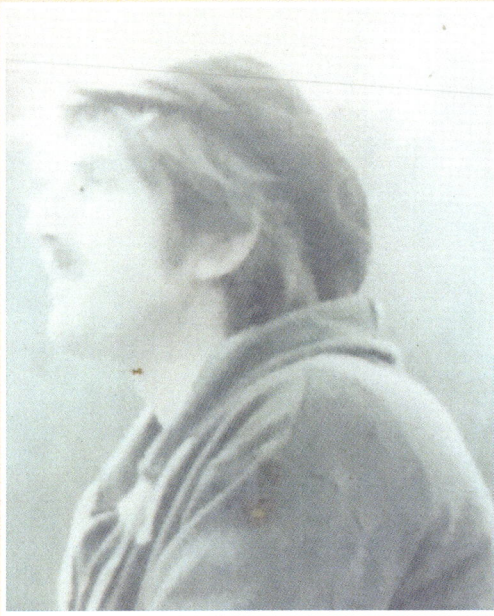

The late Peachey – Love of Eleanor's life.
Eleanor took the photograph herself.

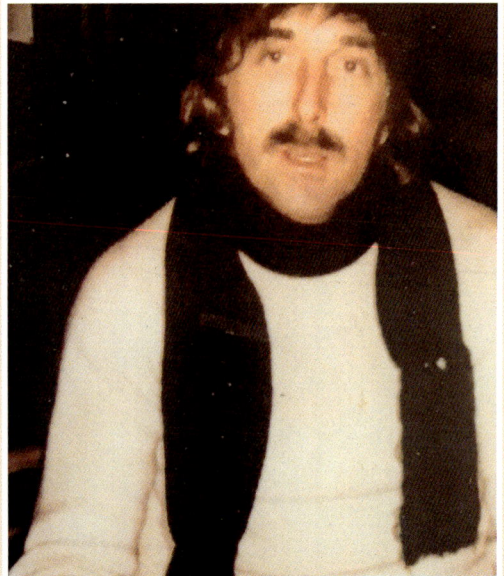

Two more photographs of
the late Peachey, Eleanor's love.

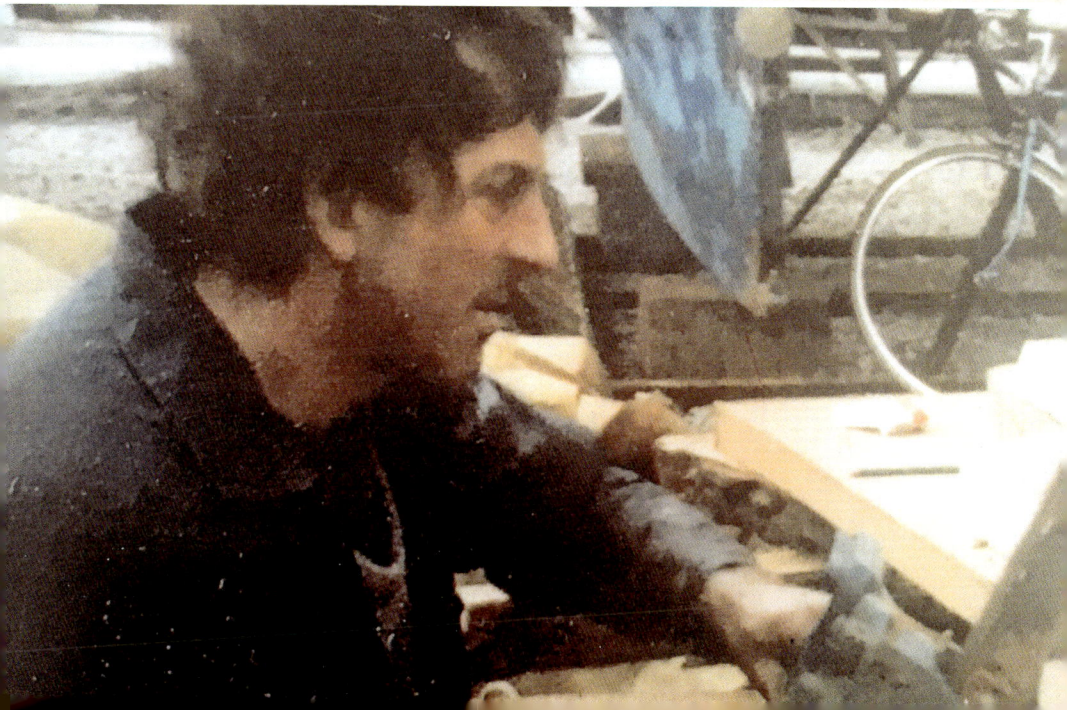

Eleanor with Robert Maxwell.

Robert Maxwell's house in Oxford, Headington Hill Hall,
where Eleanor stayed for a whole year, after being thrown out
of the Y.W.C.A.

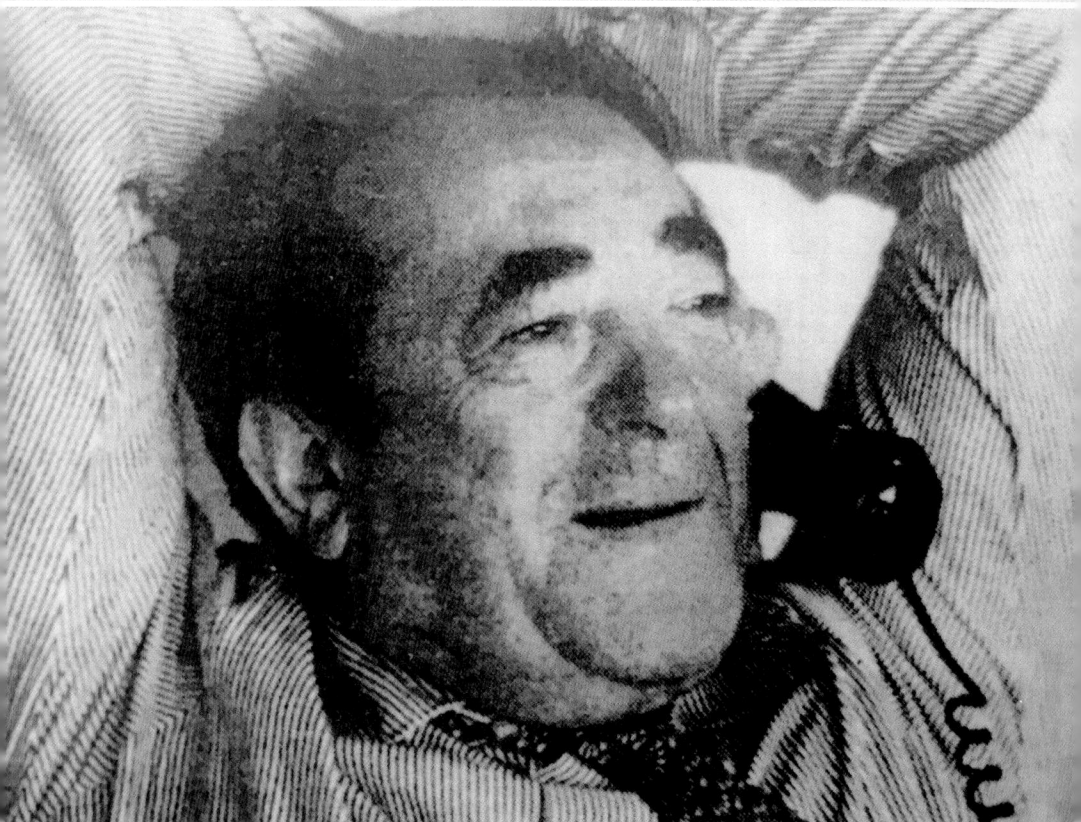

Eleanor's favourite photograph of Robert Maxwell
(looking at a ~~lady's~~ woman's legs).

The Late Rita Auden, the Niece of the Late Poet W.H. Auden

I met Rita Auden in 1984. She was staying with her sister, Anita Money. She had had trouble with her colleagues, and hence, her nerves, and had moved, from a depressing block of flats in South London, to her sister's house in Pimlico.

Rita was a surgeon at the Royal London Hospital in Whitechapel. She was a dedicated worker and was devoted to her patients. She was also an exceptionally kind-hearted woman, without a malignant bone in her body.

Very regrettably, her colleagues mocked and persecuted her without provocation. They resented her quiet mien, laughed at her vulnerability, and, in particular, they joked about her false eyelashes. They made snide remarks about her personal appearance, across the supine patients that she, and the other surgeons, operated on.

Rita was not robust enough to retaliate. On one occasion, she fainted during an operation. Fortunately, she did not fall over the patient. She fell backwards.

Her boss advised her to take three weeks off. She returned to the dismal block of flats where she had been living before.

Rita was a brilliant pianist. Because of the difficulties, which she had had at the hospital, she was unable to sleep. Her doctor refused to prescribe sleeping pills for her, which increased her torment.

To avoid going completely off her head, she threw herself into her piano-playing. She played from midnight until about eight o'clock in the morning. At nine o'clock, after she had had breakfast, she felt guilty about her piano-playing during the night, and feared that she had disturbed her neighbours.

She got hold of a large strip of canvas, a black, felt-tipped pen and some glue. She wrote a message in letters about six inches high on the canvas, apologising for having played the piano during the night. She placed her message from one wall in the lobby to the other.

This was not all. She found a step ladder, climbed up it and stated precisely what pieces of music she had been playing and at what times!

"At 12:15, I played Chopin's *Prelude* in A major. At approximately one o'clock in the morning, I played what I could of the first movement of Rachmaninoff's *Second Piano Concerto in C Minor*. This took me quite some time, I'm afraid, and sometimes I had to go back to the beginning and start all over again. After that, I played Beethoven's *Für Elise in A Minor.*"

I don't know exactly what happened after that. I think the porter, a singularly disagreeable man called Mr Lilly, rang up Rita's sister, Anita, who hurried onto the scene, and persuaded her sister to stay in her house once more.

There is no doubt at all that Rita is somewhat eccentric, however, but her talents are legion. She was also beautiful, kind and was forever searching for knowledge. She worshipped her uncle, the poet, W.H. Auden, and often referred to him as "my only friend".

She could read both the Greek classics and Dostoevsky in the original, and had a memory like an elephant. She could also recite reams of Virgil without tiring. She was a truly great scholar, who was disgracefully maligned by her catty, and jealous, surgical colleagues. I wish a bust could be erected in the hallway of the Royal London Hospital in her memory.

I would also like to mention the kindness of her sister, Anita Money, towards me, and the many dinners which she cooked for me, asking nothing in return.

I Shared a Corridor with Baroness Thatcher at the Cromwell

I can't remember what year it was, only that it was winter. I was taken ill with pneumonia in both lungs, although I normally enjoy rude health, particularly in the respiratory tract. I took a black cab to my GP's consulting rooms, and he sent me to the Cromwell Hospital, having told me I was "dangerously ill". The only complication was the venue of the hospital. I had once walked out of there, without paying, because the staff had refused to give me a copy of *The Daily Mirror*. The staff told me it had folded but I informed them that I had spent the previous weekend in the proprietor's house. I put up a tremendous fight and these dickheads then told me it had sold out. I still refused to pay.

There were a lot of cameramen outside the hospital, as Baroness Thatcher was incarcerated there. I was admitted and rang my housekeeper, Mary Rothwell, as well as Harriet.

I sat up in bed while Harriet and Mary installed themselves in other parts of the room. I tried hard to breathe. Harriet suffers from asthma and sometimes has difficulty getting air into her lungs. She knows how to control her problem, however, with the aid of a Ventolin inhaler.

"Just husband your resources!" she kept saying. As I have never suffered from breathing disorders, I lacked her self-control.

A consultant chest physician, called Dr Brian O'Connor, came into the room. He then spoke peremptorily to the nurses at the nursing station. I could hear him shouting the words, "Get that patient down to intensive care immediately, and put an oxygen mask on her face!"

While I was being wheeled towards the lift, I saw Baroness Thatcher, who was walking down the corridor between two nurses. She was unmade-up and was wearing a dressing gown and slippers. She was undergoing "physiotherapy". I thought I was having a hallucination.

Once I arrived in intensive care, I tried to stand up but fell backwards. Two nurses caught me. If they hadn't, I would have fallen and cracked my skull.

There were a lot of patients in intensive care. The place reminded me of a ward occupied by Florence Nightingale's patients.

The nurses were efficient and kind-hearted, unlike some of the nurses I had come across on staying in different hospitals in the past.

I usually abide by the axiom: "Put a woman into a nurse's uniform and she becomes like Hitler!"

I lay on my back all the time and breathed through a mask. Harriet brought her lunch in every day. She was dressed from head to foot in black on one occasion.

"Isn't your choice of colour somewhat premature?" I asked her.

"Sorry, I've just been to a funeral," she replied.

There was a dying Arab among the patients, and a cacophony of his weeping relatives were standing round his bed. A male relative, dressed in what looked like a white nightgown, read aloud passages from what I assumed was *The Koran*.

Among the dying man's relatives were a number of women, who chanted loudly and wept even more loudly! All in all, they sounded like a load of wasps, buzzing round and round a plate.

Eventually, the Arab died, but the chanting and weeping continued. His body was removed from intensive care in a coffin covered by green cloth. All his relatives left intensive care. Harriet was relieved because she was able to speak without having to shout.

I stayed in intensive care for six weeks. After that I was guided back to the ward. Mary, my housekeeper, was waiting in my room.

I opened the cupboard, but it was empty. The suitcase, which Mary had brought, had disappeared. I still felt ill, not to mention, very angry.

"Where the fucking hell are my things?" I shouted. It transpired that my suitcase and its contents had been put into storage.

I found out that Baroness Thatcher, who, like myself, had been very ill, had heard my furious words through the thin wall, which divided her room from mine.

"Who on earth is that horrible old man, using that filthy, disgusting language?" she asked one of the nurses.

Somehow, the story got into *The Daily Mail* and I was referred to as "the eccentric writer, Eleanor Berry".

I was sent home within a week or so. Baroness Thatcher was not so fortunate, however. She died after a few weeks. She was transferred to the Ritz, where she breathed her last. I can't deny that she was a great Prime Minister, though, despite the fact that she completely changed her accent, and sounded phoney.

"I'm Not Leaving Your House Until I've Had My Way with You!"

I once had a relationship with a man called Luke Wilson (name changed). Luke was very good-looking and always laughed at my jokes. He and I met several times a week, and went to his house in London.

Regrettably, a heavily made-up, peroxide blonde called Jo-Jo (surname withheld) chatted him up in a pub one evening. Both were very much the worse for wear, and she asked him, in an extremely fast manner, if she could move in with him.

He lived in a large house. His address was 33 Chelsea Square, which was just off the King's Road. As Jo-Jo was a social climber, his address appealed to her. Luke had a weak character, and he said she could move in with him straight away. Most men are babies. They tend to be far weaker than women.

Jo-Jo was emotionally insecure. This was because her favourite uncle had died when she was twelve, and she didn't have any siblings. She was also very highly sexed. In fact, the bloody woman couldn't get enough of the stuff! She demanded sex at least four times a day. Sometimes, even that was not enough for her. She forced Wilson to drive her to Shepherd's Market, in his Rolls, so that she could pick up prostitutes after dinner every evening.

On her instructions, he drove the prostitutes back to 33 Chelsea Square, where she performed sexual acts on them. Wilson was not particularly interested, though. He went to bed early every evening.

"I'm only doing this for kicks, Lukey," she explained. When she had satisfied herself, she sent the women back to Shepherd's Market in taxis without paying them! So dumbfounded were they by her behaviour that it never occurred to any of them to ask her for payment.

I heard about these goings on from Wilson's ex-wife, Connie, who was a friend of mine at the time, and who kept me informed about every facet of Jo-Jo's insane behaviour. Wilson used to talk to Connie regularly. Although they were separated, he liked to confide in her, particularly about sexual matters, to make her jealous.

One day, Connie heard that Jo-Jo had planned to stay with her parents for the weekend. Also, I heard that Wilson would be alone at 33 Chelsea Square.

I took advantage of the situation, dressed provocatively and knocked on Wilson's front door, at nine o'clock on the Sunday morning.

He opened the door, wearing a dressing gown and pyjamas.

"I'm not leaving your house, until I've had my way with you!" I said, my voice raised.

He paused for a moment, leant nervously to one side, and suddenly smiled broadly. "Oh, *do* come in," he said. He rang Jo-Jo up, in her parents' house, and told her what had happened. She never returned to the house.

Unfortunately, my late brother, Adrian used to meet Wilson at pheasant shoots in Hampshire every Saturday, after a boozy lunch. Wilson was very indiscreet and told Adrian, using pretty ribald language, about his younger sister's arrival at his front door, her getting rid of his previous girlfriend and her having moved into his house, without intending to leave.

Adrian apparently slapped his thigh and let out a guffaw. Sometimes, he teased me about it. Had he not been married, he would have done the same thing himself.

The Nun Who Was Reading One of My Books

I was staying with a friend who lives in Hampshire. On this occasion, she introduced me to a nun who was staying in a house next door to hers, and who had come to tea with her.

I noticed, to my horror, that the nun was reading one of my naughtier books, namely *Help Me, Help Me, It's Red*. She was sitting in a dark corner, holding the book in her lap. In fact, she was reading it so intensely that I had trouble attracting her attention.

Because of the book's *risqué* contents, she could easily have spread the word round the neighbourhood that I was the author of perverse literature.

Help Me, Help Me, It's Red is about a schizophrenic doctor's relationship with his father, a Harley Street psychiatrist. The book is a black comedy and, very regrettably, it contains a lot of swear words, to brighten things up.

The schizophrenic doctor had severe psychological issues during his childhood, when he was bullied by his father.

Strangely, his father reforms by the time his son reaches adulthood, and the two go to the other extreme and have an almost incestuous relationship.

This is too late, however. The younger man never recovers. His behaviour has been brought on by his experiences at a very young age, when he had been saddled with solitary confinement, freezing air temperatures, near starvation and the sight of his dead nanny lying on the floor to boot. He has become a serial killer and a sex maniac.

My prose is pretty graphic throughout the book, which is only intended for a strictly selective audience.

I spoke to the nun as tactfully as possible. I said, "Oh, Sister, I don't really think this book is suitable for your eyes. Allow me to ease it gently out of your hands." I continued, "I have read quite a few reviews about it, and they all

186

suggest that this is not the book for you. Mind you, I have no idea who wrote it, but even the reviews I have read lead me to fear that there is a risk that it could shake your faith."

"I've finished it, actually," said the nun abruptly.

"Indeed? Are you OK?" I ventured inanely.

"The book is about sin. I enjoy reading about sin. Did you write it yourself?" asked the nun.

I suddenly felt very hot and agitated. I looked at the mirror facing me. My cheeks were red. "Why, no! No, I didn't write it! No, of course not!" I lied.

There was a silence.

"We've been having particularly nice weather, lately, haven't we?" I eventually managed to mutter.

Edgar Allan Poe's Birthday

Edgar Allan Poe's birthday was on the 19th of January (he was born in 1809). Regrettably, the date of his birth coincided with that of a boat trip I had been invited on by two men from London. The boat was a cruise ship and was bound for somewhere in the Mediterranean. I had no idea that the sea was going to be so rough.

I remembered that it was Edgar Allan Poe's birthday, however, and I intended to persuade the two men to celebrate it with me. I went to the bar and consumed a number of gin and tonics, by which time I was fairly merry, and in the mood for partying. Somehow, I found the two men and forcefully asked them to come over to the bar.

I climbed onto a barstool and produced a paperback copy of Poe's poems. I started to read *"The Raven"* aloud, as it was his most favourite famous poem. I only managed to read half of it.

By two o'clock in the morning, I was legless, as were the two men from London. A pissed-off barman reluctantly agreed to guide us back to our cabins.

The sea was really rough, due to the time of year. The boat was rocking and causing us to fall over all the time. We had different cabins. My friends shared cabins with other men. I went into my cabin, which I shared with two women, neither of whom I knew. The lights had been turned off. I cannot sleep in the dark, because of the nightmares I suffer when I see my beloved Peachey dead.

One of the women snored loudly and the other, who was sleeping by the window, had drawn the curtains, shutting out all the light, even that provided by the moon and stars. I ran my fingers up and down the wall, in an effort to find the light switch. I turned the light back on.

The two women woke up. Both had heavy Irish accents.

"Turn that bloody light off!" said one of them.

I was still intoxicated and shouted, although I was under the impression that I was whispering. "All my psychiatrists, occupying rooms the whole way up and down Harley Street, are absolutely adamant that I sleep with the light on, at all times!"

"Why?" asked one of the Irish women.

"Because I'm terrified of the dark. I've had a bereavement."

Unfortunately, I had woken up most of the occupants of the cabins in the corridor. They staggered out of their cabins, despite the inclement weather, which was getting even worse.

"Shut up!" some of them shouted.

"You shut up!" I replied.

The two men from London also told me to shut up. They said they would not be travelling on a cruise ship with me again.

I was glad to be back on shore and made up my mind that I would never be celebrating Edgar Allan Poe's birthday again, because of the inconvenient time of year. Looking back on the matter, I thought it was really inconsiderate of Edgar Allan Poe to have a birthday on 19th January.

Knee Replacement

I underwent a left knee replacement recently, in a London hospital.

Instead of asking for a general anaesthetic, I insisted on having a local to avoid depression after the operation.

I assumed I would be given a customary morphine injection, and I did not realise, for one moment, that the anaesthetist would be giving me a colossal heroin injection, or a diamorphine injection, as it is referred to as a rule.

It would have been courteous of the consultant surgeon had he asked my permission before authorising the anaesthetist to give me the heroin injection, but he failed to do so.

Soon, I sensed that something was very much amiss. I experienced an extraordinary feeling of euphoria. In fact, my spirits went so fantastically high, that I felt as if I were hitting the moon.

As a result, I became exceptionally talkative. I addressed all the surgeons collectively and at length, at the top of my voice.

"There's something you all should know, boys!" I shouted. "I need to tell you a bit about Robert Maxwell's relationship with his father."

"Will you be quiet, please!" shouted the consultant surgeon. The temperature in the operating theatre was quite warm. His assistant mopped his brow.

"I don't see why I should be quiet," I replied. "A member of your staff has just given me what seems to have been a massive heroin injection, without having had the decency to ask my permission first, so you are all to listen to me, boys, whether you wish to do so or not.

"There was this bare-footed, ragged and impoverished Czechoslovakian boy, walking down a village street, accompanied by his father, a burly, unemployed peasant.

"Suddenly, the boy bent over and was sick in the gutter for some reason. His father, a certain Mehel Hoch, grabbed him savagely by the hair and rubbed his son's face in the vomit."

The enormous quantity of heroin which I had been given, caused me to repeat this unfortunate story over and over again.

"Will you please be quiet!" shouted the consultant surgeon, even more loudly than before.

"No, I most certainly will not be quiet!" I shouted back. I continued to speak, my voice raised. "The experience must have traumatised the boy for the rest of his life. It is often the case that boys have undesirable relationships with their fathers, just as Robert Maxwell suffered from a terrible relationship with his own father. What about you, Sir, did you have a satisfactory relationship with your father?"

"Mind your own business, Miss Berry," shouted the consultant surgeon. "Another thing, if I hear one more word from you about Robert Maxwell's relationship with his father, you are going to lose a leg!"

"I find you quite unnecessarily rude," I replied.

Shortly after the operation, I became really low-spirited, just as I would imagine a habitual heroin addict becomes when his "fix" wears off, and he hits the floor. No doubt he feels as if he has fallen down a deep, dark well and is unable to get out of it.

I was taken to my room on a trolley and got into bed. My spirits got lower and lower. I lay on my back for a good two hours or so.

I watched a bit of television. Gradually, I felt fractionally better. I couldn't help being very angry, however, because my permission had not been sought regarding the heroin injection.

I decided to report this frightful man to the GMC (General Medical Council), on leaving the hospital. Predictably, they did sweet FA.

An Unfortunate Phone Call

I have a cousin called Simon Scott who works in the film industry. One morning, I rang him up to cancel a dinner date, and was in a very impatient mood for some reason. At the time, he was working on a film called *Eyes Wide Shut*. I rang his number.

"Can I speak to Simon Scott, please?" I asked.

"I'm afraid he's very busy right now," said a man with a lazy, Eastern Seaboard, American accent. He was very curt and uncooperative.

"I don't care if he's got his hand up a fucking horse's arse! I want to speak to him, and I want to speak to him now." I don't normally use such disgusting language, unless I am really provoked.

The American repeated his words, this time in an exceptionally irritated tone of voice. "I've just told you, he's very busy right now. You can't speak to him."

"When can I speak to him?"

"Tomorrow maybe."

By this time, I was really pissed off. I said, "I feel the time has come for me to take your name, so that I can report you to your superiors, for being so difficult and awkward on the telephone."

"This is Stanley Kubrick speaking," said the American suddenly.

I was dumbfounded. "*You* are Stanley Kubrick? I grovel on trembling, bended knee!" I eventually managed to mutter.

I hung up pretty smartish.

Moscow

I went to Moscow alone when I was about eighteen. My parents did not approve of my going there alone, so I told them I was going to stay with friends in Cornwall. Brezhnev was in charge at the time. I had taught myself Russian and was pretty well bilingual. I had taught myself the language on my own steam. My parents were against the idea. They wanted my third language to be Italian.

I was fascinated by Russian literature and indeed all things Russian. I was also a card-carrying member of the Communist Party. I had managed to book myself into a hotel, using a travel agent. The hotel was called the *Rossia*. It was close to Red Square, near the legendary *Stenka Razin* Street.

I went to Moscow in order to meet Russians. I walked across Red Square to visit Lenin's tomb. It was pouring with rain. I had on a leopard skin raincoat and thigh-high, patent white boots. My attire was somewhat eccentric. I was soaking wet. I approached a policeman outside the tomb and spoke to him in my best Russian. Admittedly, I sounded rather verbose. "I'm sorry to bother you, comrade. I have come all the way from London to see Vladimir Ilyich." (Lenin was known as Vladimir Ilyich by Communist diehards in Russia at the time.)

I added, "I am a card-carrying member of the British Communist Party, so could you please be very kind and let me go to the head of the queue, comrade?" I made a point of addressing him as "comrade". I thought it would sound more polite.

The policeman was singularly bad-tempered, however. He was about five foot eight inches tall and had severe acne. He shouted, "*Ochered! Ochered! Rada Christi!*" which means, "Go to the end of the queue, for Christ's sake!"

I didn't argue with him, because I was in someone else's country. I went to the end of the queue, and eventually, I saw the old stiff. I had waited for about two hours. Lenin looked serene and not unattractive. He seemed like someone in a mortuary who had recently died. Some old ladies crossed themselves on walking past his body. Most of them were shabbily dressed.

I had been warned by friends in London never to speak to anyone outside my hotel room late at night. This was because members of the KGB had a tendency to button-hole foreigners, invite them to parties, give them spiked drinks and photograph them in sexually compromising situations. I longed to be approached. I had rehearsed my quip several times in front of a mirror.

A bald-headed man, aged about fifty, and wearing a grey raincoat, tightly belted in at the waist, came up to me in the corridor, just outside my room. He looked the epitome of Khrushchev. He had an artificially civil manner and invited me to a party.

I repeated what I had rehearsed in front of the mirror, in Russian once more. "I am really sorry, comrade. It's now five to twelve, and if I don't get back to my room by twelve o'clock, I'll miss the unique experience of hearing your *glorious* national anthem being played on the radio." (God knows how I would have said this today!)

The man whitened and looked a bit staggered. "Goodnight, comrade," he eventually managed to splutter.

Apart from this Gestapo-like figure, I made friends with quite a few Russians. My purpose was to go to Moscow alone, and, not only to find out about Russian poetry and go to the Bolshoi, but also frequent cafes, restaurants, and places where beautiful folk music would be played on rippling balalaikas.

For a short time, I modelled myself on Isadora Duncan, although I have never been able to dance. I made inquiries about clubs, where I didn't have much luck, due to the Cold War.

Finally, I went to the bar at the *Rossia* hotel, quite late at night, where I met two sex-obsessed male students of about my age. They kept teasing each other. They had travelled from the Black Sea, where they lived in a flat overlooking the sea, intending to visit the capital.

They were both very good-looking and had short, black hair, and bright, green eyes. One had his hair parted in the centre, but the other's was parted at the side. They were about the same height: 5' 6".

They had quite a few drinks and I accompanied them. We spoke about

Russian poetry and Russian literature at length, but it was not long before I felt slightly inebriated.

Both men were anxious to come into my room so that they could have some "vigorous hanky-panky". As I had made friends earlier with the *Babushka* (or "grandmother") who sat outside foreigner's rooms, to prevent Russians from going into them, I thought there would be an excellent chance of my bribing the *Babushka*, whom I had got on so well with. I thought, in my drunken state, that I could easily get away with oiling her palm, with at least 40 roubles. Also, I was taking the pill, and in the mood for adventure.

After a considerable time, however, my alcohol intake began to wear off and I sensed danger. I thought about the *Babushka* in depth, and the terrible perils I would be getting myself into. Also, I like to make a lot of noise during sexual activity, which would have reverberated down the whole corridor.

The 40 roubles would definitely not have satisfied the *Babushka* and I soon got bored with the two men. They were as keen as mustard, however, and had become like a couple of fucking three-year-old boys. I explained once more to them, that it would be really dangerous to do what they wanted. I parted with them amicably and kissed them on the cheek. I'm bound to say I didn't know either of their names. I thought once more about the dangers of inviting Russians to foreigner's rooms, and the terrible consequences of so doing, particularly during the Cold War.

No doubt, I would have ended up in the *Lubyanka**. I have heard that conditions in this prison are horrendous. Temperatures are too cold in the winter and too hot in the summer. Also, the cells are completely dark and damp.

Whether I would have been let out early is neither here nor there. My father would certainly have cut me out of his will!

I often chattered to the *Babushka* who sat near my room, and who was on the verge of being bribed on that drunken night. I practised my Russian on her and she turned out to be really friendly. She had a small television on her desk, and she allowed me to watch it before bedtime.

She asked me where I was from, and I told her I was from London. She said her daughter was learning English and asked me when I would be going home. I said that, unfortunately, I was going home the following morning.

"There is nothing unfortunate about returning to one's motherland!" she said sternly.

*The *Lubyanka*: A deadly Moscow prison in which inmates stay for infinite periods of time.

By and large, the Russians really are a pretty batty lot, but that does not alter the fact that they are fascinating, and that, last but not least, they are totally unspoilt.

On another occasion, I was having breakfast in the dining room of the *Rossia*. All they provided was black bread and lemon tea. A man aged about thirty, sat down opposite me. He looked rather like Nureyev.

"You have such beautiful, big brown eyes. Tell me about your soul," he said in Russian.

"Not now, comrade," I replied as politely as I could. "After I've finished my breakfast, maybe."

He stared at me while I continued to eat my breakfast. He had a beaming ear-to-ear smile, which never left my face. I was rather embarrassed.

I don't like black bread or lemon tea. I yearned for bacon, eggs, toast and milky English tea. One morning, I hailed a taxi and asked the driver to take me to the British Embassy, where I demanded a "civilised English breakfast".

The staff at the British Embassy were most disagreeable. I made a point of telling them that the income tax I paid "through the nose" enabled them to enjoy the luxury of living at the British Embassy. They refused to give me a civilised English breakfast and asked me to leave the premises. They wouldn't even hail a taxi for me. I became very aggressive and asked them to refer me to the British Ambassador's office, but to no avail. I was left in the company of a sentry in a street very near the embassy, on whom I was able to practise my Russian once more. To please him, I waved a copy of *Pravda* in his face, causing him to clap. "Very good!" he said in English. Within about ten minutes, I got a taxi back to the hotel.

On the whole, I had a good time in Moscow. It was particularly exciting, as my visit was during the Cold War, and everyone walked suspiciously in the streets, looking over their shoulders, to see whether they were being followed. I found these people intriguing. They inspired me to write a book at a later date.

I was walking down Gorki Street, towards Red Square, one afternoon. Gorki Street is so wide that many vehicles can travel up and down it abreast.

A nondescript-looking man recognised from my clothing that I was a foreigner, and approached me.

"You ought to be in a group. Why are you wandering about alone?" he asked officiously in Russian.

"I'm very sorry, comrade. I don't wish to be in a group. I wish to be alone. Is there anything else you want to know?"

"Yes. How much money have you got?"

"Mind your own business, comrade," I replied.

The man buggered off.

It was experiences such as these which caused me to enjoy Cold War Russian life on a short-term basis, but nothing would have induced me to live in Russia permanently. I value my freedom too much.

I passionately wanted to stay in Moscow for another week. Somehow, I don't remember how, I found my way to Frank Taylor's office to seek help. He was my father's Moscow correspondent. At first, due to my extreme enthusiasm, he was terrified, because he thought I was intending to defect to Russia, and had no idea what he was going to say to my father (his boss). He took me to an office next door to his, in which a very unhelpful woman kept repeating the words, "If you don't leave my office, I will send for Ivan Petrovich."

Mr Taylor promptly rang my father, and explained that I was sitting in his office in Moscow, refusing to leave. All this time, my father thought I was staying with friends in Cornwall.

"Why did you have to lie to us?" he asked, mildly, on my return to London.

"Because I didn't want you to know the truth!" I replied. It would be an understatement to say that my father wasn't very pleased. Nor, for that matter, was my mother.

* * *

My mother did not get on as well as I did, when she went to Russia, years before I was born. Stalin was in charge at the time of her visit. She was accompanied by her brother, Freddie, her sister-in-law, Sheila, and my father.

She was walking down a Moscow street with her singularly embarrassed companions, shouting loudly. Her voice, as always, was unbelievably carrying. Some ragged, shabbily-dressed children were playing, with a ball, on the pavement.

"I thought this was meant to be a socialist country!" she shouted. "Why are all these children running about in rags?"

My mother and her party travelled on the Trans-Siberian Railway. Very regrettably, an English-speaking guide was sitting next to her throughout the journey. She continued to raise her voice as she commented adversely about the monotonous, passing Steppe-lands: "God, this is such an ugly country! Oh, this is such an ugly country! Can you beat the phenomenal ugliness of this country?" Her voice reverberated along most of the train, and any unfortunate English-speaking travellers understood every world she uttered.

Worse was to come. She got out at Vladivostok, where she had a man shot! Apparently, the man had removed her gold initials from her vanity case. God knows what he wanted them for!

"Mind you, if a Soviet citizen is shot dead in Stalin's Russia, he wouldn't have much to live for anyway, would he?" said my mother. Once more, her voice was overheard. My father was mortified with embarrassment.

* * *

At the time of my mother's Russian visit, her sister, Eleanor Smith, was dead and her brother, Freddie, was her only living sibling.

Freddie had married Sheila, my father's younger sister. When I was a child, Sheila was upright but very kind, and was always smiling. She often read aloud to me. She was also a prolific writer, who didn't suffer fools gladly. I was once in a car with her, aged eight. I begged her to drive me to some derelict house in the country, and pleaded with her, over and over again. Still I would not accept her refusal to grant my wish. Eventually, she said, "Do shut up! You're the biggest bore in Buckinghamshire!"

My mother's elder brother, Freddie, was good-looking and closely resembled his father. His sense of humour was mischievous, but he was very melancholic and was inclined to hit the bottle, as I've said before. This did nothing other than to increase his depressions.

Sheila and Freddie, who were both prolific writers, had two children, a boy (Robin) and a girl (Juliet). Both are dead.

When they grew up, they were phenomenally witty and had their listeners in stitches. Like their parents, they, too, were writers.

Juliet, like my maternal grandmother, had a taste for the macabre and could recite reams of Oscar Wilde's *The Ballad of Reading Gaol* and *Old Grindrod Was Hanged on the Gibbet High* by Harrison Ainsworth.

She was also very musical and could sing *"Land of my Fathers"* in Welsh. I was so enthralled by her renditions that I asked her to repeat the hymn over and over again. Eventually, she gave me the record.

She knew some terrifying ghost stories and told me many of these when I was about ten. One of them, entitled *The Red Hair in the Horse Meat*, was so frightening that it kept me awake all night. This was the night before I was due to go to Godstowe.

Robin, her brother, was delightful beyond belief. On one occasion, he took me to a restaurant in Jermyn Street, London, and he made me laugh so much that a lump of steak got stuck in my throat.

My life was at risk. I was faced with the choice of putting my hand down my throat and bringing everything up, or dying. I decided to do the former, and I brought up everything I had eaten, even the prawn cocktail I had had for my first course. Waiters hovered round the table, their white napkins flapping in the air.

Robin was very squeamish and edged away from me as the anxious waiters continued to hover. "You could at least have made an effort to go to the lavatory," he said eventually.

"How could I have done so? I was dying!"

Robin died on a tennis court at the age of forty-eight. It was thought that his death had been due to too much caffeine and too many cigarettes. He never drank alcohol, because he was terrified of becoming like his father.

He had been walking from one side of a tennis court to the other. He was struck down unexpectedly by a massive heart attack. Adrian absolutely adored Robin and was gutted by the news. They had grown up together, like brothers. He never really recovered from Robin's death. They were as close as Siamese twins. Once, on visiting Venice, they had a spectacular swordfight in the lobby of the *Gritti Palace Hotel*. Visitors to and from the hotel staggered past them in terror.

In 1973, Robin offered me a hundred pounds to get into White's all-male Club, disguised as a twelve-year-old boy. It was a bet. Robin was convinced I would fail to pull it off.

I took him up on his offer and hired a schoolboy's uniform from a theatrical shop on the Charing Cross Road. I coiled my then waist-length hair under a wig, on top of which I wore a grey schoolboy's cap. The rest of the uniform was grey, and I had on men's shoes as well.

A friend of Robin's reluctantly accompanied me to White's, and we went to the bar, my fingers covered in ink. He posed as my uncle, to whom I said in a loud, deep, voice, "I'm afraid I'm really bad at Latin. Will you test me on '*hic, haec, hoc*'?"

He looked at my inky fingers disapprovingly. "Not now. Later, maybe," he said.

I started to talk about rugger, maintaining my deep voice. "I had a lot of trouble getting out of that scrum, and then squitty little Jones, minor, pulled a fast one!" I boomed. Under a rolled-up sleeve, I had written the words "Wilcox minor is a twit," with a felt pen.

My "uncle" told me to roll down my sleeve and ushered me into White's rather depressing dining room. I was determined to play the part of a boy throughout lunch. I grabbed an elderly waitress's boobs.

"Cor, you haven't half got a smashing pair of knockers!" I said.

We were thrown out. Not because I was a woman, but because I was behaving in a rude and unruly manner. I won the bet. When we reached Robin's house afterwards, he gave me a hundred pounds in cash and the wonderful audience that I craved. Whenever he laughed, he scratched his head and shook it at the same time. His laughter was unique, extraordinary and more than infectious. He was the most wonderful company imaginable and I still miss him to this day.

* * *

While I was at Sussex University, I got on better with the tutors than the students, many of whom kept posters of bloody Che Guevara on the walls of their rooms, and tended to be copper-bottomed left-wingers. In order to hide my original accent, I spoke with a heavy Irish accent all the time. Eventually, this came naturally to me.

I once had tea with my aunt, Sheila, who, though kind-hearted, was quite conservative, particularly as she got older. "Oh, I do wish you'd stop speaking to me with that that dotty Irish accent!" she said forcefully, as she poured out Yorkshire tea from a Meissen teapot.

There was a particularly pleasant tutor, at the university, called Stephen Metcalfe who taught English literature. Regrettably, he is no longer with us. He entertained us in his house every Saturday, from nine thirty in the morning, until about one o'clock, and offered us sandwiches and wine. Sometimes, he took us to a restaurant in Lewes, afterwards, and everyone went Dutch.

The most important thing about Stephen was that he dispelled the shyness that students sometimes suffered from. The copper-bottomed left-wingers seldom attended his gatherings. They considered them boring.

I really appreciated these Saturday mornings, which enabled me to enjoy my life at university far more than I would have done without Stephen's help. However, because the university library was so crowded, I wrote all my essays in the London Library in Saint James's Square. Eventually, I was thrown out, however, because I was seen writing in the margins of Samuel Richardson's *Clarissa*.

* * *

Once I had graduated, I took an agency job as a commercial translator, using French and Russian.

I was also asked to translate verbally, still using these languages. Unfortunately, I couldn't keep up. I lost my head and shouted at the parties concerned, and, for want of better words, I was bunged out.

Shortly after that, I worked as a temporary medical secretary for many years in a number of London hospitals, as I stated earlier. Provided the personnel managers didn't double book me, which was rarely the case, I stayed in the same departments for at least six months on the whole.

The permanent medical secretaries resented the "temps", and frequent arguments between the permanents and the "temps" took place.

The "temps" earned twice as much as the permanents, although the "temps" could be sacked at a minute's notice. I have mentioned the situation in my story about the job I took in the Royal Free Hospital. Because of the distasteful atmosphere in a lot of National Health hospitals, I eventually asked one of my employment agencies to send me to a different hospital every week, so that no one would get to know me, or find out what I was earning.

I made a lot of money temping. When I was sent to the gynaecology department at Guy's Hospital, I failed to get on with my supervisor, who was at least ten years younger than me. Despite the age difference, she kept complaining, as I was always trying to do two things at once, and couldn't keep up with her.

"You chit of a girl! Kindly refrain from speaking to me like that, when I am old enough to be your mother!" I shouted.

The supervisor was civil to me after that, although the work I had to do in her office was drawing to a close. The following week, I was transferred to an abortion clinic in the same hospital. The job in the abortion clinic was even more stressful than the one in the gynaecology department. I was alone in the office and had to work around the times of all the patients' menstrual periods. If they'd been gone for three months, I had to put them on the Monday afternoon list. If they'd been gone for between three and five months, I was told to put them on the Wednesday morning list. If they had been gone for more than six months, I had to ring up their GPs, whose lines were often either engaged or unavailable. I then had to speak to the GPs' secretaries. These women were either stupid, offensive or in the habit of hanging up all the time.

I went home with a heavy heart one evening, and on the following day, my ordeal was even worse. Five bad-tempered prostitutes thronged my office, and none of them could remember when her last bleed had taken place. What is more, few of them could speak proper English, and the only words they were able to use were "fuck" and "cunt". I burst into tears and walked out, without even handing in my notice.

* * *

I had been so traumatised by the strain of temporary medical secretarial work, that I did voluntary work for a while, to pass the time and also to add points to my CV. I read Dostoevsky to blind patients in a dingy old people's home in South London. The patients were aged from about eighty-eight to ninety-eight.

I was asked to read to a ninety-six-year-old woman who mistook my voice for that of her seventy-five-year-old son. She hadn't seen her son for at least five years.

There was a shortage of *Diazepam* in the home, and the supervisor asked me to read to some of the patients, because of what he rudely considered to be my deep, monotonous voice.

I sat on the ninety-six-year-old woman's bed, facing away from her, and read an interminable passage from *Crime and Punishment*.

The passage describes a certain Luzhin's unwillingness to meet the main protagonist (Raskolnikov) at a railway station, because of his alleged "rudeness" when they had last met. The passage lasts for at least two hundred words!

I continued to read aloud, but someone tapped me on the shoulder. It was the supervisor. "I'm sorry, Miss Berry, but I'm afraid the lady you've been reading to has just died," he said curtly, adding, "You will have to leave the premises now."

I found the whole situation very depressing. Also, the supervisor failed to thank me for my services and was unpardonably offensive.

"I'm going to the cinema," I said angrily. "Be sure to inform the old lady's son about his mother's death. Incidentally, I don't intend to return to this ghastly place. I find you too rude."

* * *

I will go forward in time.

There were two general elections in 1974, one in about February of that year and one in the autumn.

Labour won both the elections.

Just before the campaign leading to the early 1974 election, my mother was terrified of a Labour victory. She rang me up hysterically, and said, "In no circumstances are you to dye your hair and in no circumstances are you to go skiing. You're to stay in England and work for the Conservative Party!"

I disobeyed all her orders. I dyed my hair a sort of carrot colour. I went skiing with Nicky, and on returning to England, I got in touch with Bob Maxwell and worked fervently for the Labour Party in his offices and in the streets. While I was canvassing for Labour, I had no idea that they would win. I felt that Ted Heath (the Conservative leader) would win on a landslide.

As was the case in all the elections, when I was working for Bob, I took the train to London on polling day and voted Conservative. I only wanted Bob to win in his own constituency.

Bob and some members of his family were staying in the "Wharf" house, near the Labour Party headquarters. It was the eve of poll. I was sitting in the dining room with the late Judy Ennals, one of Bob's argumentative secretaries. She had worked for him for about twenty years. We were by ourselves talking in a rather manic manner about Russian literature.

I was convinced that the Tories were going to win on a landslide, and I didn't bother to go into Bob's study. It was there that the results were coming through on the television.

Suddenly, like a bat out of hell, Betty (Bob's wife) rushed into the dining room. I thought, for a minute, that the building was on fire.

"Eleanore! Come on!" she said, her voice raised in excitement. "We're going to have a Labour government!"

I pretended to be elated. After all, I had become a Tory and had only done all this work to please Bob and to annoy my mother. I sat on the floor in his study, and tried to screw a smile onto my face, without the aid of a spanner.

We stayed in the study until about four o'clock in the morning.

Judy Ennals had her own room and was putting on her nightclothes.

I knocked on her door. "Sorry to bother you, Judy, now that Labour have got in, do you think the government's going to be awfully left-wing?" I ventured nervously.

"It depends on what you call left-wing," she replied tersely. "As far as I'm concerned, I fear it may not be nearly as left-wing as I'd like it to be."

"Oh? Just how left-wing is that?" I asked.

"The first thing I'd like to see happen is complete press censorship."

I thought immediately about my father and his two newspapers. I felt sick. I went to my room and took my pills.

Worse was to come. As always, but without being fully aware of it, I had kept an extremely high profile during the campaign, and my name had got into the papers. It had been stated that I had been working for Robert Maxwell. Also, my age was given, together with a lot of other details, including a rather unflattering photograph.

My mother was absolutely furious because I had disobeyed her and helped Labour to win. She wrote me a letter, which began with the words, "*We are all punch drunk with gloom because of the election results. It really was a time for you NOT to go working for Labour.*"

Added to this, my father's favourite brother, Seymour, banned me from staying in his house. It was ironic that, for once, Seymour and my mother were on the same side.

Adrian even went so far as to comment that what I had been doing was the same as fighting for the wrong side during the Civil War!

To make amends, I wrote Seymour a very long letter, in which I stated that my relationship with Robert Maxwell had made me feel very confused, because he had once saved my life, and in no way could I betray a man who had done that.

I added that I had taken the train to London on polling day and had voted Conservative. Not only had I voted Conservative, I had also become a Conservative.

The letter was fifteen pages long! In the end, Seymour very kindly forgave me and allowed me to stay in his house once more. It's possible that he didn't get round to reading the whole letter.

I showed the letter to my aunt, Sheila, who, for some reason, laughed like a drain. "I do wish you'd spoken to me first, instead of writing a long, boring letter like this!" she said obscurely.

* * *

In about 2000, a "yellow" journalist called Alexis Parr wrote a seedy and sordid article about my books in general. The article was published in the satirical magazine, *Punch*.

The article suggested that I was a necrophiliac. A necrophiliac is a person who has sexual intercourse with either a dead body or more than one dead body.

I consulted an upmarket solicitor, who read the article and said it showed the worst example of libel that he had ever encountered in his career! I started proceedings.

I had a row with Adrian, who said I was to drop the proceedings, due to bad publicity effecting the family. I said I would, but I went ahead with them.

Before the solicitor had had a chance to write to *Punch*, I was in such a temper that I stormed into the editor's office, having found out his name.

I introduced myself and waved the offending piece in front of him.

"What can I do for you?" he asked.

"I am in a rage, and when I am in a rage, by Christ, I'm like a bull!" I shouted.

"Do please take a seat, Miss Berry. Would you care for a bottle of port?"

"No," I replied. "This article by Alexis Parr is totally unacceptable. I intend to sue you!"

I sued *Punch* and won, although Adrian was furious because I had gone back on my word.

"I had no choice but to go back on my word!" I shouted. "The article could easily have got into the *News of the World*!"

Nicky then came onto the scene at my request. He was wonderfully calm, as usual.

Miguel (Harriet's eldest son) wrote me such a sweet letter about Alexis Parr's article. He said it smacked of gutter journalism at its worst and that I would, one day, be a great writer. God bless him!

Court Cases That Have Interested Me,
and a Few Doctors Whom I Have Known
Dr Crippen

I have listed attending sensational court cases as being among my interests. Let's call it a hobby. This is definitely germane to my autobiography. I have also spoken about members of the medical profession whom I have known.

I'll start with the infamous Dr Crippen. Naturally, I did not know him.

His wife, Cora, was an irritating and monotonous piano-player. Crippen found her hobby intolerable. She was also offensively obese, loud-mouthed, vulgar and possessed a considerable number of other faults, which I have not got time to list. Dr Crippen himself was feeble and frail

Cora's piano-playing persisted from one night to the next and also continued throughout the day. In the end, her effete husband could no longer tolerate this habit. He killed her, chopped her body into pieces, threw the pieces into his cellar and covered them with lime. He told his inquisitive neighbours that she was ill and that she had gone to America for a "rest".

He fell in love with his secretary, Ethel le Neve, and eloped with her. He told her to dress like a twelve-year-old boy. The two boarded a boat, bound for Canada, I think, but they were alerted by wireless. He touched her body in such a way, that he gave the impression that the "boy" accompanying him was a woman.

Not only was his strange behaviour noticed by other passengers, Ethel looked outrageously feminine throughout the trip.

F.E. Smith, my maternal grandfather, defended her brilliantly and got her off, by playing on her crippling anaemia. Although he protected her from the gallows, she failed to thank him for his services. Her behaviour left much to be desired.

When the pieces of Cora's chopped-up body were being passed from one jury member to the next, F.E., for such was he known sometimes, saw his mawkish and morbid wife, Margaret (my maternal grandmother), in a prominent part of the visitor's gallery. He scowled at her in fury. Once he arrived home, he gave her a terrific ticking-off!

* * *

As a child, I revelled in seeing the contents of the Chamber of Horrors at Madame Tussauds in London. On being taken to the Tower of London, I asked my luckless nanny to show me the chopping block, over and over again. I also attended strangers' funerals.

My parents arranged for me to see a paediatric psychiatrist when I was about ten. The examination took a boringly long time. The three of us were interviewed at length by a shabby-looking, middle-aged woman who was wearing a dowdy, green dress. Her untidy red hair was coiled on top of her head.

First, she interviewed me sympathetically. Then my father was interviewed. There was a silence in the room, while the psychiatrist browsed through her notes.

My father looked questioningly at my mother, whose head was lowered.

"I'm afraid it's all been coming from your mother," he said. "The gene is quite prominent. It's not the little girl's fault."

There was another silence. My father looked sternly at my mother, and commented, "You, yourself, are a fine one to talk. When you were a young woman, you asked the Home Secretary to arrange for you to be shown round the Black Museum at Scotland Yard, didn't you?"

My mother failed to reply. She sighed irritably.

I, too, had later written to the Right Hon Roy Jenkins, the Labour Party's Home Secretary, when I was in my early twenties. I asked him whether he would kindly arrange for me to be shown round the Black Museum as well, and I thanked him profusely for the trouble he had taken.

My mother kept a thick album, containing cuttings describing gory court cases. I found it on a shelf in her house. "This trend certainly hasn't skipped a generation," commented Harriet.

It cannot be denied that my mother shook off her morbidity as she grew older.

On another subject, my motto is "I am not a Smith for nothing." This has always applied to the desire of the Smiths to take revenge when injury has been committed, either against themselves or their loved ones. How on earth do you think Sir Winston Churchill won the war, as opposed to the Germans?

Dennis Nilsen

I attended part of the trial of the late Dennis Nilsen. He was as gay as a cricket. He was a Scotsman and was what appeared to be a cannibal and someone who, according to all the newspapers, killed "for company". He was also known to be a crashing bore. He was arrested in 1983. He had once been a policeman and a photograph of him wearing a policeman's uniform, appeared on the front pages of all the newspapers.

He picked up a series of homeless men, who were not likely to be missed, took them, one by one, to his small, foul-smelling flat in north London, and drowned them by pushing their heads under bathwater.

He then washed their bodies, put their clothes back onto them, God knows how, and sat them down on chairs, so that he could speak to them at length without being interrupted. Apparently, he had a problem where making conversation was concerned. Young men, with whom he started conversations in pubs, tended to interrupt him all the time.

I can well understand why! As I said, he was accounted for as being a paralysing bore!

After the bodies had decomposed, Neilson removed their flesh with a meat-cleaver and flushed them down his lavatory.

What was even more unbelievable, was the fact that he called the police to complain, in his own words, that "an unpleasant smell had permeated the building in which he lived!"

The police investigated the problem, and told Nilsen that his drains had been blocked by human remains.

"Good grief! That's awful!" quipped Nilsen.

"Don't mess about. Are we talking about one body or two?"

"Well, sixteen, actually," ventured Nilsen.

Once he had been taken to a police station and made to sit in the interview room, Nilsen spoke for two and a half hours about the necessity of reading *The Guardian* from cover to cover every day.

He also asked the police to give him a copy of *The Guardian* and requested that it be brought to his cell regularly, so that he could read it before he went to bed every night. The police told him he was a "fucking bore!" – as many other farts had.

He refused to give evidence at the Old Bailey. Only three of his psychiatrists did so, one of whom was very giggly.

Throughout his trial, Nilsen sat motionless in the dock, reading *The Guardian*. Occasionally, he smiled at nothing in particular. God knows what, considering what an uninspiring rag it is and always has been.

Strangely, his clothing was extremely dapper, and his hair was neatly brushed. He wore glasses, which gave him a professorial look.

The most fascinating aspect of this case, was that his behaviour was totally incomprehensible. I don't think there has ever been such a disordered personality as Dennis Nilsen's in existence in the 1980s – that is to say, a personality quite as batty as his invariably had been

I have often asked myself and others whether this profoundly eccentric man has ever owned shares in *The Guardian*, or has had familial connections with the paper in the past. Clearly, there is no connection between this dour, dreary newspaper, and cutting up corpses in order to use them as speaking companions! "What does it all mean?" I have asked myself repeatedly.

I queued outside the Old Bailey to witness part of the case, and to ask other visitors for their opinions about this fruitcake.

I queued in the cold for almost twenty-four hours. The queue was endless.

While I was waiting my turn, I decided to continue teaching myself German, as I thought at the time, that I needed to learn another language besides French and Russian. My head was buried in my German primer.

A woman standing next to me was about five years my senior. She had a thick Cockney accent and was very friendly.

"'Ere, your German's going to be as good as Adolf 'Itler's by the time this case is over!" she said.

Among us, was a reporter from *The News of the World*. He seemed affable, but I was cautious and refrained from giving him my name. He asked me for my name, however. I changed the subject: "I say, that editor of yours, is he a pretty tough egg?" I asked him.

"It's a she, actually," replied the reporter. "Come on, love. What's your name?" he insisted.

"Mae West," I replied spontaneously. That name was not familiar to him.

"Do you come up to the Bailey a lot, Mae?" he asked in a friendly tone of voice.

"Only when there's a really gory, gruesome trial taking place," I replied. I smiled at him because of his friendliness.

"You've certainly picked a grisly one today!" commented *The News of the World* reporter. "Do you take *The Guardian* by any chance?" he added.

"I sometimes use it as lavatory paper," I replied.

We both let out a guffaw. Incidentally, I once asked my father who owned *The News of the World*.

"A round, red, rude man," my father replied obscurely.

Neville George Cleverley Heath

Just after World War II, there emerged an airline pilot called Neville George Cleverley Heath. It was claimed that he was never particularly successful as a pilot, during the war, but that he was by no means incapable.

Although he was a loner, he was well-spoken, handsome, and almost always wore uniforms and medals to which he was not entitled.

He liked living the "high life", and to spend his time drinking heavily, picking up loose women and taking them to hotels, where he used assumed names. He then took them to a chosen room, before torturing and murdering them. At one of these hotels, he called himself "Rupert Brooke". Why not William Shakespeare?

He had a pretty laid-back attitude towards his crimes, after he had murdered his victims. He sat near their bodies, chain-smoking and staring vacantly into space, before disposing of them.

Although Neville Heath was amoral, he was a most devoted son. When he knew his time was up, he wrote to his parents, apologising, in his own words, for "having been so damned unworthy of them both!" I can't deny, I liked his choice of words.

He was definitely a bad boy but was not without a certain amount of style, in that he asked for a double whisky before the noose was tightened round his neck. Also, just before he was led to the gallows, he asked for a copy of *The Daily Telegraph*. (My father *would* have been pleased, even if it had meant that his paper had only gained one extra copy.)

At least, unlike boring old Dennis Nilsen, he didn't ask for the bloody *Guardian*.

Reggie Kray

I'd like to mention the late Reggie Kray. I never witnessed his performance in court, but I got to know him well, I thought he was quite a character, as well as being a genuine gentleman. I do not intend to describe his career as a gangster, however.

I sent him some red roses after his twin brother, Ronnie, had died. He mentioned me on the television, which was a great honour.

"A very kind lady, called 'Eleanor Berry', sent me some red roses," he said, in a quiet, gentle tone of voice.

We were friends thereafter. He rang me up repeatedly and said, "I wanna speak to Elayna Burree."

"My name is Eleanor Berry," I replied forcefully.

"Yeah, that's right, Elayna Burree," he repeated.

I changed the subject. "What did you think of my first book about Robert Maxwell?" I asked him. (I had written more than one.)

"With respect, and I repeat, with very great respect, as I know you're a lady, but all you ever do is just go on and on and on and on about this *bleeding bloke*!" he replied.

The man had actually referred to me as a "lady". He was always tops with me, until he was laid in earth.

The Black Panther

I can't remember the exact name of the notorious Black Panther. He was a northerner. I think his name was Donald Neilson. His trial took place in Oxford, sometime in the 1970s. I attended part of it.

He was evil to the core. He robbed people, left, right and centre, and brutally grabbed hold of a young woman called Lesley Whittle, because she was wealthy.

He broke into her parents' house, and he snatched her from her bed, and kidnapped her, to gain what riches she possessed. He was totally amoral and had no conscience at all.

He asked her brother for a substantial amount of money, which he said he wanted delivered somewhere on a stretch of wasteland. His instructions were muddled and deliberately vague.

Lesley's brother went out of his way to get hold of the money demanded by Neilson, who finally murdered Lesley and pushed her body down a damp drain, in which he had kept her for days on end. In the end, he tightened a wire round her neck, strangling her.

The defendant wept pathetically throughout the trial, including the time when he was in the witness box. It was impossible to gauge who of the two was the most half-witted and, at the same time, the most evil: the Black Panther or his sickeningly stupid defence barrister.

In no circumstances could anyone have sympathised with this vile man. He had a daughter, called "Kathryn", who was roughly the same age as Lesley.

Apparently, he was devoted to his daughter, although she informed newspaper reporters that she despised her father. In fact, she didn't have a complimentary word to say about the bastard. Most of all, she said he was a professional bully and a selfish control freak. An article in one of the tabloids was headed, "*The Dad I Hated*, by Kathryn Neilson".

Neilson's treatment of Lesley was, without doubt, the most despicable since that of the Moors murderers towards small, innocent children. He was a coward, a murderer, a sadist, a bully and a thief, as well as many other things. He even treated his wife appallingly, and when he tried to teach his daughter, Kathryn, the time, he banged her violently onto a lavatory seat.

His main regret was that Kathryn was born a girl, instead of a boy. When she was growing up, he forced her to play military games with tanks, and he made her wear boys' tin helmets. She hated every minute of it.

Mercifully, the bastard is dead now, and with a bit of luck, he is rotting in hell.

The Cambridge Rapist: Peter Samuel Cook

I attended the trial of the Cambridge Rapist, Peter Samuel Cook, in the autumn of 1975. It took place in Norwich. I didn't realise how far Norwich is from London at the time.

The Judge presiding over the case was the late Melford Stevenson, a notoriously fierce Judge, who, for some reason, was unusually bad-tempered that morning. Stevenson was in favour of murderers being hanged in abundance, before the abolition of capital punishment. He really was a right swinger!

Cook was brought into the dock. He was dapper and was wearing a pale-blue suit, a dark mauve shirt and a fairly smart tie. Boringly, he had nothing to say, other than, "Guilty," and, in one instance, "Guilty, without intent to wound."

He spoke with a regional accent which was not unattractive.

Melford Stevenson began proceedings by peremptorily demanding a map of Cambridge. He found it difficult to pinpoint a street which he was looking for. He shook the map in the air, as if it were a dishcloth impregnated with varnish, and inadvertently dropped it on the floor.

Cook's unfortunate defence counsel, though he had nothing to say in favour of his pathetic and perverted client, bounded forward, like a starving dog, scooped up the map and obsequiously handed it to the Judge, who snatched it from his hand. Comic relief indeed!

Stevenson theatrically compared Cook to Jack the Ripper, and gave him two life sentences. Some would say this punishment was ridiculously harsh. Some people on the other hand, complained that it was not at all severe, given that Cook was sick in the head.

He also described the defendant's *modus operandi*, which was "terrifying". During his attacks, Cook broke into solitary women's rooms, with his face covered by a black leather balaclava and the word, "RAPIST" painted on its forehead in large, white letters. Added to this, he carried a sharp knife on most occasions, in order to terrify his victims even more.

Invariably, his opening words were: "Don't scream and no harm will come to you. I have a sharp knife!"

On one occasion, on attacking a woman, whose name I will not give, he savagely bit off part of one of her breasts.

On yet another occasion, he sodomised one of his victims.

The end of Cook's short trial was an anti-climax. "Put him away!" commanded Stevenson. It was after that that a few newspaper reporters interviewed the defendant's wife, Margaret Rose, an enormously fat, sadly unprepossessing-looking woman, who had lived with her husband in a shabby white caravan at the end of a dirt track, surrounded by monotonous, dirty countryside. The caravan was strangely named Costa del Sol!

She admitted to reporters that her marriage had not been consummated, and that she was responsible for Cook's unacceptable behaviour. "Blame me," she said. "Our life was sexless," stated one of the newspaper's headlines.

Her husband had bought her a see-through nightgown for her birthday, and had suggested that she wear it. She ungraciously refused to grant his request, which I thought was most unreasonable and incommoding of her.

Cook frequently visited a sex shop and bought pornographic videos, to relieve himself of his frigid wife's behaviour. "Have you got any blues, governor?" he apparently used to shout to the shop's manager. His approach to this man was always manic and hysterical, as if sex had been denied to him for a long time.

The Cooks were often seen by their neighbours, who described them as being the perfect couple, despite their unfortunate looks. I hardly think their neighbours were able to congratulate them on their choice of partner.

They were on a bus once. Cook pulled out a copy of a newspaper, which showed a police photo-fit of the rapist on its front page.

"Don't you think the rapist looks like me?" he asked his wife, Margaret Rose.

"Well, not really," she replied.

"Have another look. Can't you see the resemblance?"

"Are you the rapist, Peter?" asked Margaret Rose.

"No, of course not," he said.

Cook found out that he was developing female hormones. When he had been in prison for some time, he applied for early parole on these grounds. His request was turned down, however.

Also, he was a copper-bottomed left-winger.

"I'm dead against these people, who've got pots of money," he said to a "friend" on one occasion. That did not deter him from robbing countless innocent women of their savings.

Although there were times when his personal appearance could be quite striking, he was still a right regular bad 'un at the times of his crimes.

However, it cannot be denied that he felt genuinely guilty about what he had done, once he was incarcerated in prison. It was known, that until his death, he was interested in architecture.

Lastly, I enjoyed the "evidence" of Cook's defence counsel, who kept repeating that his client had the "decency" to plead guilty and the "courtesy" to ask whether his victims were all right, the day after he had raped them. The words "decency" and "courtesy" sounded almost Dickensian.

Cook died in 2004 of "unknown causes".

Peter Sutcliffe: The Yorkshire Ripper

I attended the trial of the late Peter Sutcliffe, the Yorkshire Ripper, at the Old Bailey in 1981. I didn't fancy the idea of queuing outside the court for two days and nights. Besides, the trial had come to the point of showing Sutcliffe giving evidence himself.

I was very pleased with myself. I made up a forged press card. On it was a statement that I was French and that I was working for *France Dimanche*, a downmarket French newspaper, and the French equivalent of the *The News of the World* (which has now folded).

Mercifully, I was escorted into the building and was guided to the press benches. I had spelt my name as "Mlle Eléanore Berri," and there was a small photograph of me, in which I looked very French. I had inserted a stamp above the photograph, which I had smudged. Whenever I spoke, which was seldom, I used a bogus French accent.

"You're going to end up sharing a cell with Mr Sutcliffe," commented my sister-in-law, Marina, when I showed her and Adrian the card.

The Judge entered the courtroom. I can't remember his name. Everybody rose. "Bring up Peter Sutcliffe," he said.

Sutcliffe bounded up the steps from the cells below with a strange spring in his step.

I needn't describe his height, but he was casually dressed in a denim suit and rather worn-out cowboy boots. I won't describe his unusually thick, wiry black hair or his facial features, which are known to the British public. One thing I did notice, however, was a pair of beautiful big, brown eyes. Many women would have referred to them as "come to bed" eyes. No doubt, it was they that had attracted the prostitutes getting into his car.

He crossed the well of the court, still maintaining a spring in his step, jauntily ascended the witness box and took the oath.

I don't intend to describe his extraordinary voice, because, as was universally known, it was abnormally high-pitched.

Sir Michael Havers, the Attorney General, cross-examined him. Havers raised his voice in a rage, dramatically produced a noose and thrust it in front of Sutcliffe's face at one point. Sometimes, he addressed him simply as "Sutcliffe".

"Did God tell you to hit a woman on the head with a brick in a sock?" Havers demanded aggressively. (It is known that Sutcliffe claimed to have been influenced by celestial voices.)

The question was so obscure that almost everyone in the courtroom, including Sutcliffe himself, laughed out loud. The Judge banged the gavel in front of him and threatened to clear the court.

Havers repeated the question.

"Ee don't noo," replied Sutcliffe. "Ee don't think ee made ees instrooctions very clear." (I don't know. I don't think he made his instructions very clear.)

It seemed to me that Sutcliffe was either absolutely half-witted or was doing his best to be funny, without succeeding.

In either event, he was not very entertaining. I became bored stiff but stayed in the courtroom until it was time to leave.

I did note one thing, however, something which was published in all the newspapers. Sutcliffe was absolutely devoted to his wife, Sonia, although she had always been very strict with him. She made him take his shoes off, as soon as he came into the house. Sometimes, she pulled the television socket out of the wall, while he was waiting for his evening meal! Perhaps, it was she whom he really meant to kill. No one knows.

Sutcliffe as a Painter

According to the newspapers, Sutcliffe was, and always had been, a talented painter. I have seen copies of his work and have been impressed by them. He also painted the faces of some of the women who visited him in prison.

I wanted him to paint my portrait, for macabre reasons, of course, so I sent him a flattering photograph of myself, accompanied by a complimentary letter. About a week later, I received an extremely curt letter, which read as follows:

> *"I act as one of Mr Peter Sutcliffe's psychiatrists. Mr Sutcliffe has instructed me to tell you that he wants nothing whatsoever to do with you."*

I considered this man's behaviour to be incomprehensible, as well as being nothing short of disgraceful. I wrote him the following letter:

> *"Sutcliffe,*
>
> *"I am in possession of an exceptionally insolent letter from one of your many psychiatrists, stating that you wish to have nothing whatsoever to do with me.*
>
> *"You have the manners of a concentration camp lavatory attendant, the sex appeal of a menstruating housemaid, and the voice of a boy who has been forced to sing alto."*

I did not receive a reply.

Mind you, many of the inhabitants of Yorkshire tend to be very rude for some reason, and I am sure the Yorkshire Ripper was no exception to this rule.

The Ratner Case

In 1994, I was involved in what was referred to as "the Ratner case". First, I gave evidence in a Magistrates' Court. Later, in December of that year, I appeared as Chief Prosecution Witness at the Knightsbridge Crown Court.

Dr Victor Ratner (or "Ratty", as I called him) had died in suspicious circumstances, in August, 1994. He choked on his own vomit, while his wife, Gida, lay beside him, apparently not noticing anything! I was shattered because he had been a wonderful friend to me for many years. Also, I had been working for him as a debt collector, which was most enjoyable. He commented that I had the right kind of voice for the job!

I'll refer to my appearance at the Magistrates' Court in London. I opened my briefcase and produced a pile of papers.

"We don't allow witnesses to refer to notes in court," said the magistrate, a big, burly woman in royal blue.

"One of the Yorkshire Ripper's psychiatrists was allowed to refer to his notes in court," I protested.

"Miss Berry, you are *not* one of the Yorkshire Ripper's psychiatrists, thank the Lord!"

"When did Dr Ratner die?" she then asked.

"Between 1:00 and 1:15 in the morning of Saturday the 7th day of August last," I replied.

"All you really need to say is the 7th of August," said the magistrate crisply.

I wasn't asked to give further evidence in the Magistrates' Court, although I was somewhat inebriated and she must have noticed.

Eleanor in Court

My next subject comes under the heading, "Eleanor in Court". The following is an edited extract from the cross-examination I endured, for three days, at the Knightsbridge Crown Court, in December, 1994.

I had accused the late Dr Ratner's widow, Gida, of robbing me of £16,000. I got some of the money back. Gida had a particularly accomplished barrister, whom I shall refer to as "Mr Cox", although that is not his real name. In the end, she was acquitted.

I enjoyed my cross-examination, nevertheless. I felt as if I were playing a vigorous game of tennis, without having to do any running. Also, I made a point of addressing the Judge as "my lord" throughout, although I was only giving evidence in a Crown Court.

On the first day of my appearance, I drove past the house, which had once been inhabited by my maternal grandfather, F.E. Smith. I got out of the car and spoke out loud to the bright blue plaque on the wall. I asked my grandfather to help me by giving me his brilliant gift for words. Had he not helped me from beyond the grave, I would not have been able to answer the cross-examining barrister's questions in such an articulate manner.

My exact words, when addressing the plaque, were, "Help me, Grandfather. Help the youngest child, of your youngest child. Give me your wonderful gift for words!"

I can't deny that I was also helped by a flask of gin and tonic, which I was carrying in my briefcase. However, my grandfather's presence, which I felt so powerfully by my side, while I was answering the cross-examining barrister's questions, was by far the greatest aid of all, despite the fact that the defendant was discharged eventually.

Gida Ratner had passed my notes to her lawyers, in an attempt to get me to back down. I knew that F.E. Smith considered her action to be both corrupt and evil. I have always believed that the dead can watch the living, and help them, provided they have been related to them at some time.

COX	(Cross-examining barrister, and Gida Ratner's counsel) From what I have heard, you seem to be a vindictive and dishonest woman.
BERRY	Back up your statement with facts, sir.
COX	You are, nevertheless, a vindictive woman.
BERRY	(Shouts) I will tolerate your disgusting insolence no longer! That is a filthy, reprobate lie, as well as being totally unworthy of your profession.
COX	(Changes subject) You call yourself a writer, do you not?
BERRY	I do not *call* myself a writer, sir. I *am* a writer, and a prolific one at that.
COX	One of your books is entitled, *Your Father Had to Swing, You Little Bastard.*
BERRY	That is correct.
COX	There is a character in this book, called Geraldine Myer
BERRY	Myers, sir!
COX	Do you identify with her?
BERRY	Hardly, sir. She was a professional opera singer. I only sing in my bath.
COX	I have here another book which you have written, *My Old Pal Was a Junkie.* You have written two books, have you not?
BERRY	Those are not the only books I have written, sir. Your library is incomplete.
COX	Have you ever served on the bench as a magistrate?
BERRY	No.
COX	Your character, Geraldine Myers, tells people she is a magistrate. The documents I have before me indicate that you do the same. Is it not dishonest to pose as a magistrate?
BERRY	Who are you to talk about dishonesty, when you know very well that you are using stolen documents for financial gain?
COX	Would you please answer my question.
BERRY	I'm not answering your question, until you answer my question!

COX	You have posed as a magistrate in the past, have you not?
BERRY	Certainly, I have written to a few people in the past, calling myself a magistrate. I did so as a joke. Do you really think that anyone hearing me speak, would believe that I was a magistrate? Jesus, sir, where is your sense of humour?
COX	You do have a rather curious sense of humour, do you not, Miss Berry?
BERRY	Humour is not a category that can be defined easily. For the sake of emotional survival, I try to see that there is a funny side to all things grave.
COX	May I put it to you that you have identified with Geraldine Myers, on another occasion? For instance, she pays an artist to paint lines of age on her rival's face. Have you ever done that?
BERRY	No. Besides, writers do not necessarily commit the actions of the characters in their books, or condone them either. For instance, would you accuse the writer, Daphne du Maurier, of being an accessory to the fact that Max de Winter shot his first wife?
COX	Would you call your book, *Your Father Had to Swing, You Little Bastard* a comedy?
BERRY	Most definitely, sir.
COX	I hardly see it as a comedy.
BERRY	(Exasperated) It is a *black* comedy, sir. Also, it seems you have read it extremely carefully, so much so that you have broken its back and caused most of its pages to fall out. It appears that you have neither absorbed nor understood its contents, however.
COX	I also understand that, when you were at university, where you gained a 2.2 in English, you completed a contextual thesis on the infamous Comte de Sade. Is this correct?
BERRY	No, sir. It is incorrect. He was not a comte. He was a marquis.
COX	(Loses it) There is a spirit of ghoulishness in your books. If you had been alive at the time of the French Revolution, would you have been a *tricoteuse*?
BERRY	No, sir. I can't knit.

COX	Put it this way, Miss Berry. If there were public hangings in England today, would you attend one?
BERRY	(Long pause) That would depend entirely on whether or not I could find a parking space within fifty yards of the gallows.
COX	You were sacked from St Bartholomew's Hospital, were you not?
BERRY	Yes.
COX	Why?
BERRY	I had had a bereavement and my boss, who had once adulated me, was very jealous of my affection for the gentleman who had just died.
COX	You are referring to Maxwell, are you not?
BERRY	(Shouts) *Mister* Maxwell to you!
THE JUDGE	Will you please stop shouting, Miss Berry.
BERRY	I apologise, my lord. I am very distressed. May I please trouble you for a glass of water.
THE JUDGE	Yes, certainly, Miss Berry.
COX	(Plays his final card) Do you know someone called Dr Larry Baker?
BERRY	Yes.
COX	It was he who dismissed you from St Bartholomew's Hospital, was it not?
BERRY	Yes. He committed an evil deed, for which he had to be punished.
COX	You mean a deed for which *you* thought he had to be punished?
BERRY	If you say so.
COX	(Repeats sarcastically) *If you say so.* I have here some papers relating to the manner in which you are said to have punished Dr Larry Baker.

Cox then accuses Berry of having done the following things to Dr Larry Baker:

1. Sending taxis to his house every fifteen minutes of the night,
2. Sending representatives of the Communist Party to his house, late at night,

3. Sending a Jehovah's Witness to his house, late at night,
4. Informing Customs and Excise at Heathrow Airport that he had been carrying heroin and crack cocaine rectally,
5. Having anonymous leaflets about impotence, premature ejaculation and erectile dysfunction sent both to his house and his office.

COX   Let's begin with the last of all the punishments which you planned to inflict on Dr Larry Baker. Miss Berry, I will read aloud a letter, written by you, relating to what you did.

Judge does fuck all. Cox reads aloud the following:

"Dear sir,

"Re: Problems with my cock

"I am having a lot of trouble with my cock. I have let down a large number of men and women alike, because I finish before I am able to start."

(The letter is passed round the jury.)

COX   This very letter is proof of your vindictive personality, is it not?
BERRY   It would have been, if I had posted it, but I did not do so.
COX   Do you usually write letters which you do not post?
BERRY: Frequently.
COX: Why?
BERRY: To get them off my chest, obviously.
COX: I am going to read aloud another of your letters, this time to the Communist Party.

"Dear Sirs,

"I wish to join the Communist Party. Perhaps you would care to send someone round to my house to discuss this. If someone does call, could they be sure to make it latish, 'cos of darts?"

Would you like it if representatives of the Communist Party were to come round to your house late at night?

BERRY	That would surely depend on whether or not I were living in a communist country.
COX	Miss Berry, you are an exhibitionist and a consummate liar. This has been proved.
BERRY	(Pause) Do you think I am intimidated by a silly little man in a wig?
COX	I don't think anyone would be capable of being intimidated by you, Miss Berry.

I do not see the point of continuing to record the extracts from my cross-examination. Enough is enough. In short, Gida Ratner was discharged, as I stated earlier. It was a bloody good game, though. It was like a game of tennis, without having to do any running.

* * *

Although my period of employment under Ratty's roof was lamentably short, he and I had a lot of fun, when he was not seeing patients.

Gradually, Gida, who was much younger than we were, was squeezed out of the equation.

When Ratty wasn't busy, and when I didn't have any work to do, we behaved like children. We often went upstairs to his bedroom and had pillow fights.

On some occasions, we went to his consulting room and played off-ground-he. The person caught had to jump on top of the desk, before being tapped on the arm or shoulder.

Sometimes, Ratty invited other Harley Street consultants to tea at about three o'clock in the afternoon, when the room was brimming with doctors, most of whom were wearing pinstripe suits and red carnations.

Ratty treated me in the same way as he did these consultants, although they all uttered incomprehensible medical jargon for much of the time. I listened to them, though, and sometimes heard about operations, which fascinated me.

Ratty treated members of the royal family regularly, although I had no idea which royals were attending his rooms. I suggested to him that my books be distributed amongst them and circulated round Buckingham Palace.

One day, when I was a bit confused, due to a little too much alcohol consumption, I placed a basket of my books into the hands of a lady, whom I assumed was a royal. She accepted the basket graciously.

"Would you like me to carry these books out to your chauffeur?" I ventured.

The woman was Peter O'Toole's sister.

"*Tu est incroyable!*" exclaimed Ratty. (You are unbelievable!)

Gradually, Ratty's clientele began to dwindle. This did not prevent him from treating animals and birds with broken wings, however. He had a slight drinking problem because he was unhappily married, and often drank vodka before breakfast! As was always his habit, he injected himself regularly with a drug called *Pethidine*. This was something he had done all his life, in the same way as his father had.

I spoke to his friend, and former partner, the late Dr Peter Stephan, after his death.

"He was a desperately unhappy man," said Dr Stephan. "But he was too proud to allow his unhappiness to show. All his wife did was mock him, and this hurt him enormously, particularly as she did so in front of his patients."

* * *

Although many years have passed, I still miss Ratty terribly. After all, it was he who had given me lithium carbonate to heal my bipolar disorder in 1972, and it was he who had shown such extraordinary modesty throughout his short but wonderful life.

Not only do I tell doctors my problems; I like to hear their problems as well. Their problems are often infinitely more complicated and sadder than mine, and I like to give them my undivided attention, as they tell me about their pains and anxieties.

I have spoken about the late Dr Carl Heinz Goldman on many occasions.

I went into his consulting room one day and he was sobbing convulsively.

"Oh? Dr Goldman? Whatever is the matter?" I asked.

"I vant to die!" he replied, in his pronounced Leipzig accent.

"Why do you want to die?" I asked him banally.

"I went into my wife's bedroom last night, and she wouldn't even let me kiss her!"

"Couldn't you have forced yourself onto her? She's your wife, damn it! You've got every right," I said stupidly.

"That would constitute rape. I'd have to go to prison."

I thought for a while, walked round his desk and put my arm round him.

"Oh, well, you can still kiss me," I said.

"You're my patient, I can't have sex with my patients. I'd be struck off. I'd have nowhere to live, and no money."

My consultations with these doctors followed roughly the same pattern. Many of them said I was an absolute brick, which is exactly what Peachey said to me, just before he died, God rest his soul.

Sometimes, it was difficult for me to witness the sadness of the doctors whom I visited. There were times, however, when many of them helped me and I really cherished my consultations with them. I loved to psychoanalyse them as well, instead of being at the receiving end of their questions.

In short, I have had a very varied life, more so than most people. The many books that I have written, and am still writing, are a great comfort to me. My books are my children.

I have suffered much sadness in my life, namely the loss of my two brothers, but most of all, the loss of my beloved Peachey, in a period of about a month!

At that horrible time, I was able to tell, just who my true friends are, and who they are not.

I have not given names, due to libel laws, but there are two individuals, previously posing as my friends, who have hurt me more deeply that I can say in words, particularly with regard to Peachey's death. I have named these individuals Jenny and Cynthia already.

I was exposed to a degree of cruelty and callousness, of which I would be totally incapable myself. I do not claim to be perfect, but I have never, in my life, been cruel to anyone, without massive provocation.

No doubt, the two individuals will recognise themselves, on reading this book's last paragraphs. I believe in an eye for an eye and a tooth for a tooth, and had Sir Winston Churchill not done so, the Germans would have won the war.

I strongly disapprove of unprovoked cruelty, as I have said on more than one occasion. I will end this book with my chosen words: I am not a Smith for nothing.